应用型本科通用教材

创新应用英语教程

（第二册）

宋宝梅　主编

中国林业出版社
China Forestry Publishing House

内 容 简 介

随着高等学校大学外语教学指导委员会制定的《大学英语教学指南》等文件的正式公布，要求高等院校提供分类的高质量大学英语教学的趋势就更加明显。《创新应用英语教程》是一套内容涉及广泛、话题趣味性强的应用系列教程。其选材新颖，题材广泛，内容丰富，强调在真实环境下的语言应用。同时考虑到学生有通过大学英语四、六级考试的需求，本教材能使学生们顺利进入大学英语四、六级考试的前期准备阶段的学习。

本教材内容有较强的时代特点，注重知识性、趣味性、可读性、针对性和系统性的融合。本教材内容涉及自然、健康、食物、情绪、社交媒体、文化、休闲娱乐等方面。学生既可以学习到相关话题的地道英语，增加话题相关的词汇量，还可以通过课后形式多样的练习题，由浅入深地巩固词汇，增进阅读理解能力，练习地道的英文翻译和表达，循序渐进地提升英语应用能力。本教材还根据应用型本科院校的学生特点，增加了语法和应用文写作等专项讲解练习，让学生扎实掌握英文用词造句的规则，更好地进行听、说、读、写等语言实践活动。此外，本教材创新性地在每个单元都融入了与中国传统文化相关的英文表达，如谚语的翻译、古诗词鉴赏、与文化相关的短文翻译等，既能提升学生的爱国情怀和文化修养，也能在英语日常交际中，使学生学会表达中国的文化。

图书在版编目（CIP）数据

创新应用英语教程. 第二册 / 宋宝梅主编. -- 北京 : 中国林业出版社, 2024.8. -- (应用型本科通用教材).
ISBN 978-7-5219-2776-4

Ⅰ. H319.39

中国国家版本馆 CIP 数据核字第 2024XU0113 号

责任编辑：高红岩　王奕丹
责任校对：苏　梅
封面设计：睿思视界视觉设计

出版发行：中国林业出版社
　　　　　（100009，北京市西城区刘海胡同 7 号，电话 83223120）
电子邮箱：cfphzbs@163.com
网　　址：https://www.cfph.net
印　　刷：北京中科印刷有限公司
版　　次：2024 年 8 月第 1 版
印　　次：2024 年 8 月第 1 次印刷
开　　本：787mm×1092mm　1/16
印　　张：12.75
字　　数：318 千字
定　　价：45.00 元

《创新应用英语教程》(第二册)编写人员

主　　编：宋宝梅

副 主 编：栾　巍

编写人员：(按姓氏拼音排序)

　　　　　栾　巍　　(哈尔滨信息工程学院)

　　　　　宋宝梅　　(东北农业大学)

　　　　　孙佳丽　　(哈尔滨信息工程学院)

　　　　　王　影　　(吉林动画学院)

前 言
Preface

　　《创新应用英语教程》系列教材的编写以提高学生英语综合运用能力为教学目标，以培养应用型本科人才为定位，根据应用型本科院校生源、办学定位、人才培养目标等因素，遵循语言教学和学习规律，合理安排相应的英语教学内容，以强调真实环境下的语言运用为重点，既考虑到学生有通过国家英语应用能力考试统考的需求，也兼顾其能够顺利进入大学英语四、六级考试的前期准备阶段的学习。在编写过程中，我们遵循"实用为主，够用为度，以运用为本"的原则，充分考虑学生实际的英语运用能力，在单元安排、内容取舍、体例结构上注意区分教学层次，根据由浅入深、循序渐进、方便教学的原则安排教学内容。

　　在本教材中，学生可以欣赏地道的英语文章，在学习语言的同时开拓视野，锻炼创新思维和独立思考能力，培养自主学习与合作式学习能力。在提高阅读能力的同时，学生的思辨能力和人文素养也将有较大的提升。课后练习的设计包含了语法和应用文写作等专项练习，练习形式多样、题量适中，以全面提高学生的英语综合运用能力，为今后的终身学习打下坚实的基础。此外，学生通过本教材的学习，可如同亲身游历各国一般，感受异域文化及各国风土人情，体会多元文化的存在。

　　本册主编宋宝梅负责课题设计、编写规划等，并编写了第 14～15 章；栾巍编写了第 1～6 章；孙佳丽编写了第 7～10 章；王影编写了第 11～13 章。

　　由于时间仓促，水平有限，错误及疏漏之处在所难免，恳请广大读者和同行提出宝贵意见，以便日后对本教材做出修订，使之更加完善。

编　者
2023 年 11 月

目 录
Contents

前言 Preface

Unit 1 Diversity and Inclusion ········ 1
- Part A   Interracial Roommates ········ 1
- Part B   New Jersey School District Eases Pressure on Students — Baring an Ethnic Divide ········ 5
- Part C   Grammar ········ 9
- Part D   Workshop ········ 13

Unit 2 Nature ········ 15
- Part A   The Growth of Forest Area in Rich Countries ········ 15
- Part B   The Quiet Heroism of Mail Delivery ········ 18
- Part C   Grammar ········ 23
- Part D   Workshop ········ 27

Unit 3 Obesity ········ 28
- Part A   Obesity and Disease ········ 28
- Part B   Is Breakfast Really the Most Important Meal of the Day? ········ 31
- Part C   Grammar ········ 36
- Part D   Workshop ········ 39

Unit 4 Online Education ········ 41
- Part A   Online Classes ········ 41
- Part B   Make Stuff, Fail, and Learn While You're at It ········ 44
- Part C   Grammar ········ 49
- Part D   Workshop ········ 52

Unit 5 Animal ········ 53
- Part A   Cats ········ 53
- Part B   How to Eat Well ········ 56
- Part C   Grammar ········ 60
- Part D   Workshop ········ 63

Unit 6 Health ········ 64
- Part A   Effect of Health on Marital Status in Old Age ········ 64
- Part B   How Work Will Change When Most of Us Live to 100 ········ 67

	Part C	Grammar	71
	Part D	Workshop	75

Unit 7　Spirit and Mood · 77
	Part A	The State of Boredom Experienced by Man	77
	Part B	The Start of High School Doesn't Have to Be Stressful	80
	Part C	Grammar	84
	Part D	Workshop	90

Unit 8　Social Media · 92
	Part A	Facebook	92
	Part B	Fake Holiday Villa Websites Prompt Warning	95
	Part C	Grammar	99
	Part D	Workshop	103

Unit 9　Culture · 105
	Part A	Writing on It All	105
	Part B	Why Are Asian Americans Missing from Our Textbooks?	108
	Part C	Grammar	113
	Part D	Workshop	117

Unit 10　Internet security · 118
	Part A	Internet-Connected Security Camera	118
	Part B	Can Burglars Jam Your Wireless Security System?	121
	Part C	Grammar	125
	Part D	Workshop	128

Unit 11　AI in Education · 130
	Part A	Artificially Intelligent Teaching Assistant	130
	Part B	Some College Students Are Angry That They Have to Pay to Do Their Homework	134
	Part C	Grammar	138
	Part D	Workshop	140

Unit 12　Food · 142
	Part A	How to Affect Calories Consumption?	142
	Part B	The History of the Lunch Box	146
	Part C	Practical Writing	150
	Part D	Workshop	153

Unit 13　Recreation and Entertainment · 155
	Part A	A Growth Mindset of Internet Can Spark Innovative Thinking	155
	Part B	Team Spirit	159
	Part C	Practical Writing	163
	Part D	Workshop	166

Unit 14　Travelling · 169
	Part A	The Olympic Class Ships	169

	Part B	As Tourists Crowd Out Locals, Venice Faces "Endangered" List	173
	Part C	Practical Writing	177
	Part D	Workshop	180
Unit 15	**Digital Age**		182
	Part A	Dilemma of Textbook Publishing in the Digital Age	182
	Part B	When a Language Has No Words for Numbers	186
	Part C	Practical Writing	190
	Part D	Workshop	192

Unit 1　Diversity and Inclusion

Interracial Roommates

Several recent studies have found that being randomly assigned to a roommate of another race can lead to increased tolerance but also to a greater likelihood of conflict.

Recent reports found that lodging with a student of a different race may decrease prejudice and compel students to engage in more ethnically diverse friendships.

An Ohio State University study also found that black students living with a white roommate saw higher academic success throughout their college careers. Researchers believe this may be caused by social pressure.

In a *New York Times* article, Sam Boakye — the only black student on his freshman year floor — said that "if you're surrounded by whites, you have something to prove."

Researchers also observed problems resulting from pairing interracial students in residences.

According to two recent studies, randomly assigned roommates of different races are more likely to experience conflicts so strained that one roommate will move out.

An Indiana University study found that interracial roommates were three times as likely as two white roommates to no longer live together by the end of the semester.

Grace Kao, a professor at Penn said she was not surprised by the findings. "This may be the first time that some of these students have interacted, and lived, with someone of a different race," she said.

At Penn, students are not asked to indicate race when applying for housing.

"One of the great things about freshman housing is that, with some exceptions, the process throws you together randomly," said Undergraduate Assembly chairman Alec Webley. "This is the definition of integration."

"I've experienced roommate conflicts between interracial students that have both broken down stereotypes and reinforced stereotypes," said one Penn resident advisor (RA). The RA of two years added that while some conflicts "provided more multicultural acceptance and melding ," there were also "jarring cultural confrontations."

The RA said that these conflicts have also occurred among roommates of the same race.

Kao said she cautions against forming any generalizations based on any one of the studies, noting that more background characteristics of the students need to be studied and explained.

Words & Expressions

randomly/'rændəmli/*adv.* 随机地，任意地
tolerance/'tɒlərəns/*n.* 宽容，容忍
likelihood/'laɪklihʊd/*n.* 可能，可能性
prejudice/'predʒədɪs/*n.* 偏见
compel/kəm'pel/*v.* 强迫，迫使
ethnically/'eθnɪkli/*adv.* 人种上，民族上
diverse/daɪ'vɜːs/*adj.* 形形色色的，不同的
observe/əb'zɜːv/*v.* 观察，看到
interracial/ˌɪntə'reɪʃl/*adj.* 人种间的，人种混合的
residence/'rezɪdəns/*n.* 住处，住宅
interacted/ˌɪntər'æktɪd/*v.* 相互作用
assembly/ə'sembli/*n.* 议会，集会
integration/ˌɪntɪ'ɡreɪʃ(ə)n/*n.* 结合，融合
stereotype/'steriətaɪp/*n.* 老套，模式化的见解
reinforced/riːɪn'fɔːst/*adj.* 使更具说服力的
jarring/'dʒɑːrɪŋ/*adj.* 刺耳的，不和谐的
generalization/ˌdʒen(ə)rəlaɪ'zeɪʃ(ə)n/*n.* 概论
engage in （使）从事，参与
result from 起因于；由…造成
according to 据…所说
apply for 申请
break down 打破，消除

Notes

1. Penn

宾夕法尼亚大学（University of Pennsylvania），简称宾大（UPenn，Penn），位于宾夕法尼亚州最大的城市费城，是一所私立研究型大学，8 所常春藤盟校之一，美国大学协会14所创始成员之一。全球大学校长论坛成员。宾大由本杰明·富兰克林创建于1740年，是美国第四古老的高等教育机构，也是美国第一所从事科学技术和人文教育的现代高等学校。

2. New York Times

《纽约时报》有时简称为"时报"（*The Times*），是一份在美国纽约出版的日报，在全世界发行，有相当高的影响力，是美国高级报纸、严肃刊物的代表，长期以来拥有良好的公信力和权威性。由于风格古典严肃，它有时也被戏称为"灰色女士"（The Gray Lady）。它最初的名字是《纽约每日时报》（*The New York Daily Times*），创始人是亨利·贾维斯·雷蒙德和乔治·琼斯。

Unit 1 Diversity and Inclusion

Exercises

I. Comprehension of the Text

There are 5 questions in this section. For each of them there are four choices marked A, B, C and D. You should choose the best answer for each question.

1. What can we learn from some recent studies?
   A. Conflicts between students of different races are unavoidable.
   B. Students of different races are prejudiced against each other.
   C. Interracial lodging does more harm than good.
   D. Interracial lodging may have diverse outcomes.
2. What does Sam Boakye's remark mean?
   A. White students tend to look down upon their black peers.
   B. Black students can compete with their white peers academically.
   C. Black students feel somewhat embarrassed among white peers during the freshman year.
   D. Being surrounded by white peers motivates a black student to work harder to succeed.
3. What does the Indiana University study show?
   A. Interracial roommates are more likely to fall out.
   B. Few white students like sharing a room with a black peer.
   C. Roommates of different races just don't get along.
   D. Assigning students' lodging randomly is not a good policy.
4. What does Alec Webley consider to be the "definition of integration"?
   A. Students of different races are required to share a room.
   B. Interracial lodging is arranged by the school for freshmen.
   C. Lodging is assigned to students of different races without exception.
   D. The school randomly assigns roommates without regard to race.
5. What does Grace Kao say about interracial lodging?
   A. It is unscientific to make generalizations about it without further study.
   B. Schools should be cautious when making decisions about student lodging.
   C. Students' racial background should be considered before lodging is assigned.
   D. Experienced resident advisors should be assigned to handle the problems.

II. Languages Focus

A. *Match the following words in left with their explanations in right.*

1. ethnically   a. given added strength or support
2. diverse   b. many and different
3. integration   c. the probability of a specified outcome

4. randomly   d. act together or towards others or with others
5. reinforced   e. with respect to ethnicity
6. likelihood   f. force somebody to do something
7. compel   g. in a random manner
8. interracial   h. the act of tolerating something
9. tolerance   i. between races
10. interacted   j. the action of incorporating a racial or religious group into a community

B. *Fill in the blanks with the words or expressions given below. Change the form where necessary.*

| likelihood | ethnically | integration | engage in | interracial |
| observe | randomly | apply for | prejudice | result from |

1. There is very little _____ of that happening.
2. She _____ that all the chairs were already occupied.
3. His music is an _____ of tradition and new technology.
4. Historically, there has been a lot of deep-seated prejudice against _____ mixed people.
5. The world would be better off if there were more _____ marriages.
6. The winning numbers are _____ selected by computer.
7. Students are given the fullest opportunity to _____ class discussions.
8. Their decision was based on ignorance and _____.
9. If you want to _____ a job at the office where I work, I'll put in a good word for you.
10. That is to say, most cases of diabetes _____ the unhealthy lifestyle.

Ⅲ. Translation

Translate the following sentences into Chinese.

1. Recent reports found that lodging with a student of a different race may decrease prejudice and compel students to engage in more ethnically diverse friendships.

_____

_____

2. An Ohio State University study also found that black students living with a white roommate saw higher academic success throughout their college careers.

_____

_____

3. Researchers also observed problems resulting from pairing interracial students in residences.

_____

4. Students are not asked to indicate race when applying for housing.

___

5. I've experienced roommate conflicts between interracial students that have both broken down stereotypes and reinforced stereotypes.

___

IV. Discussion

Can you give some suggestions to foreigners who have settled in China on how to live a comfortable life here?

New Jersey School District Eases Pressure on Students — Baring an Ethnic Divide

A) This fall, David Aderhold, the chief of a high-achieving school district near Princeton, New Jersey, sent parents an alarming 16-page letter. The school district, he said, was facing a crisis. Its students were overburdened and stressed out, having to cope with too much work and too many demands. In the previous school year, 120 middle and high school students were recommended for mental health assessments and 40 were hospitalized. And on a survey administered by the district, students wrote things like, "I hate going to school," and "Coming out of 12 years in this district, I have learned one thing: that a grade, a percentage or even a point is to be valued over anything else."

B) With his letter, Aderhold inserted West Windsor-Plainsboro Regional School District into a national discussion about the intense focus on achievement at elite schools, and whether it has gone too far. At follow-up meetings, he urged parents to join him in advocating a "whole child" approach to schooling that respects "social-emotional development" and "deep and meaningful learning" over academics alone. The alternative, he suggested, was to face the prospect of becoming another Palo Alto, California, where outsize stress on teenage students is believed to have contributed to a number of suicides in the last six years.

C) But instead of bringing families together, Aderhold's letter revealed a divide in the district, which has 9,700 students, and one that broke down roughly along racial lines. On one side are white parents like Catherine Foley, a former president of the Parent-Teacher-Student Association at her daughter's middle school, who has come to see the district's increasingly pressured atmosphere as opposed to learning. "My son was in fourth grade and told me, 'I'm not going to amount to anything because I have nothing to put on my resume.'" she said. On the other side are parents like Mike Jia, one of the thousands of Asian-American professionals who have moved to the district in the past decade, who said Aderhold's reforms would amount to a "dumbing down" of his children's education. "What is happening here reflects a national anti-intellectual trend that will not prepare our children for the future," Jia said.

D) About 10 minutes from Princeton and an hour and a half from New York City, West Windsor and Plainsboro have become popular bedroom communities for technology entrepreneurs, researchers and engineers, drawn in large part by the public schools. From the last three graduating classes, 16 seniors were admitted to MIT. It produces Science Olympiad winners, classically trained musicians and students with perfect SAT scores.

E) The district has become increasingly popular with immigrant families from China, India and Korea. This year, 65 percent of its students are Asian-American, compared with 44 percent in 2007. Many of them are the first in their families born in the United States. They have had a growing influence on the district. Asian-American parents are enthusiastic supporters of the competitive instrumental music program. They have been huge supporters of the district's advanced mathematics program, which once began in the fourth grade but will now start in the sixth. The change to the program, in which 90 percent of the participating students are Asian-American, is one of Aderhold's reforms.

F) Asian-American students have been eager participants in a state program that permits them to take summer classes off campus for high school credit, allowing them to maximize the number of honors and Advanced Placement classes they can take, another practice that Aderhold is limiting this school year. With many Asian-American children attending supplementary instructional programs, there is a perception among some white families that the elementary school curriculum is being sped up to accommodate them.

G) Both Asian-American and white families say the tension between the two groups has grown steadily over the past few years, as the number of Asian families has risen. But the division has become more obvious in recent months as Aderhold has made changes, including no-homework nights, an end to high school midterms and finals, and an initiative that made it easier to participate in the music program.

H) Jennifer Lee, professor of sociology at the University of California, Irvine, and an author of the *Asian American Achievement Paradox*, says misunderstanding between first-generation Asian-American parents and those who have been in this country longer are common. What white middle-class parents do not always understand, she said, is how much pressure recent immigrants feel to boost their children into the middle class. "They don't have the same chances to get their children internships or jobs at law firms," Lee said. "So what they believe is that their children must excel and beat their white peers in academic settings so they have the same chances to excel later."

I) The issue of the stresses felt by students in elite school districts has gained attention in recent years as schools in places like Newton, Massachusetts, and Palo Alto have reported a number of suicides. West Windsor-Plainsboro has not had a teenage suicide in recent years, but Aderhold, who has worked in the district for seven years and been chief for the last three years, said he had seen troubling signs. In a recent art assignments, a middle school student depicted an overburdened child who was being scolded for earning an A, rather than an A+,

Unit 1 Diversity and Inclusion

on a math exam. In the image, the mother scolds the student with the words, "Shame on you!" Further, he said, the New Jersey Education Department has flagged at least two pieces of writing on state English language assessments in which students expressed suicidal thoughts.

J) The survey commissioned by the district found that 68 percent of high school honor and Advanced Placement students reported feeling stressed about school "always or most of the time." "We need to bring back some balance," Aderhold said. "You don't want to wait until it's too late to do something."

K) Not all public opinion has fallen along racial lines. Karen Sue, the Chinese-American mother of a fifth-grader and an eighth-grader, believes the competition within the district has gotten out of control. Sue, who was born in the United States to immigrant parents, wants her peers to dial it back. "It's become an arms race, an educational arms race," she said. "We all want our kids to achieve and be successful. The question is, at what cost?"

Words & Expressions

ease/iːz/ v. 减轻，缓和
bare/beə(r)/ v. 使暴露，使露出
ethnic/ˈeθnɪk/ adj. （有关）种族的，民族的
alarming/əˈlɑːmɪŋ/ adj. 令人担忧的，令人恐惧的
assessment/əˈsesmənt/ n. 评估，评价
administered/ədˈmɪnɪstə(r)/ v. 管理，治理；执行
elite/eɪˈliːt/ n. 尖子，精英
advocate/ˈædvəkeɪt/ v. 拥护，提倡
alternative/ɔːlˈtɜːnətɪv/ n. 可供选择的事物，替代物
atmosphere/ˈætməsfɪə(r)/ n. 气氛，环境
dumbing down/ n. 肤浅，低能化
enthusiastic/ɪnˌθjuːziˈæstɪk/ adj. 热心的，热情的
competitive/kəmˈpetətɪv/ adj. 竞争的，好胜的
supplementary/ˌsʌplɪˈmentri/ adj. 补充的，附加的
instructional/ɪnˈstrʌkʃ(ə)n(ə)l/ adj. 教学的；指导的
perception/pəˈsepʃ(ə)n/ n. 看法，认识
accommodate/əˈkɒmədeɪt/ v. 顺应，适应
initiative/ɪˈnɪʃətɪv/ n. 措施，倡议
boost/buːst/ v. 使增长，推动
internships/ˈɪntɜːnʃɪps/ n. 实习生；实习期
excel/ɪkˈsel/ v. 精通，擅长；超过
depicted/dɪˈpɪktɪd/ v. 描述，描绘
scold/skəʊld/ v. 责骂，训斥

Notes

1. Princeton

普林斯顿，是美国东北部城市，位于新泽西州（State of New Jersey）。有著名的普林斯顿大学和普林斯顿高等研究院。普林斯顿地处纽约和费城之间，是一座别具特色的乡村都市。

2. the University of California, Irvine

加利福尼亚大学尔湾分校，又译加州大学尔湾分校或欧文分校，创建于 1965 年，隶属于加利福尼亚大学系统，是公立研究型大学，美国大学协会、环太平洋大学联盟、国际公立大学论坛成员，被誉为"公立常春藤"。加州大学尔湾分校有 8 位诺贝尔奖得主、7 位普利策奖得主，学校位列美国最佳大学排名第 35 位，公立大学第 7 位；2019 年华盛顿月刊美国最佳大学排名全美第 18 位。

Exercises

Ⅰ. Comprehension of the Text

Read the text and answer the following questions. Write the answers on the lines.

1. Why did David Aderhold send parents an alarming 16-page letter?
_____
2. What is a "whole child" approach to schooling?
_____
3. What was the result of David Aderhold's letter?
_____
4. What is Aderhold's reform?
_____
5. What kind of issue has caught people's attention?
_____

Ⅱ. Main Details Comprehension

Each of the following statement contains information given in one of the paragraphs. Identify the paragraph from which the information is derived. You may choose a paragraph more than once. Each paragraph is marked with a letter. Answer the questions by marking the corresponding letter in the blanks.

____1. Aderhold is limiting the extra classes that students are allowed to take off campus.

____2. White and Asian-American parents responded differently to Aderhold's appeal.

____3. Suicidal thoughts have appeared in some students' writings.

Unit 1 Diversity and Inclusion   9

____4. Aderhold's reform of the advanced mathematics program will affect Asian-American students most.

____5. Aderhold appealed for parents' support in promoting an all-round development of children, instead of focusing only on their academic performance.

____6. One Chinese-American parent thinks the competition in the district has gone too far.

____7. Immigrant parents believe that academic excellence will allow their children equal chances to succeed in the future.

____8. Many businessmen and professionals have moved to West Windsor and Plainsboro because of the public schools there.

____9. A number of students in Aderhold's school district were found to have stress-induced mental health problems.

____10. The tension between Asian-American and white families has increased in recent years.

Ⅲ. Translation

Translate the five following sentences into English, using the words or expressions given in brackets.

1. 健康的人较能应付压力。（cope with）

_____

2. 我相信我们每一个人都能为世界的未来做出贡献。（contributed to）

_____

3. 发言人强调说，这些措施并不等于全面禁止。（amount to）

_____

4. 他的费用与广播的实际成本相比是沧海一粟。（compared with）

_____

5. 有些学生觉得很难适应新的环境。（accommodate to）

_____

Part C

Grammar
基本句子类型（Basic Types of Sentences）

按照句子结构划分，句子可以分为3种类型：简单句、并列句和复合句。

一、简单句（Simple Sentence）

简单句只有一个主语（或并列主语）和一个谓语动词（或并列谓语动词）。英语简单句由于所用的主要动词（即系词、不及物动词和及物动词）不同，产生了不同的句子类型。在简单句中主语和谓语是句子的主干，是句子的核心。

按照动词的性质来划分，英语句子有5种基本句型（Basic Patterns）

1．主谓：主语＋不及物动词。例如：

I walked and laughed.

在此结构中有两个不及物动词 walked 和 laughed 充当谓语动词。

2．主谓宾：主语＋及物动词＋宾语。例如：

Agriculture needs water.

在此结构中，谓语动词具有实际意义，是主语产生的动作，但不能表达完整的意思，需要后面跟一个宾语，即动作的承受者，才能使意思完整。

3．主谓双宾：主语＋及物动词＋间接宾语＋直接宾语。例如：

I bought you a book.

在此结构中，谓语动词是 bought，you 是间接宾语，a book 是直接宾语。

4．主谓宾补：主语＋及物动词＋宾语＋宾语补语。例如：

I keep our room clean.

在此结构中，谓语动词是 keep，our room 是宾语，clean 是宾语补语。

5．主系表：主语＋系动词＋表语。例如：

This kind of food tastes delicious.

在此结构中，this kind of food 是主语，taste 是系动词，delicious 是表语。

系动词包含：be 动词（am，is，are），表示感官（feel，look，smell，sound，taste），表示似乎（seem，appear），表示变化（get，become，turn，grow，make，come，go，fall，run），表示保持（remain，keep，stay，continue，stand，rest，lie，hold）。

有一种"there＋be＋主语＋状语"的特殊句型表示存在。或"有…"。句中的 be 可换成 live，exist，appear 等表示存在、出现、消失等意思的不及物动词。引导词 there 可换成 here 或表地点、方向的副词或介词短语等。例如：

There is a coffee shop around the corner.

街角处有一个咖啡厅。

Here is a message for you.

有你一条消息。

二、并列句（Compound Sentence）

并列句是由两个或两个以上并列而又相互独立的简单句连接起来的句子。并列句的结构为：简单句＋并列连词＋简单句，或者中间有"；"连接。

1．表示连接

常用的连接词有：and（和），not only...but also（不仅…而且），neither...nor（既不…也不），so（所以，因此），therefore（因此，所以）。例如：

Right now it's the summer vacation, and I'm helping my dad on the farm.

现在是暑假，我在农场帮爸爸干活。

She's not only a great dramatic actress but she's also very funny.

她不仅是一位伟大的女戏剧演员，而且也很幽默。

2．表示转折

常用的连接词有：but（但是），still（仍然），yet（然而），however（然而），while（而，然而）whereas（反过来）。例如：

Unit 1   Diversity and Inclusion

I'd asked everybody but only two people came.
每个人我都请了，却只来了两个人。

I sat on the chair to unwrap the package while he stood behind me.
我坐在椅子上打开包裹，当时他就站在我身后。

3．表示选择

常用的连接词有：or（或者），or else（否则），either...or（不是…就是），otherwise（否则）。例如：

You are either a total genius or else you must be totally crazy.
你要么是个纯粹的天才，要不然你准是完全疯了。

I'm lucky that I'm interested in school work, otherwise I'd go mad.
我很庆幸自己对学习怀有兴趣，不然我会疯掉的。

4．表示因果

常用的连接词有：for（为了，因为），so（因此，所以）。例如：

She was confused，for she didn't know French.
她很疑惑，因为她不懂法语。

It's time of year for the rice harvest, so every day I work from dawn until dark.
这是一年收割稻谷的时期，因此我每天都从早工作到晚。

易错提醒：because 和 so 不能连用。例如：

I was hungry，so I made a sandwich. 我饿了，所以做了一个三明治。
＝Because I was hungry, I made a sandwich. 因为我饿了，所以做了一个三明治。

三、复合句（Complex Sentence）

从属复合句由一个主句和一个或一个以上的从句构成。"简单句＋引导词＋简单句"结构，其中简单句是主句，"引导词＋简单句"是从句。根据从句在句子中所充当的成分，可以分为主语从句、表语从句、状语从句、宾语从句、定语从句、同位语从句 6 类。例如：

Parents shouldn't give their children whatever they want.
父母不应该给孩子任何他们想要的东西。

I worked for a foreign company when I was in Shanghai.
我在上海时为一家外企工作。

I like the book which your mother gave you.
我喜欢你妈妈给你的那本书。

Exercises

Choose the best answer to the following sentences.

1. _____ does he do his work well, _____ he helps others with their work.
   A. Not only; but also   B. Neither; nor   C. Either; or   D. Both; and

2. There _____ two new beds and an old desk in the room.
   A. is   B. are   C. have   D. has

3. There _____ a clock and two pictures on the wall.

  A. is   B. are   C. has   D. have

4. I could speak _____ French _____ Chinese, but luckily, I could talk with them in English.

  A. both; and   B. neither; nor   C. either; or   D. not only; but also

5. Jack often uses his computer at home, _____ he never plays games on it.

  A. and   B. but   C. so   D. or

6. - Alice, how do your parents like pop music?

  - _____ my dad _____ my mom likes it. But they both prefer Beijing Opera.

  A. Either; or   B. Neither; nor   C. Not only; but also   D. Both; and

7. -Hurry up, _____ you will be late for school.

  - OK. I'm coming.

  A. and   B. but   C. or   D. so

8. -Mike, what were your parents doing at 8:00 last night?

  -My mother was reading _____ my father was playing computer games.

  A. while   B. when   C. unless   D. as long as

9. Getting a right job can be difficult _____ the students _____ prepared to deal with the job interview.

  A. if; won't   B. unless; will   C. unless; are   D. if; are

10. Li Fang is very busy, _____ she's always helping others with their lessons.

  A. but   B. although   C. so   D. for

11. Hold your dream, _____ you might regret some day.

  A. and   B. or   C. but   D. so

12. _____ Li Ping _____ Wu Fang _____ League members.

  A. Neither; nor; are   B. Either; nor; is   C. Both; and; are   D. Neither; or; is

13. She is American, _____ she knows little about American history.

  A. so   B. yet   C. and   D. therefore

14. There is plenty of rain in the south _____ there is little in the north.

  A. while   B. as   C. when   D. so

15. Peter can play the piano, _____ he can't play it well.

  A. and   B. but   C. or   D. so

16. You'd better wake up Tom at 6:30 _____ he will be late for the match.

  A. if   B. or   C. and   D. but

17. He must have thought Jane was worth it _____ he wouldn't have wasted time on her, I suppose.

  A. or   B. and   C. so   D. but

18. You told me it was so, _____ as a matter of fact it is not so.

  A. or   B. whereas   C. so   D. but

19. He was a businessman, and _____ he always has an eye out for any opportunity to make money.

    A. or   B. whereas   C. otherwise   D. therefore

20. The two companies decided to work together _____ they had common interest.

    A. because   B. unless   C. but   D. or

Workshop
Cultural Introduction

Ⅰ. Appreciation of Proverbs

1．物以类聚，人以群分。《战国策》

Birds of a feather gather together.

释义：比喻同类的东西常聚在一起，志同道合的人相聚成群，反之就分开。

2．远亲不如近邻。《东堂老》

Near friend is better than a far-dwelling kinsman.

释义：指遇有急难，远道的亲戚不如近旁的邻居那样能及时帮助。

3．四海之内皆兄弟。《英烈传》

All men are brothers.

释义：世界各国的人民都像兄弟一样。

4．合即立，分即垮。

United we stand, divided we fall.

5．与众同乐，其乐更乐。

Joys shared with others are more enjoyed.

Ⅱ. Appreciation of Chinese poetry

Calming the Waves
Su Shi

On the 7th day of the 3rd month, we were caught in rain on our way to the Sandy Lake. The umbrellas had gone ahead, my companions were quite downhearted, but I took no notice. It soon cleared, and I wrote this.

    Listen not to the rain beating against the trees.
    Why don't you slowly walk and chant at ease?
    Better than saddled horse I like sandals and cane.
    O I would fain
    Spend a straw-cloaked life in mist and rain.
    Drunken, I'm sobered by vernal wind shrill

And rather chill.
In front I see the slanting sun atop the hill;
Turning my head, I see the dreary beaten track.
Let me go back!
Impervious to wind, rain or shine, I'll have my will.

定风波·莫听穿林打叶声
苏轼

三月七日沙湖道中遇雨。雨具先去，同行皆狼狈，余独不觉。已而遂晴，故作此。

莫听穿林打叶声，何妨吟啸且徐行。
竹杖芒鞋轻胜马，谁怕？一蓑烟雨任平生。
料峭春风吹酒醒，微冷，山头斜照却相迎。
回首向来萧瑟处，归去，也无风雨也无晴。

Ⅲ. Cultural Tips

竹子与中国诗歌书画和园林艺术有源远流长的关系，从竹子与人们生活的息息相关中不难看出，中国不愧被誉为"竹子文明的国度"。没有哪一种植物能够像竹子般对人类的文明产生如此深远的影响，甚至可以称为竹文化。而诸如"竹报平安""衰丝豪竹""青梅竹马""日上三竿"一类的成语也都包含着与竹子有关的有趣典故。对于"芒鞋竹杖"来说，芒鞋为一种草鞋；竹杖指手杖，比喻随身使用的东西。宋朝陈师道在《绝句四首》写道："芒鞋竹杖最关身。"自古多少文人雅士以布衣芒鞋，云游三山五岳四海，潇洒自在如神仙。苏东坡词"竹杖芒鞋轻胜马，谁怕一蓑烟雨任平生"，表达了诗人高尚的品格、自在的身影。事实上，那广大的士农工商、三教九流，多着芒鞋布衣，他们行走在外，暑日寒冰，雨晴烟晚，没有骏马、没有轺车、"竹杖芒鞋轻胜马"，安步当车，在人生的旅途中，是那么坚毅、那么安然自在。

Unit 2 Nature

The Growth of Forest Area in Rich Countries

Forests in countries like Brazil and the Congo get a lot of attention from environmentalists, and it is easy to see why South America and sub-Saharan Africa are experiencing deforestation on an enormous scale: every year almost 5 million hectares are lost. But forests are also changing in rich Western countries. They are growing larger, both in the sense that they occupy more land and that the trees in them are bigger. What is going on?

Forests are spreading in almost all Western countries, with the fastest growth in places that historically had rather few trees. In 1990, 28% of Spain was forested; now the proportion is 37%. In both Greece and Italy, the growth was from 26% to 32% over the same period. Forests are gradually taking more land in America and Australia. Perhaps most astonishing is the trend in Ireland. Roughly 1% of that country was forested when it became independent in 1922. Now forests cover 11% of the land, and the government wants to push the proportion to 18% by the 2040s.

Two things are fertilizing this growth. The first is the abandonment of farmland, especially in high, dry places where nothing grows terribly well. When farmers give up trying to earn a living from farming or herding, trees simply move in. The second is government policy and subsidy. Throughout history, governments have protected and promoted forests for diverse reasons, ranging from the need for wooden warships to a desire to promote suburban house-building. Nowadays forests are increasingly welcome because they suck in carbon pollution from the air. The justifications change, the desire for more trees remains constant.

The greening of the West does not delight everyone. Farmers complain that land is being taken out of use by generously subsidised tree plantations. Parts of Spain and Portugal suffer from terrible forest fires. Others simply dislike the appearance of forests planted in neat rows. They will have to get used to the trees, however. The growth of Western forests seems almost as unstoppable as deforestation elsewhere.

environmentalist /ɪnˌvaɪrən'mentəlɪst/ n. 环境保护主义者
deforestation /ˌdiːˌfɒrɪ'steɪʃn/ n. 毁林，滥伐森林

hectare/'hekteə(r)/n. 公顷（土地丈量单位）
occupy/'ɒkjupaɪ/v. 使用，居住；占据
proportion/prə'pɔːʃ(ə)n/n. 部分，份额，比例
astonishing/ə'stɒnɪʃɪŋ/adj. 惊人的，令人惊讶的
independent/ˌɪndɪ'pendənt/adj. 自治的，独立的；自立的
fertilize/'fɜːtəlaɪz/vt. 使肥沃
abandonment/ə'bændənmənt/n. 抛弃；放纵
herding/hɜːrdɪŋ/n. 集中畜群；畜牧
subsidy/'sʌbsədi/n. 补贴，津贴
warship/'wɔːʃɪp/n. 战船，军舰
carbon/'kɑːbən/adj. 碳的，碳处理的
justification/ˌdʒʌstɪfɪ'keɪʃ(ə)n/n. 正当理由，合理解释
delight/dɪ'laɪt/v. 使高兴，以…为乐
generously/'dʒenərəsli/adv. 慷慨地；宽大地
range from…to 从…到…变动
suck in 吸收；使卷入
suffer from 忍受，遭受

Exercises

I. Comprehension of the Text

There are 5 questions in this section. For each of them there are four choices marked A, B, C and D. You should choose the best answer for each question.

1. What is catching environmentalists' attention nowadays?
   A. Rich countries are stripping poor ones of their resources.
   B. Forests are fast shrinking in many developing countries.
   C. Forests are eating away the fertile farmland worldwide.
   D. Rich countries are doing little to address deforestation.
2. Which countries have the fastest forest growth?
   A. Those that have newly achieved independence.
   B. Those that have the greatest demand for timber.
   C. Those that used to have the lowest forest coverage.
   D. Those that provide enormous government subsidies.
3. What has encouraged forest growth historically?
   A. The government's advocacy.
   B. The use of wood for fuel.
   C. The favorable climate.
   D. The green movement.

4. What accounts for our increasing desire for forests?
   A. Their unique scenic beauty.
   B. Their use as fruit plantations.
   C. Their capability of improving air quality.
   D. Their stable supply of building materials.
5. What does the author conclude about the prospects of forestation?
   A. Deserts in sub-Saharan Africa will diminish gradually.
   B. It will play a more and more important role in people's lives.
   C. Forest destruction in the developing world will quickly slow down.
   D. Developed and developing countries are moving in opposite directions.

II. Languages Focus

A. *Match the following words in left with their explanations in right.*

1. deforestation   a. a unit of surface area equal to 100 ares
2. hectare   b. the act of giving something up
3. generously   c. the state of being clear of trees
4. astonishing   d. free from external control and constraint
5. proportion   e. a feeling of extreme pleasure or satisfaction
6. justification   f. surprising greatly
7. delight   g. in a generous manner
8. independent   h. a statement in explanation of some action or belief
9. abandonment   i. a group of wild mammals of one species that remain together
10. herding   j. the quotient obtained when the magnitude of a part is divided by the magnitude of the whole

B. *Fill in the blanks with the words or expressions given below. Change the form where necessary.*

| herding | proportion | deforestation | astonishing | generously |
| delight | justification | abandonment | independent | hectare |

1. Rich countries are doing little to address _____.
2. Constant rain forced the _____ of the next day's competitions.
3. Even sheep are no longer big business: farmers now favor dairy _____.
4. The head is out of _____ with the body.
5. This news will _____ his fans all over the world.
6. All I can say in _____ of her actions is that she was under a lot of pressure at work.
7. Language is the most _____ behavior in the animal kingdom.
8. We aim to help the less able in society to lead an _____ life.
9. It was the people with the least money who gave most _____.

10. Since 2000, yields per _____ have risen by nearly two-thirds.

Ⅲ. Translation

Translate the following sentences into Chinese.

1. Forests are spreading in almost all Western countries, with the fastest growth in places that historically had rather few trees.
_____
_____

2. South America and sub-Saharan Africa are experiencing deforestation on an enormous scale: every year almost 5 million hectares are lost.
_____
_____

3. The growth of Western forests seems almost as unstoppable as deforestation elsewhere.
_____

4. Throughout history, governments have protected and promoted forests for diverse reasons, ranging from the need for wooden warships to a desire to promote suburban house-building.
_____
_____

5. Nowadays forests are increasingly welcome because they suck in carbon pollution from the air.
_____

Ⅳ. Discussion

Forest is the ecological barrier of nature and the cradle of human survival and reproduction. To protect the forest is to protect the human living environment. Can you give some suggestions to protect the forest?

The Quiet Heroism of Mail Delivery

A) On Wednesday, a polar wind brought bitter cold to the Midwest. Overnight, Chicago reached a low of 21 degrees Fahrenheit below zero, making it slightly colder than Antarctica, Alaska, and the North Pole Wind chills were 64 degrees below zero in Park Rapids, Minnesota and 45 degrees below zero in Buffalo, North Dakota, according to the National Weather Service. Schools, restaurants, and businesses closed, and more than 1,000 flights were canceled.

B) Even the United States Postal Service (USPS) suspended mail delivery. "Due to this arctic outbreak and concerns for the safety of USPS employees," USPS announced Wednesday morning, "the Postal Service is suspending delivery Jan. 30 in some 3-digit ZIP Code locations." Twelve regions were listed as unsafe on Wednesday, on Thursday, eight remained.

C) As global surface temperatures increase, so does the likelihood of extreme weather. In 2018 alone, wildfires, volcanic, eruptions, hurricanes, mudslides, and other natural disasters cost at least $49 billion in the United States. As my colleague Vann Newkirk reported, Puerto Rico is still confronting economic and structural destruction and resource scarcity from 2017's Hurricane Maria. Natural disasters can wreck a community's infrastructure, disrupting systems for months or years. Some services, however, remind us that life will eventually return, in some form, to normal.

D) Days after the deadly 2017 wildfires in Santa Rosa, California, a drone caught footage of a USPS worker, Trevor Smith, driving through burned homes in that familiar white van, collecting mail in an affected area. The video is striking: The operation is familiar, but the scene looks like the end of the world. According to Rae Ann Haight, the program manager for the national-preparedness office at USPS, Smith was fulfilling a request made by some of the home owners to pick up any mail that was left untouched. For Smith, this was just another day on the job. "I followed my route like I normally do," Smith told a reporter. "As I came across a box that was up but with no house, I checked, and there was mail — outgoing mail — in it. And so we picked those up and carried on."

E) USPS has sophisticated emergency plans for natural disasters. Across the country, 285 emergency management teams are devoted to crisis control. These teams are trained annually using a framework known as the three Ps: people, property, product. After mail service stops due to weather, the agency's top priority is ensuring that employees are safe. Then it evaluates the health of infrastructure, such as the roads that mail carriers drive on. Finally, it decides when and how to re-open operations. If the destruction is extreme, mail addressed to the area will get sent elsewhere. In response to Hurricane Katrina in 2005, USPS redirected incoming New Orleans mail to existing mail facilities in Houston. Mail that was already processed in New Orleans facilities was moved to an upper floor so it would be protected from water damage.

F) As soon as it's safe enough to be outside, couriers start distributing accumulated mail on the still-accessible routes. USPS urges those without standing addresses to file change-of-address forms with their new location. After Hurricane Katrina hit in 2005, mail facilities were set up in dozens of locations across the country in the two weeks that USPS was unable to provide street delivery.

G) Every day, USPS processes, on average, 493.4 million pieces of mail—anything from postcards to Social Security checks to medicine. Spokespeople from both USPS and UPS told me all mail is important. But some mail can be extremely sensitive and timely. According to data released in January 2017, 56 percent of bills are paid online, which means that just under half of payments still rely on delivery services to be completed.

H) It can be hard to identify which parcels are carrying crucial items such as Social Security checks, but USPS and UPS try their best to prioritize sensitive material. They will coordinate with the Social Security Administration to make sure that Social Security checks reach the right people in a timely fashion. After Hurricane Florence and Hurricane Michael last fall, USPS worked with state and local election boards to make sure that absentee ballots were available and received or time.

I) Mail companies are logistics companies, which puts them in a special position to help when disaster strikes. In a 2011 USPS case study, the agency emphasized its massive infrastructure as a "unique federal asset" to be called upon in a disaster or terrorist attack. "I think we're unique as a federal agency," USPS official Mike Swigart told me, "Because we're in literally every community in this country…We're obligated to deliver to that point on a daily basis."

J) Private courier companies, which have more dollars to spend, use their expertise in logistics to help revitalize damaged areas after a disaster. For more than a decade, FedEx has supported the American Red Cross in its effort to get emergency supplies to areas affected by disasters, both domestically and internationally. In 2012, the company distributed more than 1,200 MedPacks to Medical Reserve Corps groups in California. They also donated space for 3.1 million pounds of charitable shipping globally. Last October, the company pledged $1 million in cash and transportation support for Hurricanes Florence and Michael. UPS's charitable arm, the UPS Foundation, uses the company's logistics to help disaster-struck areas rebuild. "We realize that as a company with people, trucks, warehouses, we needed to play a larger role," said Eduardo Martinez, the president of the UPS Foundation. The company employs its trucks and planes to deliver food, medicine, and water. The day before I spoke to Martinez in November, he had been touring the damage from Hurricane Michael in Florida with the American Red Cross. "We have an obligation to make sure our communities are thriving," he said.

K) Rebuilding can take a long time, and even then, impressions of the disaster may still remain. Returning to a normal life can be difficult, but some small routines mail delivery being one of them may help residents remember that their communities are still their communities. "When they see that carrier back out on the street," Swigart said, "that's the first sign to them that life is starting to return to normal."

Words & Expressions

Antarctica/æn'tɑ:ktɪkə/*n.* 南极洲
Fahrenheit/'færənhaɪt/*n.* 华氏温度计；华氏温标
suspend/sə'spend/*v.* 暂停，中止
arctic/'ɑ:ktɪk/*adj.* 北极的；严寒的

Unit 2　Nature 21

eruption/ɪˈrʌpʃ(ə)n/*n.* 喷发；（战争、怒气等的）爆发
mudslide/ˈmʌdslaɪd/*n.* 塌方；山崩；
scarcity/ˈskeəsəti/*n.* 不足，缺乏
infrastructure/ˈɪnfrəstrʌktʃə(r)/*n.* 基础设施，基础建设
disrupt/dɪsˈrʌpt/*v.* 中断，扰乱
preparedness/prɪˈpeərɪdnəs/*n.* 有准备；做好准备
drone/drəʊn/*n.* 无人驾驶飞机
footage/ˈfʊtɪdʒ/*n.* 连续镜头
sophisticated/səˈfɪstɪkeɪtɪd/*adj.* 见多识广的；先进精密的
annually/ˈænjuəli/*adv.* 每年，一年一次地
redirected/ˌriːdəˈrektɪd/*v.* 重新传入，重新寄送
couriers/ˈkʊriəz/*n.* 邮递员
accessible/əkˈsesəb(ə)l/*adj.* 可到达的；可使用的
absentee/ˌæbsənˈtiː/*n.* 缺席者
logistics/ləˈdʒɪstɪks/*n.* 后勤，组织工作；物流
federal/ˈfedərəl/*adj.* 联邦（制）的
obligated/ˈɒblɪɡeɪtɪd/*adj.* 有义务的
revitalize/ˌriːˈvaɪtəlaɪz/*v.* 使恢复生机，使复兴
domestically/dəˈmestɪkli/*adv.* 国内地；家庭式地
charitable/ˈtʃærətəbl/*adj.* 慈善的；仁慈的
pledged/pledʒd/*v.* 保证；抵押
concerns for　为…担心，关心
in some form　以某种形式
devote to　将…奉献给；把…专用于
in response to　响应；回答
coordinate with　使协调；配合

Notes

1. Hurricane Maria
飓风"玛利亚"。2017 年 9 月 17 日，"玛利亚"由热带风暴升级为飓风。19 日，"玛利亚"已经升级为 5 级飓风，风速为每小时 160 千米。19 日晚，风速达到每小时 249 千米。沿着此前飓风"艾尔玛"的路径推进，再度横扫加勒比海。同一时间，热带风暴"李"（Lee）在远离陆地的大西洋上形成。此外，飓风"荷西"（Jose）在美国东岸外海向北推进。

2. the United States Postal Service
美国邮政服务公司，美国国有运递企业。前身是 1775 年成立的美国邮政部，1971 年改称现名。公司是一家独立的联邦政府代理机构，实行董事会管理制度。业务涵盖邮件投递、包裹传送、货物运输、邮政服务等，并可提供网上服务。其总部设在华盛顿。

3. American Red Cross

美国红十字会，是全球最大的救援组织之一，但它只是全球灾民救援和应急防备体系的一个分支。美国红十字会创建于 1881 年，美国国会在 1990 年正式承认这一组织，并给它制定了正式章程。

Exercises

I. Comprehension of the Text

Read the text and answer the following questions. Write the answers on the lines.

1. How much money did natural disasters cost the U.S. in 2018?
_____

2. What kind of damage can natural disasters cause?
_____

3. What will be the agency's top priority after mail service stops?
_____

4. What donations did FedEx make?
_____

5. What is the 3p framework?
_____

II. Main Details Comprehension

Each of the following statement contains information given in one of the paragraphs. Identify the paragraph from which the information is derived. You may choose a paragraph more than once. Each paragraph is marked with a letter. Answer the questions by marking the corresponding letter in the blanks.

_____1. The United States Postal Service has a system to ensure its employees' safety.

_____2. One official says USPS is unique in that it has more direct reach to communities compared with other federal agencies.

_____3. Natural disasters can have a long-lasting impact on community life.

_____4. Mail delivery service is still responsible for the completion of almost half of payments.

_____5. The sight of a mailman on the street is a reassuring sign of life becoming normal again.

_____6. After Hurricane Katrina interrupted routine delivery, temporary mail service points were set up.

_____7. Postal service in some regions in the U.S. was suspended due to extreme cold weather.

Unit 2　Nature

_____8. Private postal companies also support disaster relief efforts by distributing urgent supplies

_____9. A dedicated USPS employee was on the job carrying out duties in spite of extreme conditions.

_____10. Postal services work hard to identify items that require priority treatment.

Ⅲ. Translation

Translate the five following sentences into English, using the words or expressions given in brackets.

1. 与财务部门合作，完成进口税费的缴纳工作。（coordinate with）

_____

2. 然而她对未来流露出的希望和担心，也与一般人并无二致。（concern for）

_____

3. 我们资源上的最大限制是我们可以投入某件事情上的时间。（devote to）

_____

4. 这只是一个概念，但是现在这种技术确实以某种形式存在。（in some form）

_____

5. 这种产品是为了满足顾客的需要而开发的。（in response to）

_____

Grammar
一致关系（Agreement）

一致关系就是在英语句子中各个成分之间必须在人称、性、数等方面保持一定的语法关系。一致关系必须遵循3个原则，即语法一致原则、意义一致原则和就近一致原则。

一、语法一致原则

语法一致原则指谓语动词与其主语在人称和数方面要保持一致。一般情况下，主语为单数形式时，谓语动词也要用单数形式；主语为复数时，谓语动词也用复数形式。

例如：The children were in the classroom three hours ago.

当主语有其他情况时，判断谓语动词用单数还是复数的方法有以下几种：

（1）由 and 或 both...and...连接两个名词作主语时，一般谓语动词用复数形式；但是，由 and 连接的并列主语如果指的是同一个人、同一事物或同一概念，谓语动词则用单数形式。注意，这时后面可数名词没有冠词。例如：

The singer and the dancer are beautiful.

The singer and dancer is beautiful. 这个既是歌手也是舞者的人很漂亮。

（2）由 and 连接并列主语，且每一个并列主语都被 each，every 或 no 修饰时，谓语动词用单数形式。例如：

Every boy and every girl likes to go swimming.

（3）就前原则。当句子的主语后面带有 with, together with, along with, rather than, as much as, no less than, in addition to, except, but, as well as, including 等修饰语时，谓语动词的数要与前面的名词保持一致。例如：

John, together with his wife and two daughters, has just left and will return at four o'clock.

（4）由代词 each, everyone, no one, either, neither, another, the other 作主语，以及由 something, any one, every body, nothing 等复合不定代词作主语时，谓语动词要用单数形式。例如：

Nothing but trees was to be seen.

Neither of them wants to come.

（5）由动词不定式、动名词或从句作主语时，谓语动词用单数形式。例如：

Eating more fruits is good for our health.

（6）只有复数形式的名词作主语时，谓语动词应用复数形式，如 pants, shoes, chopsticks, glasses 等，但如果主语由 kind of, series of, pair of, type of, sort of＋名词作主语时，谓语动词要和 kind, pair 等词保持一致，与 of 之后的名词或代词无关。例如：

A pair of shoes was in the box.

Some new forms of art were discussed at the meeting.

（7）A number of＋名词复数做主语时，谓语动词用复数，意为"一群，许多"。The number of＋名词复数作主语时，谓语动词用单数，意为"…数量"。A little, much, a great deal of, a large amount of 修饰不可数名词，其短语作主语时，谓语动词用单数。例如：

A number of students are playing football on the playground.

The number of teachers in our school is 26.

A large amount of damage was done in a very short time.

（8）A lot of, lots of, "plenty of＋名词" "分数/百分数＋of＋名词" 作主语时，谓语动词的单复数取决于名词。如果所修饰的名词是不可数名词，则谓语动词用单数。如所修饰的名词是可数名词复数，则谓语动词用复数。例如：

Lots of people have been to the great wall.

About three fourths of the earth is covered with water.

二、意义一致原则

意义一致原则指谓语动词的数必须和主语的意义一致，即谓语动词的单复数主要看主语所表达的概念。

（1）集体名词 class, family, group 等作主语时，如果指一个不可分割的整体时，谓语动词用单数；如果强调整体中的每一个成员，则谓语动词用复数。例如：

My family is a happy one and my family are watching TV now.

（2）集体名词 people, police 形单意复，作主语时，谓语动词用复数；而 news, physics, maths, works（工厂）等形复意单，作主语时，谓语动词用单数（policeman 作主语时，指个体，谓语动词用单数）。例如：

The people there are very friendly.
Physics is my favorite subject.

（3）表示度量、时间、价格等的名词复数或词组作主语时，看作一个整体，谓语动词用单数形式。例如：
Eight dollars is enough.
Thirty minutes is short.

（4）从句作主语，看作一个整体，谓语动词用单数形式。例如：
What he said is important for us.

（5）"the＋形容词"表示一类人，作主语时，谓语动词用复数。例如：
The old are more likely to catch cold than the young.

（6）乘法算式或加法算式作主语，谓语动词可以用单数也可以用复数；但除法算式或减法算式作主语，谓语动词必须用单数。例如：
Four times five is（或 are）twenty.
Six divided by two is three.

（7）主句中有 all，half，most，the rest 等修饰时，都要根据其后面的名词来判断单复数。例如：
The rest of the books are on the desk.
The rest of the water is on the table.

三、就近一致原则

有时候谓语动词的形式与主语并不一致，却与邻近它的名词一致，这种原则就叫就近一致原则。

（1）在 There be 句型中，be 动词的形式由其后最近的名词决定。例如：
There is a girl and several boys in the reading room.
There are three boys and a girl in the reading room.

（2）Or，either…or…，neither…nor…，not only…but also…等连接的并列成分作主语时，谓语动词的形式由离它最近的名词决定。例如：
Not only you but also she likes swimming.

Exercises

Choose the best answer to the following sentences.

1. Library with three thousand books _____ to the nation as a gift.
   A. is offered　　　B. has offered　　　C. are offered　　　D. have offered

2. -What will Lucy do this Sunday?
   -She as well as her family _____ go camping by a small lake.
   A. am going to　　　B. is going to　　　C. are going to　　　D. were going to

3. Professor Smith, along with his assistants, _____ on the project day and night to meet the deadline.
   A. work　　　B. working　　　C. is working　　　D. are working

4. -How soon can you finish this job?

   -Two days _____ enough for me to finish the work.

   A. isn't　　　　B. aren't　　　　C. is　　　　D. are

5. Both Li Lei and Han Meimei _____ interested in the TV program *the Voice of China*.

   A. are　　　　B. am　　　　C. was　　　　D. is

6. He as well as his parents _____ rock music. That _____ really surprising!

   A. likes; sound　　　B. like; sounds　　　C. like; sound　　　D. likes; sounds

7. Nobody but Jane _____ the secret.

   A. know　　　　B. knows　　　　C. have known　　　　D. is known

8. My friends and I are interested in drawing, but none of us _____ good at it.

   A. do　　　　B. does　　　　C. is　　　　D. has

9. Nowadays, each of the students _____ a new dictionary in the countryside.

   A. has　　　　B. had　　　　C. have　　　　D. have had

10. -The number of the students in our class _____ fifty-six.

    -How many of _____ are girls?

    A. is; them　　　B. are; them　　　C. is; they　　　D. are; they

11. Nine plus three _____ twelve.

    A. are making　　　B. is making　　　C. make　　　D. makes

12. One and a half bananas _____ on the table.

    A. are left　　　B. is left　　　C. have left　　　D. has left

13. About 60 percent of the students _____ from the south, the rest of them _____ from the north and foreign countries.

    A. are; is　　　B. are; are　　　C. is; are　　　D. is; is

14. Everybody except Mike and Linda _____ there when the meeting began.

    A. is　　　　B. are　　　　C. was　　　　D. were

15. Not only Jim but also my parents and I _____ a few places of interest since we came to China.

    A. has visited　　　B. will visit　　　C. visited　　　D. have visited

16. Neither my sister nor I _____ been to America before.

    A. have ever　　　B. have never　　　C. has ever　　　D. has never

17. Two days _____ enough for me to finish the work. I need a third day.

    A. isn't　　　　B. is　　　　C. aren't　　　　D. are

18. Three-fourth of the buildings _____ in the earthquake.

    A. was destroyed　　　B. is destroyed　　　C. were destroyed　　　D. have destroyed

19. Not only Tom but also Alice and Mary _____ busy.

    A. is　　　　B. was　　　　C. are　　　　D. has

20. Many species of animals which once lived on the earth _____ no longer in existence.

    A. is　　　　B. are　　　　C. was　　　　D. were

Workshop
Cultural Introduction

Ⅰ. Nature in Poetry

Lake Dongting Viewed from Afar
Liu Yuxi

The autumn moon dissolves in soft light of the lake,
unruffled Surface like an unpolished mirror bright.
Afar, the isle amid water clear without a break,
looks like a spiral shell in a plate silver-white.

望洞庭
刘禹锡

湖光秋月两相和，潭面无风镜未磨。
遥望洞庭山水翠，白银盘里一青螺。

Ⅱ. Translate the following paragraph into English

洞庭湖位于湖南省东北部，面积很大，但湖水很浅。洞庭湖是长江的蓄洪池，湖的大小很大程度上取决于季节变化。湖北和湖南两省因其与湖的相对位置而得名，湖北意为"湖的北边"，而湖南则为"湖的南边"。洞庭湖作为龙舟赛的发源地，在中国文化中享有盛名。据说龙舟赛始于洞庭湖东岸。为的是搜寻楚国爱国诗人屈原的遗体。龙舟赛与洞庭湖及周边的美景，每年都吸引着成千上万来自全国和世界各地的游客。

Unit 3 Obesity

Obesity and Disease

With obesity now affecting 29% of the population in England, and expected to rise to 35% by 2030, should we now recognize it as a disease? Obesity, in which excess body fat has accumulated to such an extent that health may be adversely affected, meets the dictionary definition of disease, argues Professor John Wilding. He points out that more than 200 genes influence weight. "Thus body weight is strongly influenced by biology — it is not an individual's fault if they develop obesity." Yet the widespread view is that obesity is self-induced and that it is entirely the individual's responsibility to do something about it. Recognizing obesity as a chronic disease with severe complications rather than a lifestyle choice "should help reduce the stigma and discrimination experienced by many people with obesity," he adds.

Professor Wilding disagrees that labelling a high proportion of the population as having a disease removes personal responsibility or may overwhelm health services, pointing out that other common diseases, such as high blood pressure and diabetes, require people to take action to manage their condition. He suggests that most people with obesity will eventually develop complications. "But unless we accept that obesity is a disease, we are not going to be able to tackle it," he concludes.

But Dr. Richard Pile, a physician with a special interest in diabetes, argues that adopting this approach "could actually result in worse outcomes for individuals and society." He believes that the dictionary definition of disease "is so vague that we can classify almost anything as a disease" and says the question is not whether we can, but whether we should, and to what end. If labelling obesity as a disease was harmless then it wouldn't really matter, he writes. But labelling obesity as a disease "risks reducing autonomy, disempowering and robbing people of the intrinsic（内在的）motivation that is such an important enabler of change." What's more, making obesity a disease "may not benefit patients, but it will benefit healthcare providers and the pharmaceutical industry when health insurance and clinical guidelines promote treatment with drugs and surgery," he warns.

excess/ɪk'ses/*adj.* 过多的，超额的；额外的

adversely/'ædvɜːsli/*adv.* 不利地，有害地
gene/dʒiːn/*n.* 基因
self-induced/ˌself ɪn'djuːst/*adj.* 自感应的；自诱导的
chronic/'krɒnɪk/*adj.* （疾病）慢性的
complication/ˌkɒmplɪ'keɪʃ(ə)n/*n.* 使复杂化的难题；并发症
stigma/'stɪɡmə/*n.* 耻辱；（病的）外在特征
discrimination/dɪˌskrɪmɪ'neɪʃn/*n.* 歧视，区别对待
labelling/'leɪblɪŋ/*n.* 标记，贴标签
diabetes/ˌdaɪə'biːtiːz/*n.* 糖尿病
tackle/'tæk(ə)l/*v.* 应付，解决
vague/veɪɡ/*adj.* 不明确的，不清楚的
autonomy/ɔː'tɒnəmi/*n.* 自治，自治权
disempower/ˌdɪsɪm'paʊə(r)/*vt.* 剥夺权力
intrinsic/ɪn'trɪnzɪk/*adj.* 内在的，固有的
enabler/ɪ'neɪblə(r)/*n.* 促成者，赋能者
pharmaceutical/ˌfɑːmə'suːtɪk(ə)l/*adj.* 制药的
clinical/'klɪnɪk(ə)l/*adj.* 诊所的；临床的
surgery/'sɜːdʒəri/*n.* 外科手术
recognize as 承认，认可
take action to 采取行动
to what end 要达到什么目的

Exercises

Ⅰ. Comprehension of the Text

There are 5 questions in this section. For each of them there are four choices marked A, B, C and D. You should choose the best answer for each question.

1. What does Professor John Wilding argue about obesity?

    A. Its impact on society is expected to rise.

    B. It is now too widespread to be neglected.

    C. It should be regarded as a genetic disease.

    D. Its dictionary definition should be updated.

2. What is the popular view of obesity?

    A. It is difficult to define.

    B. It is a modem disease.

    C. It has much to do with one's genes.

    D. It results from a lack of self-control.

3. Why are some people opposed to labelling obesity as a disease?
   A. Obese people would not feel responsible to take any action.
   B. Obese people would not be able to afford the medical costs.
   C. Obese people would be overwhelmed with anxiety.
   D. Obese people would be discriminated against.
4. What does Dr. Richard Pile think of the dictionary definition of disease?
   A. It is of no use in understanding obesity.
   B. It is too inclusive and thus lacks clarity.
   C. It helps little to solve patients' problems.
   D. It matters little to the debate over obesity.
5. What is Dr. Richard Pile's concern about classifying obesity as a disease?
   A. It may affect obese people's quality of life.
   B. It may accelerate the spread of obesity.
   C. It may cause a shortage of doctors.
   D. It may do little good to patients

II. Languages Focus

A. *Match the following words in left with their explanations in right.*

1. adversely   a. relating to a clinic
2. excess   b. a segment of DNA
3. intrinsic   c. in an adverse manner
4. tackle   d. belonging to a thing by its very nature
5. vague   e. a quantity much larger than is needed
6. clinical   f. unfair treatment of a person on the basis of prejudice
7. surgery   g. the act or process of complicating
8. gene   h. accept as a challenge
9. complication   i. not clearly understood or expressed
10. discrimination   j. the branch of medical science that treats disease or injury by operative procedures

B. *Fill in the blanks with the words or expressions given below. Change the form where necessary.*

| surgery | gene | discrimination | tackle | adversely |
| clinical | vague | complication | intrinsic | excess |

1. We must _____ the problem with sympathy and understanding.
2. She's had laser _____ on her eye.
3. The new drug is undergoing _____ trials.
4. The _____ is only part of the causation of illness.
5. Blindness is a common _____ of diabetes.

Unit 3　Obesity 　31

6. Eventually, he came face to face with _____ again.
7. She had only a _____ notion of what might happen.
8. Let me introduce a couple of technical terms: extrinsic value and _____ value.
9. He pleaded guilty to driving with _____ alcohol.
10. Price changes must not _____ affect the living standards of the people.

III. Translation

Translate the following sentences into Chinese.

1. Thus body weight is strongly influenced by biology-it is not an individual's fault if they develop obesity.

_____

2. Yet the widespread view is that obesity is self-induced and that it is entirely the individual's responsibility to do something about it.

_____

3. He suggests that most people with obesity will eventually develop complications.

_____

4. If labelling obesity as a disease was harmless then it wouldn't really matter, he writes.

_____

5. He points out that more than 200 genes influence weight.

_____

IV. Discussion

What factors do you think contribute to obesity? Write down your suggestions for obese people.

Is Breakfast Really the Most Important Meal of the Day?

A) Along with old classics like "carrots give you night vision" and "Santa doesn't bring toys to misbehaving children", one of the most well-worn phrases of tired parents everywhere is that breakfast is the most important meal of the day. Many of us grow up believing that skipping breakfast is a serious mistake, even if only two thirds of adults in the UK eat breakfast regularly, according to the British Dietetic Association, and around three-quarters of Americans.

B) "The body uses a lot of energy stores for growth and repair through the night," explains diet specialist Sarah Elder. "Eating a balanced breakfast helps to up our energy, as well as make up for protein and calcium used throughout the night." But there's widespread disagreement over whether breakfast should keep its top spot in the hierarchy of meals. There have been concerns around the sugar content of cereal and the food industry's involvement in pro-breakfast research — and even one claim from an academic that breakfast is "dangerous".

C) What's the reality? Is breakfast a necessary start to the day or a marketing tactic by cereal companies? The most researched aspect of breakfast (and breakfast-skipping) has been its links to obesity. Scientists have different theories as to why there's a relationship between the two. In one US study that analysed the health data of 50,000 people over seven years, researchers found that those who made breakfast the largest meal of the day were more likely to have a lower body mass index (BMI) than those who ate a large lunch or dinner. The researchers argued that breakfast helps reduce daily calorie intake and improve the quality of our diet — since breakfast foods are often higher in fibre and nutrients.

D) But as with any study of this kind, it was unclear if that was the cause — or if breakfast-skippers were just more likely to be overweight to begin with. To find out, researchers designed a study in which 52 obese women took part in a 12-week weight loss programme. All had the same number of calories over the day, but half had breakfast, while the other half did not. What they found was that it wasn't breakfast itself that caused the participants to lose weight: it was changing their normal routine.

E) If breakfast alone isn't a guarantee of weight loss, why is there a link between obesity and breakfast skipping? Alexandra Johnstone, professor of appetite research at the University of Aberdeen, argues that it may simply be because breakfast-skippers have been found to be less knowledgeable about nutrition and health. "There are a lot of studies on the relationship between breakfast eating and possible health outcomes, but this may be because those who eat breakfast choose to habitually have health-enhancing behaviours such as regular exercise and not smoking," she says.

F) A 2016 review of 10 studies looking into the relationship between breakfast and weight management concluded there is "limited evidence" supporting or refuting the argument that breakfast influences weight or food intake, and more evidence is required before breakfast recommendations can be used to help prevent obesity.

G) Researchers from the University of Surrey and University of Aberdeen are halfway through research looking into the mechanisms behind how the time we eat influences body weight. Early findings suggest that a bigger breakfast is beneficial to weight control. Breakfast has been found to affect more than just weight. Skipping breakfast has been associated with a 27% increased risk of heart disease, a 21% higher risk of type 2 diabetes in men, and a 20% higher risk of type 2 diabetes in women. One reason may be breakfast's nutritional value partly because cereal is fortified with vitamins. In one study on the breakfast habits of 1,600 young people in the UK, researchers found that the fibre and micronutrient intake was better in those who had breakfast regularly. There have been similar findings in Australia, Brazil, Canada and the US.

H) Breakfast is also associated with improved brain function, including concentration and language use. A review of 54 studies found that eating breakfast can improve memory, though the effects on other brain functions were inconclusive. However, one of the review's researchers, Mary Beth Spitznagel, says there is "reasonable" evidence breakfast does improve concentration — there just needs to be more research. "Looking at studies that tested concentration the number of studies showing a benefit was exactly the same as the number that found no benefit," she says. "And no studies found that eating breakfast was bad for concentration."

I) What's most important, some argue, is what we eat for breakfast. High-protein breakfasts have been found particularly effective in reducing the longing for food and consumption later in the day, according to research by the Australian Commonwealth Scientific and Industrial Research Organization. While cereal remains a firm favorite among breakfast consumers in the UK and US, a recent investigation into the sugar content of 'adult' breakfast cereals found that some cereals contain more than three-quarters of the recommended daily amount of free sugars in each portion, and sugar was the second or third highest ingredient in cereals."

J) But some research suggests if we're going to eat sugary foods, it's best to do it early. One study recruited 200 obese adults to take part in a 16-week-long diet, where half added dessert to their breakfast, and half didn't. Those who added dessert lost an average of 40 pounds more—however, the study was unable to show the long-term effects. A review of 54 studies found that there is no consensus yet on what type of breakfast is healthier, and conclude that the type of breakfast doesn't matter as much as simply eating something.

K) While there's no conclusive evidence on exactly what we should be eating and when, the consensus is that we should listen to our own bodies and eat when we're hungry. "Breakfast is most important for people who are hungry when they wake up," Johnston says. "Each body starts the day differently — and those individual differences need to be researched more closely," Spitznagel says. "A balanced breakfast is really helpful, but getting regular meals throughout the day is more important to leave blood sugar stable through the day, which helps control weight and hunger levels," says Elder. "Breakfast isn't the only meal we should be getting right."

Words & Expressions

skipping/skɪpɪŋ/*v.* 不做（应做的事等）
regularly /ˈreɡjələli/*adv.* 定期地，有规律地
calcium/ˈkælsiəm/*n.* （化学元素）钙
hierarchy/ˈhaɪərɑːki/*n.* 等级制度
cereal/ˈsɪəriəl/*n.* 谷类食物
tactic/ˈtæktɪk/*n.* 策略；战术
fibre/ˈfaɪbə(r)/*n.* （食物的）纤维素

nutrient/'nju:triənt/n. 养分，营养物
participant/pɑ:'tɪsɪpənt/n. 参加者
guarantee/ˌgærən'ti:/n. 保证，担保
appetite/'æpɪtaɪt/n. 食欲，胃口
habitually/hə'bɪtʃuəli/adv. 习惯地；日常地
enhancing/ɪn'hɑ:nsɪŋ/v. 提高，增强
refuting/rɪ'fju:tɪŋ/v. 反驳，驳斥
recommendation/ˌrekəmen'deɪʃn/n. 正式建议，提议
mechanism/'mekənɪzəm/n. 机械装置；途径，方法
fortified/'fɔ:tɪfaɪd/adj. 加强的；防御的；增加营养的
micronutrient/ˌmaɪkrəʊ'nju:trɪənt/n. ［生化］微量营养素
inconclusive/ˌɪnkən'klu:sɪv/adj. 不确定的，非决定性的
consumption/kən'sʌmpʃ(ə)n/n. 消费，消耗
portion/'pɔ:ʃ(ə)n/n. （某物的）一部分
ingredient/ɪn'gri:diənt/n. （食品的）成分，原料
recruit/rɪ'kru:t/v. 招聘，招收
consensus/kən'sensəs/n. 一致看法，共识

Notes

BMI
Body Mass Index（BMI）为身体质量指数。BMI 计算方法是体重（公斤）除以身高（米）的平方。BMI 在 18.5～23.9 为标准（standard）；在 24～27.9 为超重（overweight）；大于 28 为肥胖（obesity）。

Exercises

Ⅰ. Comprehension of the Text

Read the text and answer the following questions. Write the answers on the lines.
1. What does diet specialist Sarah Elder say?

_____

2. What did the American researchers find?

_____

3. Why is there a link between obesity and breakfast skipping?

_____

4. What's the mechanisms behind how the time we eat influences body weight?

_____

5. What should we pay attention to if we are going to eat sugary foods?
_____

II. Main Details Comprehension

Each of the following statement contains information given in one of the paragraphs. Identify the paragraph from which the information is derived. You may choose a paragraph more than once. Each paragraph is marked with a letter. Answer the questions by marking the corresponding letter in the blanks.

_____1. According to one professor, obesity is related to a lack of basic awareness of nutrition and health.

_____2. Some scientists claim that people should consume the right kind of food at breakfast.

_____3. Opinions differ as to whether breakfast is the most important meal of the day.

_____4. It has been found that not eating breakfast is related to the incidence of certain diseases in some countries.

_____5. Researchers found it was a change in eating habits rather than breakfast itself that induced weight loss.

_____6. To keep oneself healthy, eating breakfast is more important than choosing what to eat.

_____7. It is widely considered wrong not to eat breakfast.

_____8. More research is needed to prove that breakfast is related to weight loss or food intake.

_____9. People who prioritise breakfasts tend to have lower calorie but higher nutritional intake.

_____10. Many studies reveal that eating breakfast helps people memorise and concentrate.

III. Translation

Translate the five following sentences into English, using the words or expressions given in brackets.

1. 我过去一年不曾和这个项目有关联。(associate with)
_____

2. 这个婴儿的母亲和其他两个孩子一起从火里逃了出来。(along with)
_____

3. 除考试结果外，课程作业也要计入成绩。(as well as)
_____

4. 暴露在外国文化环境中有利于我们学习当地语言。(be beneficial for)
_____

5. 根据天气预报，晚一点天应该会转晴。(according to)

Grammar
名词性从句（the Noun Clause）

在句子中起名词作用的各种从句，统称为名词性从句。根据它们在句中所起的语法作用，这类从句又可分别称为主语从句、表语从句、宾语从句和同位语从句。名词性从句可以由连接词 that 引导，也可由关系代词 what 或 whatever 引导，还可以由连接代词 who，whom，whose，which 或连接副词 when，where，why，how，whether 引导，这些词除了 that 外，其余在句中均有一定的意义。由于名词性从句和名词作用相同。因此，可用作句子主语、表语、宾语和介词宾语。

一、名词性从句的引导词

1. 从属连词

That, whether, whether…or, if，连词只起连接作用，在从句中不作任何成分，不能省略。例如：

She don't know whether (=if) the data is accurate.

2. 连接代词

Who，whom，whose，which，what，whatever，whoever 等，这些词除了起连接作用外，还可以在从句中充当主语、宾语、定语、表语等语法成分。例如：

What he sold in his articles is anxiety.

3. 连接副词

When, where, why, how，这些词在句子中除了起连接作用外，还在从句中作状语。例如：

This is where we spent our summer vocation.

注意：Whether 引导的从句常可以与连词 or 或 or not 直接连用，而 if 一般不能。Whether 可引导所有名词从句，if 仅可引导宾语从句。当宾语从句提到句首时，只能用 whether 引导，不能用 if。Whether 可以引导带 to 的不定式，if 则不能。Whether 及其引导的成分可放于介词之后，作介词的宾语，但 if 不能。

二、主语从句（the Subject Clause）

主语从句，即在复合句中充当主语成分的句子。

（1）What，who，when，where，why，how 等位于句首。例如：

When I will get married is none of your business.

What I want to know is your opinion.

Whatever we do is to serve the people.

（2）"that＋完整句子"充当整个主语，在这种用法中，that 本身没有意义，但不能省略。例如：

That you didn't go to see the film *Dear John* was a pity.

That you are so indifferent bothers me.

That they survived the accident is a miracle.

（3）用连词 whether 引导的主语从句：whether 有含义（是否）/在句中不作成分/不可以省。

注意：引导主语从句，不能用 if，只能用 whether。例如：

Whether we will hold a party in the open air tomorrow depends on the weather.

Whether she is coming or not doesn't matter too much.

Whether it will do us harm or good remains to be seen.

（4）it 作形式主语：主语从句放在句首，句子常常显得比较笨重，因此常把它移至句子末尾而用 it 作形式上的主语。常见的有下面 4 种：

① It is＋名词＋从句。例如：

It is a fact that she has done her best.

② It is＋形容词＋从句。例如：

It's necessary that we should protect ourselves from the sun damage.

③ It is＋过去分词＋从句。例如：

It was reported that another shooting took place in New York.

④ It seems/happened/appears/doesn't matter/occurred＋从句。例如：

It happened that she was there too.

（5）主语从句不可位于句首的几种情况。

① "It is said/reported that..." 结构中的主语从句不可提前。

② "It happens that..." 结构中的主语从句不可提前。

③ "It occurs to sb. That..." 结构中的主语从句不可提前。

④ "It doesn't matter how/whether" 结构中的主语从句不可提前。

注意：不要将 it 作形式主语的从句和 it 引导的强调句型弄混淆。强调句型结构为：It is（was）＋强调部分＋that（who）。在正式英语中，无论强调的是哪个部分，都要求用连接词 that。但是一般情况下，如果被强调的主语是"人"，也可以用 who。

Exercises

Choose the best answer to the following sentences.

1. ＿＿＿ makes mistakes must correct them.
   A. What   B. That   C. Whoever   D. Whatever

2. It worried her a bit ＿＿＿ her hair was turning grey.
   A. while   B. that   C. if   D. for

3. When and why he came here _____ yet.
   A. is not known B. are not known C. has not known D. have not known
4. _____ is no reason for dismissing her.
   A. Because she was a few minutes late B. Owing to a few minutes late
   C. The fact that she was a few minutes late D. Being a few minutes late
5. _____ Tom liked to eat was different from _____.
   A. That; that you had expected B. What; that you had expected
   C. That; what you had expected D. What; what you had expected
6. _____ we go swimming every day _____ us a lot of good.
   A. If; do B. That; do C. If; does D. That; does
7. It _____ Bob drives badly.
   A. thinks that B. is thought what C. thought that D. is thought that
8. It's uncertain _____ the experiment is worth doing.
   A. if B. that C. whether D. how
9. _____ the boy didn't take medicine made his mother angry.
   A. That B. What C. How D. Which
10. _____ we can't get seems better than _____ we have.
    A. What; what B. What; that C. That; that D. That; what
11. _____ you don't like him is none of my business.
    A. What B. Who C. That D. Whether
12. _____ we'll go camping tomorrow depends on the weather.
    A. If B. Whether C. That D. Where
13. _____ is going to do the job will be decided by the Party committee.
    A. That B. Why C. How D. Who
14. _____ we'll finish translating the book depends on the time.
    A. When B. Why C. What D. That
15. _____ he won't go there is clear to all of us.
    A. How B. What C. Why D. This
16. _____ the house will be built will be discussed at tomorrow's meeting.
    A. If B. Where C. That D. What
17. _____ you come or not is up to you.
    A. What B. If C. Why D. Whether
18. _____ we do must be in the interests of the people.
    A. What B. Which C. Whatever D. That
19. _____ team will win the match is a matter of public concern.
    A. Which B. That C. If D. How
20. _____ leaves the room last ought to turn off the lights.
    A. Anyone B. The person C. Whoever D. Who

Workshop
Cultural Introduction

I. TASK

Here is a short excerpt from the Goddess of the Luo. Find out the words that describe body shape in it. In groups, discuss how to describe people's appearance vividly in English.

洛神赋（节选）

曹植

其形也，翩若惊鸿，婉若游龙。荣曜秋菊，华茂春松。
髣髴兮若轻云之蔽月，飘飖兮若流风之回雪。
远而望之，皎若太阳升朝霞；迫而察之，灼若芙蕖出渌波。
秾纤得衷，修短合度。肩若削成，腰如约素。
延颈秀项，皓质呈露。芳泽无加，铅华弗御。
云髻峨峨，修眉联娟。丹唇外朗，皓齿内鲜。
明眸善睐，靥辅承权。瑰姿艳逸，仪静体闲。

The Goddess of the Luo (excerpt)
Cao Zhi

Her body soars lightly like a startled swan,
Gracefully, like a dragon in flight.
In splendor brighter than the autumn chrysanthemum,
in bloom more flourishing than the pine in spring.
Dim as the moon mantled in filmy clouds,
restless as snow whirled by the driving wind.
Gaze far off from a distance,
she sparkles like the sun rising from morning mists;
Press closer to examine,
she flames like the lotus flower topping the green wave.
In her a balance is struck between plump and frail,
a measured accord between diminutive and tall.
With shoulders shaped as if by carving,
waist narrow as though bound with white cords.
At her slim throat and curving neck,
the pale flesh lies open to view.
No scented ointments overlaying it,

no coat of leaden powder applied.
Cloud-bank coiffure rising steeply,
long eyebrows delicately arched.
Red lips that shed their light abroad,
white teeth gleaming within.
Bright eyes skilled at glances,
a dimple to round off the base of the cheek.
Her rare form wonderfully enchanting,
her manner quiet, her pose demure.

Ⅱ. Cultural Tips

洛神指洛水的女神洛滨，《辞海》中引用李善的说法，即洛滨系宓（伏）羲之女，称宓妃，因渡水淹死，成为水神。

Unit 4　Online Education

Online Classes

In the coming era of budget cuts to education, distance learning could become the norm. The temptation for those in charge of education budgets to trade teachers for technology could be so strong that they ignore the disadvantages of distance learning. School facilities are expensive to build and maintain, and teachers are expensive to employ. Online classes do not require buildings and each class can host hundreds of people simultaneously resulting in greater savings, thus increasing the temptation of distance education for those concerned more about budgets than learning. But moving away from a traditional classroom in which a living, breathing human being teaches and interacts with students daily would be a disaster. Physically attending school has hidden benefits: getting up every morning interacting with peers, and building relationships with teachers are essential skills to cultivate in young people. Moreover, schools should be more than simple institutions of traditional learning. They are now places that provide meals. They are places where students receive counseling and other support.

Those policy-makers are often fascinated by the latest technology in education and its potential to transform education overnight. But online education does not allow a teacher to keep a struggling student after class and offer help. Educational videos may deliver academic content, but they are unable to make eye contact or assess a student's level of engagement. Distance education will never match the personal teaching in a traditional classroom. In their first 18 years of life, American children spend only 9% of their time in school. Yet teachers are expected to prepare them to be responsible citizens, cultivate their social skills, encourage successful time management, and enhance their capacity to flourish in an increasingly harsh labor market. Given these expectations, schools should not become permanently "remote".

The power of the classroom is rooted in the humanity of the people gathered in the same place, at the same time. Personal teaching is about teachers' showing students a higher path and about young people going through the process together. Technology, no matter how advanced, should simply be a tool of a good teacher.

temptation/temp'teɪʃ(ə)n/*n.* 引诱，诱惑

simultaneously/ˌsɪm(ə)l'teɪnɪəsli/*adv.* 同时地
concern/kən'sɜːn/*n.* 担心，忧虑
interact/ˌɪntər'ækt/*v.* 相互交流，互动
essential/ɪ'senʃ(ə)l/*adj.* 必不可少的；基本的
cultivate/'kʌltɪveɪt/*v.* 栽培，培育
institution/ˌɪnstɪ'tjuːʃ(ə)n/*n.* 机构，团体
counseling/'kaʊns(ə)lɪŋ/*n.* 咨询服务
potential/pə'tenʃ(ə)l/*adj.* 潜在的，可能的
assess/ə'ses/*v.* 评价，评定
engagement/ɪn'ɡeɪdʒmənt/*n.* 参与，从事
enhance/ɪn'hɑːns/*v.* 增强，提高
capacity/kə'pæsəti/*n.* 能力，才能
flourish/'flʌrɪʃ/*v.* 繁荣，昌盛；茁壮成长
harsh/hɑːʃ/*adj.* （环境）恶劣的，艰苦的
permanently/'pɜːmənəntli/*adv.* 永久地
in charge of 负责
be essential to 对…至关重要
be rooted in 扎根于

Exercises

I. Comprehension of the Text

There are 5 questions in this section. For each of them there are four choices marked A, B, C and D. You should choose the best answer for each question.

1. What mainly accounts for the possibility that distance learning could become the norm?
    A. Advances in education technology.
    B. Shrinking financial resources.
    C. Shortage of school facilities.
    D. Lack of qualified teachers.
2. What does the author say is one possible benefit of students attending school physically?
    A. Developing the habit of getting up early.
    B. Eating nutritionally well-balanced meals.
    C. Growing into living and breathing human beings.
    D. Cultivating relationships with peers and teachers.
3. What does the author think of the latest technology in education?
    A. It may have potential disadvantage.
    B. It may render many teachers' jobless.

C. It may add to student's financial burden.

D. It may revolutionize classroom teaching.

4. What does the author say teachers are expected to do?

   A. Enhance student's leadership capacity.

   B. Elevate students to managerial positions.

   C. Enable students to adapt to the chances in life.

   D. Prepare students to be competitive in the future.

5. Why couldn't technology replace a good teacher?

   A. It lacks humanity.

   B. It cannot track students' growth.

   C. It is still immature.

   D. It cannot cater to personal needs.

II. Languages Focus

A. *Match the following words in left with their explanations in right.*

1. temptation   a. something or someone that causes anxiety
2. simultaneously   b. grow stronger
3. concern   c. for a long time without essential change
4. interact   d. at the same instant
5. cultivate   e. the desire to have or do something that you know you should avoid
6. institution   f. the act of sharing in the activities of a group
7. assess   g. judge the worth of something
8. engagement   h. act together or towards others or with others
9. flourish   i. train to be discriminative in taste or judgment
10. permanently   j. an organization founded and united for a specific purpose

B. *Fill in the blanks with the words or expressions given below. Change the form where necessary.*

| temptation | concern | cultivate | assess | flourish |
| simultaneously | interact | institution | engagement | permanently |

1. The stroke left his right side _____ damaged.
2. I found the _____ to miss the class too hard to resist.
3. Quite rightly, the environment is of great _____.
4. It's difficult to _____ the effects of these changes.
5. The game will be broadcast _____ on TV and radio.
6. Harmonious relationships are what many companies aim to _____.
7. The objects around you are visible because they _____ with light.
8. They're quite an _____ in these parts.

9. I was unable to attend because of a previous _____.
10. Traditional beliefs still _____ alongside a modern urban lifestyle.

Ⅲ. Translation

Translate the following sentences into Chinese.

1. In the coming era of budget cuts to education, distance learning could become the norm.

_____

2. But moving away from a traditional classroom in which a living, breathing human being teaches and interacts with students daily would be a disaster.

_____
_____

3. Physically attending school has hidden benefits: getting up every morning interacting with peers, and building relationships with teachers are essential skills to cultivate in young people.

_____
_____

4. Those policy-makers are often fascinated by the latest technology in education and its potential to transform education overnight.

_____

5. Educational videos may deliver academic content, but they are unable to make eye contact or assess a student's level of engagement.

_____

Ⅳ. Discussion

Discuss the advantages and disadvantages of distance learning with the group members and give examples of the results.

Make Stuff, Fail, and Learn While You're at It

A) We've always been a hands-on, do-it-yourself kind of nation. Ben Franklin, one of America's founding fathers, didn't just invent the lightning rod. His creations include glasses, innovative stoves and more.

B) Franklin, who was largely self-taught, may have been a genius, but he wasn't really an exception when it comes to American making and creativity.

C) The personal computing revolution and philosophy of disruptive innovation of Silicon

Valley grew, in part, out of the creations of the Homebrew Computer Club, which was founded in a garage in Menlo Park, California, in the mid-1970s. Members — including guys named Jobs and Wozniak — started making and inventing things they couldn't buy.

D) So it's no surprise that the Maker Movement today is thriving in communities and some schools across America. Making is available to ordinary people who aren't tied to big companies, big defense labs or research universities. The maker philosophy echoes old ideas advocated by John Dewey, Montessori, and even ancient Greek philosophers, as we pointed out recently.

E) These maker spaces are often outside of classrooms, and are serving an important educational function. The Maker Movement is rediscovering learning by doing, which is Dewey's phrase from 100 years ago. We are rediscovering Dewey and Montessori and a lot of the practices that they pioneered that have been forgotten or at least put aside. A maker space is a place which can be in a school, but it doesn't look like a classroom. It can be in a library. It can be out in the community. It has tools and materials. It's a place where you get to make things based on your interest and on what you're learning to do.

F) Ideas about learning by doing have struggled to become mainstream educationally, despite being old concepts from Dewey and Montessori, Plato and Aristotle, and in the American Context, Ralph Emerson, on the value of experience and self-reliance. It's not necessarily an efficient way to learn. We learn, in a sense, by trial and error. Learning from experience is something that takes time and patience. It's very individualized. If your goal is to have standardized approaches to learning, where everybody learns the same thing at the same time in the same way, then learning by doing doesn't really fit that mold anymore. It's not the world of textbooks. It's not the world of testing.

G) Learning by doing may not be efficient, but it is effective. Project-based learning has grown in popularity with teachers and administrators. However, project-based learning is not making. Although there is a connection, there is also a distinction. The difference lies in whether the project is in a sense defined and developed by the student or whether it's assigned by a teacher. We'll all get the kids to build a small boat. We are all going to learn about X, Y, and Z. That tends to be one form of project-based learning.

H) I really believe the core idea of making is to have an idea within your head — or you just borrow it from someone — and begin to develop it , repeat it and improve it. Then, realize that idea somehow. That thing that you make is valuable to you and you can share it with others. I'm interested in how these things are expressions of that person, their ideas, and their interactions with the world.

I) In some ways, a lot of forms of making in school trivialize making. The thing that you make has no value to you. Once you are done demonstrating whatever concept was in the textbook, you throw away the pipe cleaners, the cardboard tubes.

J) Making should be student-directed and student-led, otherwise it's boring. It doesn't have the motivation of the student. I'm not saying that students should not learn concepts or not learn skills. They do. But to really harness their motivation is to build upon their interest.

It's to let them be in control and to drive the car.

K) Teachers should aim to build a supportive, creative environment for students to do this work. A very social environment, where they are learning from each other. When they have a problem, it isn't the teacher necessarily coming in to solve it. They are responsible for working through that problem. It might be they have to talk to other students in the class to help get an answer.

L) The teacher's role is more of a coach or observer. Sometimes, to people, it sounds like this is a diminished rote for teachers. I think it's a heightened role. You're creating this environment, like a maker space. You have 20 kids doing different things. You are watching them and really it's the human behaviors you're looking at. Are they engaged? A they developing and repeating their project? Are they stumbling? Do they need something that they don't have? Can you help them be aware of where they are?

M) My belief is that the goal of making is not to get every kid to be hands-on, but it enable us to be good learners. It's not the knowledge that is valuable, It's the practice of learning new things and understanding how things work. These are processes that you are developing so that you are able, over time, to tackle more interesting problems, more challenging problems — problems that require many people instead of one person, and many skills instead of one.

N) If teachers keep it form-free and student-led, it can still be tied to a curriculum and an educational plan. I think a maker space is more like a library in that there are multiple subjects and multiple things that you can learn. What seems to be missing in school is how these subjects integrate, how they fit together in any meaningful way. Rather than saying, 'This is science, over here is history,' I see schools taking this idea of projects and looking at: How do they support children in higher level learning?

O) I feel like this is a shift away form a subject matter-based curriculum to a more experiential curriculum or learning. It's still in its early stages, but I think it's shifting around not what kids learn but how they learn.

Words & Expressions

innovative/'ɪnəveɪtɪv/*adj.* 革新的，新颖的
revolution/ˌrevə'luːʃn/*n.* 变革，革命
disruptive/dɪs'rʌptɪv/*adj.* 引起混乱的，破坏的
thrive/θraɪv/*v.* 茁壮成长，兴旺，繁荣
available/ə'veɪləb(ə)l/*adj.* 可用的，可获得的
defense/dɪ'fens/*n.* 防御，保卫
echo/'ekəʊ/*n.* 回声，回音
self-reliance/ˌself rɪ'laɪəns/*n.* 自力更生
individualized/ˌɪndɪ'vɪdʒuəlaɪzd/*adj.* 个人的；有个性的；具有个人特色的

distinction/dɪˈstɪŋkʃn/*n.* 差别，区分
trivialize/ˈtrɪviəlaɪz/*vt.* 使平凡；使琐碎
harness/ˈhɑːnɪs/*v.* 控制并利用
observer/əbˈzɜːvə(r)/*n.* 观察者，目击者
diminished/dɪˈmɪnɪʃt/*adj.* 减弱的；减退了的
stumbling/ˈstʌmblɪŋ/*adj.* 障碍的
challenging/ˈtʃælɪndʒɪŋ/*adj.* 富于挑战性的
curriculum/kəˈrɪkjələm/*n.* 课程
multiple/ˈmʌltɪp(ə)l/*adj.* 多个的，多种的
integrate/ˈɪntɪɡreɪt/*v.* （使）合并，成为一体
experiential/ɪkˌspɪəriˈenʃl/*adj.* 经验的
when it comes to 当提到
be available to 可被…利用或得到的
in a sense 在某种意义上
be aware of 意识到
project-based learning 基于项目的学习

Notes

1. Ben Franklin

本杰明·富兰克林（Benjamin Franklin，1706—1790年），美国政治家、科学家、印刷商和出版商、作家、发明家及外交官，美国开国元勋之一。

2. Silicon Valley

硅谷，位于美国加利福尼亚北部的大都会区旧金山湾区南面，是高科技产业云集的圣塔克拉拉谷（Santa Clara Valley）的别称。硅谷最早是研究和生产以硅为基础的半导体芯片的地方，因此得名。

3. Montessori

玛利娅·蒙台梭利（意大利语：Maria Montessori，1870—1952），意大利幼儿教育家，是意大利第一位女医生，也是第一位女医学博士，女权主义者，蒙台梭利教育法的创始人。

Exercises

Ⅰ. Comprehension of the Text

Read the text and answer the following questions. Write the answers on the lines.

1. How are maker spaces different from traditional classrooms, and what educational function do they serve?

2. What is project-based learning, and how does it differ from making?
_____

3. What should teachers aim to create in a supportive, creative environment for student-led making?
_____

4. What is the teacher's role in a maker space, according to the author?
_____

5. What is the goal of making, and how can it help students develop as learners?
_____

II. Main Details Comprehension

Each of the following statement contains information given in one of the paragraphs. Identify the paragraph from which the information is derived. You may choose a paragraph more than once. Each paragraph is marked with a letter. Answer the questions by marking the corresponding letter in the blanks.

_____1. A maker space is where people make things according to their personal interests.

_____2. The teachers' role is enhanced in a maker space as they have to monitor and facilitate during the process.

_____3. Coming up with an idea of one's own or improving one from others is key to the concept of making.

_____4. Contrary to structured learning, learning by doing is highly individualized.

_____5. America is a nation known for the idea of making things by oneself.

_____6. Making will be boring unless students are able to take charge.

_____7. Making can be related to a project, but it is created and carried out by students themselves.

_____8. The author suggests incorporating the idea of a maker space into a school curriculum.

_____9. The maker concept is a modern version of some ancient philosophical ideas.

_____10. Making is not taken seriously in school when students are asked to make something meaningless to them based on textbooks.

III. Translation

Translate the five following sentences into English, using the words or expressions given in brackets.

1. 这么大的改变将会是极具破坏性的。（disruptive）
_____

2. 我相信，在编写程序时，这一点尤其正确。（when it comes to）
_____

3. 艺术品应该以人们支付得起的价格提供给更多人。(be available to)

_____

4. 在某种意义上说，市民对陌生人的态度反映了这个城市的温度。(in a sense)

_____

5. 当你期盼最佳成绩时，要意识到这可能给孩子带来的可怕压力。(be aware of)

_____

Grammar
名词性从句（二）：宾语从句（the Object Clause）

置于动词、介词等词性后面起宾语作用的从句叫宾语从句。宾语从句的语序必须是陈述语序。谓语动词、介词、动词不定式、动词现在分词、过去式、过去分词后面都能带宾语从句。有些形容词之后也可以带宾语从句。

1. 作动词的宾语

（1）当宾语从句是陈述句时，连词由 that 引导，因为 that 在句中不作任何成分，也没有任何具体意思，在口语和非正式文体中常省略。例如：

She says (that) she won't take part in the sports meeting next Sunday.

He told us (that) they would help us through the whole work.

（2）动词短语也可以带宾语从句。常见的这些词有：make sure（确保），make up one's mind（下决心），keep in mind（牢记）。例如：

Make sure that there are no mistakes in your papers before you turn them in.

（3）有些动词带宾语从句时需要在宾语与从句前加 it。这类动词主要有 hate，take，owe，have，see to 等。例如：

I hate it when they with their mouths full of food.

（4）可运用形式宾语 it 代替的宾语从句，动词 find，feel，consider，make，believe 等后面有宾语补足语的时候，则需要用 it 作形式宾语而将 that 宾语从句后置。例如：

I think it necessary that we take plenty of hot water every day.

（5）当宾语从句是一般疑问句时，由连词 whether/if 引导，因为二者可翻译为"是否"，具有一定的意义，所以不能省略。例如：

Lucy wanted to know whether/if her grandma liked the handbag.

（6）当宾语从句是特殊疑问句时，由特殊疑问词 what，who，where，how，when 等引导。特殊疑问词不可省略。例如：

Please tell me who (whom) we have to see?

2. 作介词的宾语

例如：He was interested in whatever he saw there.

（1）有时会遇到"介词+it+that"的结构。这时，it 可看作是 that 从句的先行词。例如：

You may depend on it that they will support you.

（2）有个别动词也有这种结构"动词＋it＋that"，习惯上当作固定结构理解。例如：

I take it that they will succeed.

3．作形容词的宾语

从句可作有些形容词的宾语，如 sure，sorry，happy，surprised，excited，hopeful，proud 等。例如：

I am not certain whether/if the train will arrive on time.

4．宾语从句的时态

（1）如果主句是现在的时态，从句的时态可根据实际情况而定。例如：

I have heard (that) he will come back next week.

（2）如果主句是过去的某种时态，那么从句的时态一定要用过去的某种时态。例如：

He said（that）there were no classes yesterday.

（3）如果宾语从句表述的是客观真理、自然现象等时，不管主句是什么时态，从句都要用一般现在时。例如：

He said that light travels much faster than sound.

5．That 与 what 的选择

That 只起连接作用，在从句中不充当任何成分，也无任何词义；what 引导宾语从句时，除起连接作用外，还可在从句中作主语、宾语、表语等成分。例如：

People have heard what the president has said, they are waiting to see what he will do.（what 作及物动词 do 的宾语）

Exercises

Choose the best answer to the following sentences.

1. No one tells us ＿＿＿, so we need your help.
   A. how we should do   B. what should we do
   C. how to do it   D. what to do it

2. Could you please teach me ＿＿＿ the computer.
   A. how check   B. to check
   C. how to check   D. to how checking

3. They don't know ＿＿＿ their parents are.
   A. that   B. what   C. why   D. which

4. - Where do you think ＿＿＿ he ＿＿＿ the TV set?
   - Sorry, I've no idea.
   A. /; bought   B. has; bought   C. did; buy   D. did; bought

5. Our homework has changed a lot. Who can tell ＿＿＿ it would be like in ＿＿＿ five years.
   A. how; another   B. what; more   C. how; other   D. what; another

6. - Could you tell me _____?
   - Yes. He _____ to the USA.
   A. where is he/has been
   B. where he is/has gone
   C. where was he/has been
   D. where he was/has gone

7. - Mike wants to know if _____ a picnic tomorrow.
   - Yes. But if it _____, we'll visit the museum instead.
   A. you have; will rain
   B. you will have; will rain
   C. you will have; rains
   D. will you have; rains

8. I really don't know if she _____ it when she _____.
   A. finds; arrives
   B. finds; will arrive
   C. will find; will arrive
   D. will find; arrives

9. Miss Liu said _____ she would leave the message on the headmaster's desk.
   A. that   B. where   C. which   D. what

10. He asked me _____.
    A. who will kick the first goal in the World Cup
    B. when was the APEC meeting held
    C. when China became a member of the WTO
    D. where the 2008 Olympics will be held

11. In the bookshop, a reader asked the shopkeeper _____ *Who Moved My Cheese* was an interesting book.
    A. that   B. how   C. what   D. if

12. You must remember _____.
    A. what your teacher said
    B. what did your teacher say
    C. your teacher said what
    D. what has your teacher said

13. I don't know _____.
    A. which room I can live
    B. which room can I live
    C. which room I can live in
    D. which room can I live in

14. - Do you know when he _____ back?
    - Sorry, I don't. When he _____ back, I'll tell you.
    A. comes; comes
    B. comes; will come
    C. will come; comes
    D. will come; will come

15. The girls asked if they _____ some food and drink with them.
    A. took   B. take   C. takes   D. will take

16. Mary said that she _____ to Guangzhou.
    A. has never gone
    B. had never gone
    C. has never been
    D. had never been

17. The students want to know whether they _____ a PE class today.
    A. had   B. has   C. will have   D. are

18. Can you tell me _____ you were born, Betty?
    A. who   B. what   C. when   D. that

19. I don't know _____ they have passed the exam.
   A. what   B. if   C. when   D. where
20. Do you know _____ they listened to yesterday evening?
   A. what   B when   C why   D hows

Workshop
Cultural Introduction

Ⅰ. Appreciation of Proverbs

1. 温故而知新，可以为师矣。《论语》

Reviewing what you have acquired and learning anew, this way you can be a teacher for others.

2. 十年树木，百年树人。《管子》

It takes ten years to grow trees and a hundred years to nurture talents.

3. 一年之计，莫如树谷；十年之计，莫如树木；终身之计，莫如树人。一树一获者，谷也；一树十获者，木也；一树百获者，人也。《管子》

When planning for a year, there is nothing like growing crops; when planning for a decade, there is nothing like planting trees; when planning for a lifetime, there is nothing like nurturing talents. When you grow crops, you get one harvest; when you plant trees, you get a tenfold harvest; when you nurture talents, you get a hundredfold harvest.

4. 启蒙教育的方向将决定一个人的未来生活。——柏拉图，古希腊哲学家

The direction in which education starts a man will determine his future life. —Plato, ancient Creek philosopher

5. 教育是一个逐步发现自己无知的过程。——威尔·杜兰特，美国历史学家

Education is a progressive discovery of our own ignorance. —Will Durant, American historian

6. 知识就是力量。——弗朗西斯·培根，英国哲学家

Knowledge is power. —Francis Bacon, British philosopher

7. 读书使人充实，谈话使人敏捷，写作使人准确。——弗朗西斯·培根，英国哲学家

Reading makes a full man, conference a ready man, and writing an exact man. —Francis Bacon, British philosopher

Unit 5 Animal

Cats

The latest in cat research reveals that the lovely animal seems to have a basic grasp on both the laws of physics and the ins and outs of cause and effect.

According to a newly published study, cats seem to be able to predict the location of hiding prey using both their ears and an inborn understanding of how the physical world works.

In a recent experiment, Japanese researchers taped 30 domestic cats reacting to a container that a team member shook. Some containers rattled; others did not. When the container was tipped over, sometimes an object fell out and sometimes it didn't.

It turns out that the cats were remarkably smart about what would happen when a container was tipped over. When an object did not drop out of the bottom of a rattling container, they looked at it for a longer time than they did when the container behaved as expected.

"Cats use a causal-logical understanding of noise or sounds to predict the appearance of invisible objects," lead researcher Saho Takagi says in a press release. The researchers conclude that cats' hunting style may have developed based on their common-sense abilities to infer where prey is, using their hearing.

Scientists have explored this idea with other endearing creatures: babies. Like cats, babies appear to engage in what's called "preferential looking" — looking longer at things that are interesting or unusual than things they perceive as normal.

When babies' expectations are violated in experiments like the ones performed with the cats, they react much like their animal friends. Psychologists have shown that babies apparently expect their world to comply with the laws of physics and cause and effect as early as two months of age.

Does the study mean that cats will soon grasp the ins and outs of cause and effect? Maybe. Okay, so cats may not be the next physics faculty members at America's most important research universities. But by demonstrating their common sense, they've shown that the divide between cats and humans may not be that great after all.

prey/preɪ/ *n.* 猎物，捕获物

inborn/ˌɪnˈbɔːn/adj. 天生的
domestic/dəˈmestɪk/adj. 国内的，本国的
rattled/ˈræt(ə)l/v. （使）咯咯作响
container/kənˈteɪnə(r)/n. 容器
remarkably/rɪˈmɑːkəbli/adv. 不寻常地，惊人地
causal/ˈkɔːz(ə)l/adj. 因果关系的
appearance/əˈpɪərəns/n. 露面，演出
invisible/ɪnˈvɪzəb(ə)l/adj. 看不见的，隐形的
release/rɪˈliːs/v. 释放，放走
infer/ɪnˈfɜː(r)/v. 推断，推论
endearing/ɪnˈdɪərɪŋ/adj. 可爱的；讨人喜欢的
preferential/ˌprefəˈrenʃ(ə)l/adj. 优先的，优待的
perceive/pəˈsiːv/vt. 认为，理解
violate/ˈvaɪəleɪt/v. 违反，违背
apparently/əˈpærəntli/adv. 似乎，好像
comply/kəmˈplaɪ/v. 遵从，服从
faculty/ˈfæk(ə)lti/n. 机能；天赋
demonstrate/ˈdemənstreɪt/v. 证明；示范
ins and outs 错综复杂事物的因果

Exercises

Ⅰ. Comprehension of the Text

There are 5 questions in this section. For each of them there are four choices marked A, B, C and D. You should choose the best answer for each question.

1. What do we learn from a newly published study about cats?
   A. They can be trained to understand the physical world.
   B. They know what kind of prey might be easier to hunt.
   C. They have a natural ability to locate animals they hunt.
   D. They are capable of telling which way their prey flees.
2. What may account for the cats' response to the noise from the containers?
   A. Their inborn sensitivity to noise.
   B. Their unusual sense of direction.
   C. Their special ability to perceive.
   D. Their mastery of cause and effect.
3. What is characteristic of the way cats hunt, according to the Japanese researchers?
   A. They depend on their instincts.
   B. They rely mainly on their hearing.

C. They wait some time before attack.

D. They use both their ears and eyes.

4. In what way do babies behave like cats?

   A. They focus on what appears odd.

   B. They view the world as normal.

   C. They do what they prefer to do.

   D. They are curious about everything.

5. What can we conclude about cats from the passage?

   A. They have higher intelligence than many other animals.

   B. They interact withe the physical world much like humans.

   C. They display extraordinarily high intelligence in hunting.

   D. They can aid physics professors in their research work.

Ⅱ. Languages Focus

A. *Match the following words in left with their explanations in right.*

1. inborn	a. involving or constituting a cause
2. remarkably	b. act in accordance with someone's rules
3. causal	c. act in disregard of laws, rules, contracts, or promises
4. appearance	d. to a remarkable degree or extent
5. invisible	e. impossible or nearly impossible to see
6. release	f. normally existing at birth
7. endearing	g. free from confinement
8. perceive	h. to become aware of through the senses
9. violate	i. the act of appearing in public view
10. comply	j. lovable especially in a childlike or naive way

B. *Fill in the blanks with the words or expressions given below. Change the form where necessary.*

remarkably	release	endearing	infer	preferential
causal	inborn	perceive	comply	demonstrate

1. Scientists have explored this idea with other _____ creatures: babies.
2. What actually is the _____ relationship.
3. Inflation has decelerated _____ over the past two years.
4. Students must _____ for themselves the relationship between success and effort.
5. The government is negotiating the _____ of the hostages.
6. We have our native _____ talent, yet we hardly use it.
7. Firstborn sons received _____ treatment.
8. Some beaches had failed to _____ with environmental regulations.
9. We want to _____ our commitment to human rights.

10. We cannot _____ from which direction these robbers escaped because we could not find any trace of them.

III. Translation

Translate the following sentences into Chinese.

1. The latest in cat research reveals that the lovely animal seems to have a basic grasp on both the laws of physics and the ins and outs of cause and effect.
_____
_____

2. It turns out that the cats were remarkably smart about what would happen when a container was tipped over.
_____

3. Cats use a causal-logical understanding of noise or sounds to predict the appearance of invisible objects.
_____

4. The researchers conclude that cats' hunting style may have developed based on their common-sense abilities to infer where prey is, using their hearing.
_____
_____

5. But by demonstrating their common sense, they've shown that the divide between cats and humans may not be that great after all.
_____

IV. Discussion

Have you ever observed a cat's behavior that seemed to demonstrate their understanding of cause and effect?

How to Eat Well

A) Why do so many Americans eat tons of processed food, the stuff that is correctly called junk and should really carry warning labels?

B) It's not because fresh ingredients are hard to come by. Supermarkets offer more variety than ever, and there are over four times as many farmers markets in the US as there were 20 years ago. Nor is it for lack of available information. There are plenty of recipes, how-to videos and cooking classes available to anyone who has a computer, smartphone or television. If anything, the information is overwhelming.

C) And yet we aren't cooking. If you eat three meals a day and behave like most Americans, you probably get at least a third of your daily calories outside the home. Nearly two-thirds of us grab fast food once a week, and we get almost 25% of our daily calories from snacks. So we're eating out or taking in, and we don't sit down — or we do, but we hurry.

D) Shouldn't preparing — and consuming — food be a source of comfort, pride, health, well-being, relaxation, sociability? Something that connects us to other humans? Why would we want to outsource this basic task, especially when outsourcing it is so harmful?

E) When I talk about cooking, I'm not talking about creating elaborate dinner parties or three-day science projects. I'm talking about simple, easy, everyday meals. My mission is to encourage green hands and those lacking time or memory to feed themselves. That means we need modest, realistic expectations, and we need to teach people to cook food that's good enough to share with family and friends.

F) Perhaps a return to real cooking needn't be far off. A recent Harris poll revealed that 79% of Americans say they enjoy cooking and 30% "love it"; 14% admit to not enjoying kitchen work and just 7% won't go near the stove at all. But this doesn't necessarily translate to real cooking, and the result of this survey shouldn't surprise anyone: 52% of those 65 or older cook at home five or more times per week; only a third of young people do.

G) Back in the 1950s most of us grew up in households where Mom cooked virtually every night. The intention to put a home-cooked meal on the table was pretty much universal. Most people couldn't afford to do otherwise.

H) Although frozen dinners were invented in the '40s, their popularity didn't boom until televisions became popular a decade or so later. Since then, packaged, pre-prepared meals have been what's for dinner. The microwave and fast-food chains were the biggest catalysts, but the big food companies — which want to sell anything except the raw ingredients that go into cooking — made the home cook an endangered species.

I) Still, I find it strange that only a third of young people report preparing meals at home regularly. Isn't this the same crowd that rails against processed junk and champions craft cooking? And isn't this the generation who say they're concerned about their health and the well-being of the planet? If these are truly the values of many young people, then their behavior doesn't match their beliefs.

J) There have been half-hearted but well-publicized efforts by some companies to reduce calories in their processed foods, but the Standard American Diet is still the polar opposite of the healthy, mostly plant-based diet that just about every expert says we should be eating. Considering that the government's standards are not nearly ambitious enough, the picture is clear: by not cooking at home, we're not eating the right things, and the consequences are hard to overstate.

K) To help quantify the costs of a poor diet, I recently tried to estimate this impact in terms of a most famous food, the burger. I concluded that the profit from burgers is more than offset by the damage they cause in health problems and environmental harm.

L) Cooking real food is the best defense — not to mention that any meal you're likely to eat at home contains about 200 fewer calories than one you would eat in a restaurant.

M) To those Americans for whom money is a concern, my advice is simple: Buy what you can afford, and cook it yourself. The common prescription is to primarily shop the grocery store, since that's where fresh produce, meat and seafood, and dairy are. And to save money and still eat well you don't need local, organic ingredients; all you need is real food. I'm not saying local food isn't better; it is. But there is plenty of decent food in the grocery stores.

N) The other sections you should get to know are the frozen foods and the canned goods. Frozen produce is still produce; canned tomatoes are still tomatoes. Just make sure you're getting real food without tons of added salt or sugar. Ask yourself, would Grandma consider this food? Does it look like something might occur in nature? It's pretty much common sense: you want to buy food, not unidentifiable food like objects.

O) You don't have to hit the grocery store daily, nor do you need an abundance of skill. Since fewer than half of Americans say they cook at an intermediate level and only 20% describe their cooking skills as advanced the crisis is one of confidence. And the only remedy for that is practice. There's nothing mysterious about cooking the evening meal. You just have to do a little thinking ahead and redefine what qualifies as dinner. Like any skill, cooking gets easier as you do it more: every time you cook, you advance your level of skills. Someday you won't even need recipes. My advice is that you not pay attention to the number of steps and ingredients, because they can be deceiving.

P) Time, I realize, is the biggest obstacle to cooking for most people. You must adjust your priorities to find time to cook. For instance, you can move a TV to the kitchen and watch your favorite shows while you're standing at the sink. No one is asking you to give up activities you like, but if you're watching food shows on TV, try cooking instead.

Words & Expressions

processed /p'rəsest/ *adj.* 经过特殊加工的
junk /dʒʌŋk/ *n.* 垃圾
recipe /'resəpi/ *n.* 烹饪法，食谱
relaxation /ˌriːlæk'seɪʃ(ə)n/ *n.* 休息，消遣
sociability /ˌsəʊʃə'bɪləti/ *n.* 善于交际；社交性
outsource /'aʊtsɔːs/ *vt.* 把…外包
elaborate /ɪ'læbərət/ *adj.* 复杂的；精心制作的
modest /'mɒdɪst/ *adj.* 适中的，适度的
virtually /'vɜːtʃuəli/ *adv.* 事实上，几乎
catalysts /'kætəlɪst/ *n.* （化学）催化剂；诱因
overstate /ˌəʊvə'steɪt/ *v.* 夸大，对…言过其实
quantify /'kwɒntɪfaɪ/ *v.* 量化

offset/'ɒfset/*v.* 补偿，抵销
prescription/prɪ'skrɪpʃn/*n.* 处方，药方
unidentifiable/ˌʌnaɪ'dentɪfaɪəbl/*adj.* 无法辨认的；无法鉴定的
abundance/ə'bʌndəns/*n.* 大量，丰富
intermediate/ˌɪntə'miːdiət/*adj.* 居中的，中间的
remedy/'remədi/*n.* 解决方法
redefine/ˌriːdɪ'faɪn/*v.* 重新定义
deceive/dɪ'siːv/*v.* 欺骗，蒙骗
well-publicized 广为人知的
far off 遥远的

Exercises

I. Comprehension of the Text

Read the text and answer the following questions. Write the answers on the lines.

1. Why do so many Americans eat processed food instead of cooking at home?
_____

2. What are some factors that contribute to the decline in home-cooking in America?
_____

3. According to a recent Harris poll, what percentage of Americans enjoy cooking?
_____

4. Why is it important for young people to cook at home regularly, especially if they value healthy eating and environmental sustainability?
_____

5. What is the biggest obstacle to cooking for most people, and how can we overcome it?
_____

II. Main Details Comprehension

Each of the following statement contains information given in one of the paragraphs. Identify the paragraph from which the information is derived. You may choose a paragraph more than once. Each paragraph is marked with a letter. Answer the questions by marking the corresponding letter in the blanks.

____1. Cooking benefits people in many ways and enables them to connect with one another.

____2. Abundant information about cooking is available either online or on TV.

____3. Young people do less cooking at home than the elderly these days.

____4. Cooking skills can be improved with practice.

____5. In the mid-20th century, most families ate dinner at home instead of eating out.

_____6. Even those short of time or money should be encouraged to cook for themselves and their family.

_____7. Eating food not cooked by ourselves can cause serious consequences.

_____8. To eat well and still save money, people should buy fresh food and cook it themselves.

_____9. We get a fairly large portion of calories from fast food and snacks.

_____10. The popularity of TV led to the popularity of frozen food.

Ⅲ. Translation

Translate the five following sentences into English, using the words or expressions given in brackets.

1. 团队运动应该成为国家体育课程中的重要组成部分。（ingredient）
   _____
2. 在那些久远的日子里，绝没有人会想到一个女人可以当上首相。（far off）
   _____
3. 很难量化一个人的记忆力有多好。（quantify）
   _____
4. 在这场灾难死去的人中，大多数是无法确认身份的外来农民工。（unidentifiable）
   _____
5. 为补偿原料成本的增加而提高了价格。（offset）
   _____

Part C

Grammar
名词性从句（三）

一、表语从句（the Predicative Clause）

表语从句是在复合句中充当表语的从句，它位于主句中的连系动词之后。结构为：主语+连系动词+表语从句。常用的连系动词有：be，seem，remain，look 等。

（1）That 引导的表语从句，that 不可省略。例如：

The fact is that he escaped from the city.

（2）由 whether 引导的表语从句是疑问句语气，肯定句语序。例如：

The question is whether they will support the plan.

（3）表语从句还可以由 as if/as though，because，as 引导。例如：

It looks as if our team is going to win.

It may be because he is too young.

（4）由特殊疑问词引导的表语从句，如 who，whom，whose，what，which，whoever，whatever，whichever，where，when 等。例如：

The question is when he can arrive at the hotel.

表语从句一定要用陈述语序。

False: The question is when can he arrive at the hotel.

Right: The question is when he can arrive at the hotel.

二、同位语从句（the Appositive Clause）

同位语从句指在复合句中充当同位语的从句，属于名词性从句的范畴。同位语从句用来对前面的抽象名词进行解释说明，被解释说明的词和同位语在逻辑上是主表关系（即被解释说明的词＝同位语）。

能跟有同位语从句的往往是具有一定内容含义的抽象名词。这些名词有 news, truth, answer, doubt, order, desire, belief, condition, fact, fear, question, problem, report, dream, promise, idea 等。例如：

The girls were surprised at the fact that ocean ships can sail up the Great lakes.

（1）同位语从句有时不是紧跟在有关的名词后面，而是被其他的词分隔开了。例如：

The question came up at the meeting whether we had enough money for our research.

（2）同位语从句通常由 that 引导，但也可以由 whether, which, when, what, who, why 等引导。例如：

The question, whether she need it, has not yet been considered.

（3）同位语从句与定语从句的区别。

①同位语从句与前面的名词是同位关系，即说明它前面名词的内容；而定语从句与前面的名词是修饰与被修饰关系，即限定它前面的名词范围，或补充一些情况。例如：

The news that I have passed the exam is true. 我通过了考试这一消息是真的。

（同位语从句，即从句所表达的意思就是前面名词的内容。）

The news that he told me just now is true. 他刚才告诉我的消息是真的。

（定语从句，从句对前面名词起修饰限制作用，即"他告诉我的"那个消息，而不是别的消息。）

②引导同位语从句的 that 是连词，在从句中不充当任何成分，而引导定语从句的 that 是关系代词，除起连接作用外，还在从句中充当主语、宾语或表语等。例如：

The idea that computers can recognize human voices surprises many people. 计算机能够识别人的声音的想法使许多人感到惊奇。

（that 在从句中不充当任何成分。）

The idea that he gave surprises many people. 他提出的观点令许多人感到吃惊。

（that 在从句中作 gave 的宾语。）

Exercises

Choose the best answer to the following sentences.

1. The question is _____ we will have our sports meet next week.

    A. that   B. if   C. when   D. whether

2. The reason why he failed is _____ he was too careless.
   A. because   B. that   C. for   D. because of
3. Go and get your coat. It's _____ you left it.
   A. where   B. there   C. there where   D. where there
4. The problem is _____ to take the place of Ted.
   A. who can we get   B. what we can get
   C. who we can get   D. that we can get
5. What I want to know is _____ he likes the gift given by us.
   A. that   B. if   C. whether   D. /
6. The reason is _____ I missed the bus.
   A. that   B. when   C. why   D. what
7. That is _____ we were late last time.
   A. that   B. when   C. why   D. what
8. She looked _____ she were ten years younger.
   A. that   B. like   C. as   D. as though
9. - I fell sick!
   - I think it is _____ you are doing too much.
   A. why   B. when   C. what   D. because
10. The reason why he hasn't come is _____.
    A. because his mother is ill   B. because of his mother's being ill
    C. that his mother is ill   D. for his mother is ill
11. The fact _____ she works hard is well known to us all.
    A. that   B. what   C. why   D. which
12. The fact _____ he was successful proves his ability.
    A. that   B. what   C. which   D. why
13. The news _____ he was kidnapped surprised us greatly.
    A. what   B. that   C. why   D. when
14. His suggestion _____ the meeting be delayed was turned down.
    A. which   B. that   C. /   D. it
15. I have no idea _____ he will start.
    A. when   B. that   C. what   D. /
16. I've come from the government with a message _____ the meeting won't be held tomorrow.
    A. if   B. that   C. whether   D. which
17. The thought _____ he might fail in the exam worried him.
    A. when   B. which   C. what   D. that
18. The order _____ the prisoner be set free arrived too late.
    A. which   B. whether   C. that   D. what

19. The nurses are trying their best to reduce the patient's fear _____ he would die of the disease.

  A. that   B. as   C. of which   D. which

20. He often asked me the question _____ the work was worth doing.

  A. whether   B. where   C. that   D. when

Workshop
Cultural Introduction

Slang for Animals

1. Black sheep 害群之马
2. Straight from a horse's mouth 消息确凿
3. Don't put the cart before the horse 不要本末倒置
4. A horse of a different color 完全另一回事
5. Let the cat out of bag 泄密
6. See how the cat jumps 观望形势
7. Turn cat in the pan 背叛
8. When the cat is away, the mice will play 山中无老虎，猴子称大王
9. Love me, love my dog 爱屋及乌
10. Let sleeping dog lie 别惹是生非
11. Every dog has his day 人人皆有得意时
12. Butterflies in my stomach 紧张
13. A cat nap 打个盹儿
14. Teach fish to swim 班门弄斧
15. Fish out of water 格格不入
16. Beat a dead horse 白费力气
17. Get one's goat 惹某人生气
18. Ants in one's pants 坐立难安
19. Don't have a cow 不要大惊小怪
20. Bell the cat 冒险行为

Unit 6   Health

Effect of Health on Marital Status in Old Age

In the classic marriage vow, couples promise to stay together in sickness and in health. But a new study finds that the risk of divorce among older couples rises when the wife — not the husband — becomes seriously ill.

"Married women diagnosed with a serious health condition may find themselves struggling with the impact of their disease while also experiencing the stress of divorce," said researcher Amelia Karraker.

Karraker and co-author Kenzie Latham analyzed 20 years of data on 2,717 marriages from a study conducted by Indiana University since 1992. At the time of the first interview, at least one of the partners was over the age of 50.

The researchers examined how the onset of four serious physical illnesses affected marriages. They found that, overall, 31% of marriages ended in divorce over the period studied. The incidence of new chronic illness onset increased over time as well, with more husbands than wives developing serious health problems.

"We found that women are doubly vulnerable to marital break-up in the face of illness," Karraker said. "They're more likely to be widowed, and if they're the ones who become ill, they're more likely to get divorced."

While the study didn't assess why divorce is more likely when wives but not husbands become seriously ill, Karraker offers a few possible reasons. "Gender norms and social expectations about caregiving may make it more difficult for men to provide care to sick spouses," Karraker said. "And because of the imbalance in marriage markets, especially in older ages, divorced men have more choices among prospective partners than divorced women."

Given the increasing concern about health care costs for the aging population, Karraker believes policymakers should be aware of the relationship between disease and risk of divorce.

"Offering support services to spouses caring for their other halves may reduce marital stress and prevent divorce at older ages," she said. "But it's also important to recognize that the pressure to divorce may be health-related and that sick ex-wives may need additional care and services to prevent worsening health and increased health costs."

Unit 6 Health

Words & Expressions

vow /vaʊ/ *n.* 誓约，诺言
divorce /dɪˈvɔːs/ *n.* 离婚
diagnosed /ˈdaɪəgnəʊzd/ *v.* 诊断；被诊断为
onset /ˈɒnset/ *n.*（尤指某种坏事情的）开始，发作
incidence /ˈɪnsɪdəns/ *n.* 发生率
vulnerable /ˈvʌlnərəbl/ *adj.*（身体或精神）脆弱的，易受伤的
widowed /ˈwɪdəʊd/ *adj.* 丧偶的
imbalance /ɪmˈbæləns/ *n.* 不平衡；不安定
expectation /ˌekspekˈteɪʃ(ə)n/ *n.* 期待，预期
prospective /prəˈspektɪv/ *adj.* 有希望的，潜在的
policymaker /ˈpɒləsɪmeɪkə(r)/ *n.* 政策制定者，决策人
aware /əˈweə(r)/ *adj.* 知道的，明白的
worsening /ˈwɜːsənɪŋ/ *adj.* 日益恶化的

Exercises

I. Comprehension of the Text

There are 5 questions in this section. For each of them there are four choices marked A, B, C and D. You should choose the best answer for each question.

1. What can we learn about marriage vows from the passage?
    A. They may not guarantee a lasting marriage.
    B. They are as binding as they used to be.
    C. They are not taken seriously any more.
    D. They may help couples tide over hard times.

2. What did Karraker and co-author Kenzie Latham find about elderly husbands?
    A. They are generally not good at taking care of themselves.
    B. They can become increasingly vulnerable to serious illnesses.
    C. They can develop different kinds of illnesses just like their wives.
    D. They are more likely to contract serious illnesses than their wives.

3. What does Karraker say about women who fall ill?
    A. They are more likely to be widowed.
    B. They are more likely to get divorced.
    C. They are less likely to receive good care.
    D. They are less likely to bother their spouses.

4. Why is it more difficult for men to take care of their sick spouses according to Karraker?

   A. They are more accustomed to receiving care.

   B. They find it more important to make money for the family.

   C. They think it more urgent to fulfill their social obligations.

   D. They expect society to do more of the job.

5. What does Karraker think is also important?

   A. Reducing marital stress on wives.

   B. Stabilizing old couples' relations.

   C. Providing extra care for divorced women.

   D. Making men pay for their wives' health costs.

II. Languages Focus

A. *Match the following words in left with their explanations in right.*

1. vow	a. subject to a medical analysis
2. divorce	b. the beginning or early stages
3. incidence	c. the legal dissolution of a marriage
4. vulnerable	d. the relative frequency of occurrence of something
5. aware	e. concerned with or related to the future
6. diagnosed	f. a solemn pledge to do something or to behave in a certain manner
7. onset	g. place a value on; judge the worth of something
8. assess	h. single because of death of the spouse
9. widowed	i. capable of being wounded or hurt
10. prospective	j. bearing in mind; attentive to

B. *Fill in the blanks with the words or expressions given below. Change the form where necessary.*

vow	onset	incidence	diagnosed	prospective
assess	divorce	vulnerable	widowed	aware

1. I made a silent _____ to be more careful in the future.

2. Numerous marriages now end in _____.

3. He was eventually _____ as suffering from terminal cancer.

4. With _____ of civilization, things changed.

5. It sharply reduces the _____ of traffic accidents.

6. In cases of food poisoning, young children are especially _____.

7. His second wife, Hilary, had been _____, then exiled from South Africa.

8. The risks can be so complex that banks hire mathematicians to _____ them.

9. The story should act as a warning to other _____ buyers.

10. Smokers are well _____ of the dangers to their own health.

Unit 6 Health

Ⅲ. Translation

Translate the following sentences into Chinese.

1. In the classic marriage vow, couples promise to stay together in sickness and in health.

2. The researchers examined how the onset of four serious physical illnesses affected marriages.

3. The incidence of new chronic illness onset increased over time as will, with more husbands than wives developing serious health problems.

4. We found that women are doubly vulnerable to marital break-up in the face of illness.

5. And because of the imbalance in marriage markets, especially in older ages, divorced men have more choices among prospective partners than divorced women.

Ⅳ. Discussion

What do you think is the true meaning of marriage? What's your opinion about the phenomenon of a sick spouse experiencing the stress of divorce?

How Work Will Change When Most of Us Live to 100

A) Today in the United States there are 72,000 centenarians. Worldwide, probably 450,000. If current trends continue, then by 2050 there will be more than a million in the US alone. According to the work of Professor James Vaupel and his co-researchers, 50% of babies born in the US in 2007 have a life expectancy of 104 or more. Broadly the same holds for the UK, Germany, France, Italy and Canada, and for Japan 50% of 2007 babies can expect to live to 107.

B) Understandably, there are concerns about what this means for public finances given the associated health and pension challenges. These challenges are real, and society urgently needs to address them. But it is also important to look at the wider picture of what happens when so many people live for 100 years. It is a mistake to simply equate longevity with issues of old age. Longer lives have implications for all of life, not just the end of it.

C) Our view is that if many people are living for longer, and are healthier for longer, then this will result in an inevitable redesign of work and life. When people live longer, they are not only older for longer, but also younger for longer. There is some truth in the saying that "70 is the new 60" or "40 the new 30." If you age more slowly over a longer time period, then you are in some sense younger for longer.

D) But the changes go further than that. Take, for instance, the age at which people make commitments such as buying a house, getting married, having children, or starting a career. These are all fundamental commitments that are now occurring later in life. In 1962, 50% of Americans were married by age 21. By 2014, that milestone had shifted to age 29.

E) While there are numerous factors behind these shifts, one factor is surely a growing realization for the young that they are going to live longer. Options are more valuable the longer they can be held. So if you believe you will live longer, then options become more valuable, and early commitment becomes less attractive. The result is that the commitments that previously characterized the beginning of adulthood are now being delayed, and new patterns of behavior and a new stage of life are emerging for those in their twenties.

F) Longevity also pushes back the age of retirement, and not only for financial reasons. Yes, unless people are prepared to save a lot more, our calculations suggest that if you are now in your mid-40s, then you are likely to work until your early 70s; and if you are in your early 20s, there is a real chance you will need to work until your late 70s or possibly even into your 80s. But even if people are able to economically support a retirement at 65, over thirty years of potential inactivity is harmful to cognitive and emotional vitality. Many people may simply not want to do it.

G) And yet that does not mean that simply extending our careers is appealing. Just lengthening that second stage of full-time work may secure the financial assets needed for a 100-year life, but such persistent work will inevitably exhaust precious intangible assets such as productive skills, vitality, happiness, and friendship.

H) The same is true for education. It is impossible that a single shot of education, administered in childhood and early adulthood, will be able to support a sustained, 60-year career. If you factor in the projected rates of technological change, either your skills will become unnecessary, or your industry outdated. That means that everyone will, at some point in their life, have to make a number of major reinvestments in their skills.

I) It seems likely, then, that the traditional three-stage life will evolve into multiple stages containing two, three, or even more different careers. Each of these stages could potentially be different. In one the focus could be on building financial success and personal achievement, in another on creating a better work/life balance, still another on exploring and understanding options more fully, or becoming an independent producer, yet another on making a social contribution. These stages will span sectors, take people to different cities, and provide foundation for building a wide variety of skills.

J) Transitions between stages could be marked with sabbaticals as people find time rest and recharge their health, re-invest in their relationships, or improve their skills. At times, these breaks and transitions will be self-determined, at others they will be forced as existing roles, firms, or industries cease to exist.

K) A multi-stage life will have profound changes not just in how you manage your career, but also in your approach to life. An increasingly important skill will be your ability to deal with change and even welcome it. A three-stage life has few transitions, while a multi-stage life has many. That is why being self-aware, investing in broader networks of friends, and being open to new ideas will become even more crucial skills.

L) These multi-stage lives will create extraordinary variety across groups of people simply because there are so many ways of sequencing the stages. More stages mean more possible sequences.

M) With this variety will come the end of the close association of age and stage. In a three-stage life, people leave university at the same time and the same age, they tend to start their careers and family at the same age, they proceed through middle management all roughly the same time, and then move into retirement within a few years of each other. In a multi-stage life, you could be an undergraduate at 20, 40, or 60; a manager at 30, 50, or 70; and become an independent producer at any age.

N) Current life structures, career paths, educational choices, and social norms are out of tune with the emerging reality of longer lifespans. The three-stage life of full-time education, followed by continuous work, and then complete retirement may have worked for our parents or even grandparents, but it is not relevant today. We believe that to focus on longevity as primarily an issue of aging is to miss its full implications. Longevity is not necessarily about being older for longer. It is about living longer, being older later, and being younger longer.

Words & Expressions

centenarians /ˌsentɪ'neərɪən/ n. 百岁或百岁以上的人
expectancy /ɪk'spektənsi/ n. 期待，期望
equate /ɪ'kweɪt/ v. （使）等同
longevity /lɒn'dʒevəti/ n. 寿命；长寿
implication /ˌɪmplɪ'keɪʃn/ n. 可能的影响
inevitable /ɪn'evɪtəb(ə)l/ adj. 必然发生的
commitment /kə'mɪtmənt/ n. 忠诚，献身
milestone /'maɪlstəʊn/ n. 转折点；里程碑
characterized /'kærəktəˌraɪzd/ adj. 以…为特点的
cognitive /'kɒgnətɪv/ adj. 认识的，认知的
vitality /vaɪ'tæləti/ n. 活力，热情
persistent /pə'sɪstənt/ adj. 执意的，坚持不懈的
intangible /ɪn'tændʒəb(ə)l/ adj. 不可捉摸的，难以确定的

administer /əd'mɪnɪstə(r)/ v. 管理，治理；执行
sustained /sə'steɪnd/ adj. 持续的，持久的
reinvestment /ˌriːɪn'vestmənt/ n. 再投资
span /spæn/ v. 持续，贯穿
sector /'sektə(r)/ n. 区域，部分，小群体
sabbatical /sə'bætɪkl/ n. 休假
sequencing /'siːkwənsɪŋ/ v. 使按顺序排列

Notes

Centenarian

根据联合国《世界人口展望2022》中的方案预测结果，到2050年，中国百岁老人将接近50万人。海南省百岁老人占人口的比例居全国首位。男性百岁老人的增长率高于女性，但绝对数量仍然较低。

Exercises

Ⅰ. Comprehension of the Text

Read the text and answer the following questions. Write the answers on the lines.

1. How many centenarians will there be in the United States by 2050?
_____

2. How do you interpret this sentence: If you age more slowly over a longer time period, then you are in some sense younger for longer?
_____

3. By what age were 50% of Americans married in 2014?
_____

4. What are the factors behind these changes?
_____

5. Why does everyone, at some point in their life, have to make a number of major reinvestments in their skills?
_____

Ⅱ. Main Details Comprehension

Each of the following statement contains information given in one of the paragraphs. Identify the paragraph from which the information is derived. You may choose a paragraph more than once. Each paragraph is marked with a letter. Answer the questions by marking the corresponding letter in the blanks.

____1. An extended lifespan in the future will allow people to have more careers than now.

____2. Just extending one's career may have both positive and negative effects.

____3. Nowadays, many Americans have on average delayed their marriage by some eight years.

____4. Because of their longer lifespan, young people today no longer follow the pattern of life of their parents or grandparents.

____5. Many more people will be expected to live over 100 by the mid-21st century.

____6. A longer life will cause radical changes in people's approach to life.

____7. Fast technological change makes it necessary for one to constantly upgrade their skills.

____8. Many people may not want to retire early because it would do harm to their mental and emotional well-being.

____9. The close link between age and stage may cease to exist in a multi-stage life.

____10. People living a longer and healthier life will have to rearrange their work and life.

Ⅲ. Translation

Translate the five following sentences into English, using the words or expressions given in brackets.

1. 例如，我们都知道要求老板加薪有多难。（for instance）

_____

2. 从某种程度上说，也许这一研究结果正确与否并不重要。（in some sense）

_____

3. 总而言之，至少在现阶段，网上学习不太可能发展成为教育的主导形式。（evolve into）

_____

4. 这个世界将会不同，所以我们必须准备好适应变化。（be prepared to）

_____

5. 当今年年底来到时，他们能够完成这件工作吗？（come the end of）

_____

Part C

Grammar
定语从句（The Attributive Clause）

定语从句（也称关系从句、形容词性从句），是指一类由关系词（relative word）引导的从句，因为这类从句的句法功能多是作定语，所以称为定语从句，这类从句除了可以作定语之外，还可以充当状语等其他成分。

一、定语从句的先行词

被定语从句所修饰的词叫作先行词,定语从句通常会跟在先行词之后,由关系词引出,因此定语从句又可以称为关系分句。

二、定语从句的关系词

关系词可分为关系代词和关系副词。

1. 关系代词

That,who,which,whom,whose 等,可以代替先行词是人或者物的名词或代词,在从句中起到主语、宾语、定语等作用。

(1) 指代人的关系代词:who,在从句中多作主语或宾语,作宾语可用 whom,也可以省略。例如:

I am going to see a friend who has just come back from the US.

I will give this gift to the student whoever comes next.

(2) 指代人的关系代词:whom,可在句中作动词宾语或介词宾语。例如:

She is the person from whom you can expect good advice.

Mandela was the black lawyer to whom I went for advice.

(3) Whose (=of whom) 可代替人,也可以代替物。例如:

The club whose members are music fans meet in the school garden every Saturday afternoon.

(4) That 可以代替人,也可以代替物在句中作主语、宾语、表语。作宾语时可省略。例如:

The next day people put up shelters in the open air made with anything (that) they could find. (宾语)

The man that is speaking at the meeting is a famous scientist. (主语)

(5) Which 可以代替物品,在句中作主语、宾语、表语。例如:

She was fond of dancing, which her brother never was. (表语)

Another big earthquake which was almost as strong as the first one shook Tangshan.

注意:只能由 that 引导定语从句的几种情况:

①当先行词既包含人又包含物时,只能用引导词 that。例如:

They are talking of the stars and their appearances that interest them.

②如果有两个定语从句,其中一个关系词已经用了 which,这时另一个就用 that。例如:

The country built up a factory which produced things that have never been seen before.

③当先行词前面有 last,next,only,very 等词修饰时,只能用引导词 that。例如:

The only person that he can remember is his mother.

④当先行词是疑问代词 who,which,what 或主句以这些词开头时,只能用引导词 that。例如:

Who is the girl that is playing the guitar?

⑤当先行词为形容词最高级或被形容词最高级修饰时，只能用引导词 that。例如：

This is the most interesting story book that I have ever read.

⑥当先行词被序数词或形容词最高级所修饰，或本身是序数词、基数词、形容词最高级的时候只能用 that。例如：

This is the best movie that I've ever seen.

2．关系副词

When，where，why 等，引导定语从句的关系副词代替与其相应的先行词，并且在从句中分别起到时间、地点和原因状语的作用。

（1）When（＝at，on，in，during which）代替时间名词在句中作时间状语。例如：

The time when I first met my wife was a very difficult period of my life.

Wedding is an occasion when bride is the most beautiful.

（2）Where（＝in，at which）代替地点名词在句中作地点状语，也可以修饰表示抽象地点概念的名词。例如：

The parts of city where they had to live were decided by white people.

Teaching is a job where you are doing something serious but interesting.

I have reached a point in my life where I am supposed to make decisions of my own.

（3）Why（for which）指代原因，在句中作原因状语。例如：

I didn't get a pay rise, but that wasn't the reason why I left.

注意：

①虽然先行词是表示时间、地点的名词或表示原因的名词"reason"，但关系词在从句中不是充当状语，而是充当主语、宾语等，就不能用 when，where 和 why。也就是说选择关系词与先行词在主句中的语法地位无关，主要看代替先行词的关系词在从句中担任什么成分，其次再看先行词表示的是人、物、时间、地点还是原因。例如：

I still remember the days when I stayed in Beijing.

I have never forgotten the days which we spent together.

②副词 when 和 why 在非正式文体或口语中可以省略。例如：

I'll never forget the year (when) I graduated from college.

③在口语和非正式场合，when，where 和 why 或相当于关系副词的"介词＋which"结构，可以用 that 来代替，并可以省略。例如：

Do you know anywhere (that) I can get a drink?

三、限制性关系从句和非限制性关系从句

关系从句有限制性关系从句和非限制性关系从句之分。

1．限制性关系从句

限制性关系从句起限定作用，修饰特定的名词或名词短语；是主句不可或缺的一部分，如果去掉限制性关系从句，整个句子表意会不完整甚至不通顺；从结构上看，限制性关系从句常紧跟先行词，并且同先行词之间一般不加逗号分隔（但不是绝对的）。

限制性关系从句的关系词包括 that，which，who，whom，whose，as，than 等。例如：

All these books that had been donated by visiting professors are to be used by the postgraduates.

2．非限制性关系从句

从语义上看，非限制性关系从句主要起补充说明的作用，有时相当于一个并列分句或状语从句，可以表达原因、目的、结果、条件、让步等意义。例如：

Dr Lee, who had read through the instructions carefully before doing his experiments, did not obtain satisfactory results.（非限制性关系从句表示让步的意义，相当于 though Dr Lee had read through the instructions…）

非限制性关系从句的关系词包括 which，who，whom，whose，as 等，另外 that 在非限制性关系从句中并非绝对不可使用。例如：

All these books, which had been donated by visiting professors, are to be used by the postgraduates.

四、"as" 引导的定语从句

1．引导限制性定语从句

As 用作关系代词和关系副词引导限制性定语从句，并在从句中作主语、宾语、表语或状语，构成 the…same as, such…as, so…as 等结构。例如：

I have never seen such kind of girl as she is.

2．引导非限制性定语从句

As 引导非限定性定语从句时，代替整个主句，对其进行说明，但一般用于像 as we all know, as is known to all, as it is, as is said above, as already mentioned above, as is often the case, as is usual, as is reported in the newspaper 等句式中。As 在非限定性定语从句中作主语、表语或宾语，且导出的从句位置比较灵活，可位于句首或句末，也可插入句中，通常均有逗号将其与主句隔开。例如：

He forgot to bring his pen with him, as was often the case.

Exercises

Choose the best answer to the following sentences.

1. That is the only thing _____ I bought from the supermarket.
   A. which   B. that   C. what   D. where
2. The place _____ interested me most was the Children's Palace.
   A. which   B. where   C. what   D. in which
3. The computer _____ last week has gone wrong.
   A. which I bought it   B. I bought   C. what I bought   D. I bought it
4. That is the poor boy _____ father died in a traffic accident last year.
   A. who   B. whom   C. whose   D. which
5. Do you know the girl _____ is standing under the tree?
   A. who   B. whom   C. which   D. where
6. Is the woman _____ talked to our teacher yesterday your mother?
   A. who   B. whom   C. which   D. what

7. The young lady _____ we met yesterday is our new math teacher.
   A. what   B. whose   C. whom   D. which
8. I like to live in a house _____ is big and bright.
   A. that   B. who   C. how   D. why
9. I hate people _____ talk much but do little.
   A. whom   B. which   C. who   D. when
10. I am one of the boys _____ never late for school.
    A. that is   B. who are   C. who am   D. who is
11. Mr. Green, there is someone at the front desk _____ would like to speak with you.
    A. he   B. who   C. which   D. whom
12. I love the small village _____ I was born.
    A. that   B. which   C. where   D. whose
13. Here comes the girl _____ handwriting is the best in our class.
    A. which   B. whose   C. that   D. who
14. My parents usually buy me some simple clothes _____ can last a long time.
    A. who   B. that   C. whom   D. whose
15. - Is the girl _____ is interviewing the manager of that company your friend?
    - Yes, she is a journalist from CCTV.
    A. whom   B. which   C. who   D. whose
16. - Do you know everybody _____ came to the party?
    - No, I don't know the one _____ you had a long talk with near the door.
    A. who; /   B. whose; that   C. that; which   D. /; whom
17. The boy _____ won the first prize is called Roy.
    A. when   B. whom   C. who   D. which
18. Children like houses _____ are painted in different colors.
    A. which   B. they   C. those   D. what
19. Do you think most students prefer tests _____ have easy questions?
    A. who   B. where   C. that   D. it
20. The factory _____ his mother works is in the east of the city.
    A. that   B. which   C. on which   D. where

Workshop
Cultural Introduction

I. Images associated with longevity

1. May your fortune be as boundless as the East Sea and may you live a long and happy life! 福如东海，寿比南山。

2．仙鹤（crane）是鸟类中最高贵的一种鸟，代表长寿、富运长久。仙鹤在中国自古以来都被视为吉祥、如意、高雅飘逸，并与长寿、仙境等美好形象联系在一起。

3．鹿（deer）是长寿的仙兽，传说鹿是天上瑶光星散开时生成的瑞兽，常与神仙、仙鹤、灵芝、松柏神树在一起。

4．龟（turtle）是"四灵"之一，传说中能活千万年，古人喜欢用龟字取名以寄长寿，并常以"龟鹤之年"等寓意吉祥。

5．松树（pine tree）因其是自然界中生命力最旺盛、最长寿的树种而象征人的长寿。

6．古柏（ancient cypress）因为松柏傲霜斗雪、卓然不群、耐严寒、不凋零、生命力强、生长期长，所以我国民间把松柏作为经得起磨难和长寿的象征。

7．蟠桃（flat peach）代表长寿的仙人手中托着的大仙桃。仙桃又称寿桃，民间神话中桃子是来自天界的仙果，吃了可以保佑人健康无病。

8．a cycle of sixty years 花甲

9．seventy years of age 古稀

10．age between seventy and a hundred 耄耋

11．longevity crane 松鹤延年

12．the god of longevity 寿星

Ⅱ．Group Discussion

Write down images and poems related to longevity.

Unit 7 Spirit and Mood

The State of Boredom Experienced by Man

Boredom has become trendy. Studies point to how boredom is good for creativity and innovation, as well as mental health. It is found that people are more creative following the completion of a tedious task. When people are bored, they have an increase in "associative thought" — the process of making new connections between ideas, which is linked to innovative thinking. These studies are impressive, but in reality, the benefits of boredom may be related to having time to clear your mind, be quiet, or daydream.

In our stimulation-rich world, it seems unrealistic that boredom could occur at all. Yet, there are valid reasons boredom may feel so painful. As it turns out, boredom might signal the fact that you have a need that isn't being met.

Our always-on world of social media may result in more connections, but they are superficial and can get in the way of building a real sense of belonging. Feeling bored may signal the desire for a greater sense of community and the feeling that you fit in with others around you. So take the step of joining an organization to build face-to-face relationships. You'll find depth that you won't get from your screen no matter how many likes you get on your post.

Similar to the need for belonging, bored people often report that they feel a limited sense of meaning. It's a fundamental human need to have a larger purpose and to feel like we're part of something bigger than ourselves. When people are bored, they're more likely to feel less meaning in their lives. If you want to reduce boredom and increase your sense of meaning, seek work where you can make a unique contribution, or find a cause you can support with your time and talent.

If your definition of boredom is being quiet, mindful, and reflective, keep it up. But if you're struggling with real boredom and the emptiness it provokes, consider whether you might seek new connections and more significant challenges. These are the things that will genuinely relieve boredom and make you more effective in the process.

Words & Expressions

trendy/'trendi/*adj.* 时髦的，赶时髦的
tedious/'ti:diəs/*adj.* 冗长的；啰唆的；单调乏味的；令人厌烦的
associative/ə'səʊsiətɪv/*adj.* 联想的

daydream/'deɪdriːm/v. 白日梦；幻想；空想
stimulation/ˌstɪmjuˈleɪʃ(ə)n/n. 刺激
unrealistic/ˌʌnrɪəˈlɪstɪk/adj. 不切实际的；不实在的
valid/'vælɪd/adj. 正当的，合理的
signal/'sɪgnəl/v. 标志；表明；预示
superficial/ˌsuːpəˈfɪʃ(ə)l/adj. 肤浅的
fundamental/ˌfʌndəˈment(ə)l/adj. 十分重大的，根本的
reflective/rɪˈflektɪv/adj. 沉思的，深思的
provoke/prəˈvəʊk/v. 激起，引起，引发
mindful/'maɪndfl/adj. 记着；想着；考虑到
genuinely/'dʒenjuɪnli/adv. 真诚地；的确
be linked to 与…连接；与…有关联，与…有联系
result in 导致，结果是
keep it up 坚持；继续下去
struggle with 与…斗争
a sense of 一种…的感觉

Exercises

Ⅰ. Comprehension of the Text

There are 5 questions in this section. For each of them there are four choices marked A, B, C and D. You should choose the best answer for each question.

1. What have studies found about boredom?
    A. It facilitates innovative thinking.
    B. It is a result of doing boring tasks.
    C. It helps people connect with others.
    D. It does harm to one's mental health.

2. What does the author say boredom might indicate?
    A. A need to be left alone.
    B. A desire to be fulfilled.
    C. A conflict to be resolved.
    D. A feeling to be validated.

3. What do we learn about social media from the passage?
    A. It may be an obstacle to expanding one's connections.
    B. It may get in the way of enhancing one's social status.
    C. It may prevent people from developing a genuine sense of community.
    D. It may make people feel that they ought to fit in with the outside world.

4. What does the author suggest people do to get rid of boredom?
   A. Count the likes they get on their posts.
   B. Reflect on how they relate to others.
   C. Engage in real-life interactions.
   D. Participate in online discussions.
5. What should people do to enhance their sense of meaning?
   A. Try to do something original.
   B. Confront significant challenges.
   C. Define boredom in their unique way.
   D. Devote themselves to a worthy cause.

Ⅱ. Languages Focus

A. *Match the following words in left with their explanations in right.*

1. superficial	a. lasting or taking too long and not interesting
2. valid	b. to cause a particular reaction or have a particular effect
3. provoke	c. thinking deeply about things
4. associative	d. seeing only what is obvious
5. tedious	e. very fashionable
6. signal	f. based on what is logical or true
7. reflective	g. to try to obtain or achieve sth.
8. fundamental	h. relating to the association of ideas or things
9. trendy	i. to be a sign that sth. exists or is likely to happen
10. seek	j. serious and very important

B. *Fill in the blanks with the words or expressions given below. Change the form where necessary.*

seek	result in	tedious	provoke	fundamental
trendy	valid	signal	associative	reflective

1. We had to listen to the _____ details of his operation.
2. The scandal surely _____ the end of his political career.
3. Such a war could _____ the use of chemical and biological weapons.
4. I enjoy being able to go out and buy _____ clothes.
5. There is a _____ difference between the two points of view.
6. She had _____ reasons for not supporting the proposals.
7. The article was intended to _____ discussion.
8. The _____ guilt was ingrained in his soul.
9. We are currently _____ new ways of expanding our membership.
10. Intuition may affect _____ tasks.

Ⅲ. Translation

Translate the following sentences into Chinese.

1. Studies point to how boredom is good for creativity and innovation, as well as mental health.

2. These studies are impressive, but in reality, the benefits of boredom may be related to having time to clear your mind, be quiet, or daydream.

3. Feeling bored may signal the desire for a greater sense of community and the feeling that you fit in with others around you.

4. It's a fundamental human need to have a larger purpose and to feel like we're part of something bigger than ourselves.

5. If your definition of boredom is being quiet, mindful, and reflective, keep it up.

Ⅳ. Discussion

Can you give some suggestions about how to relieve boredom?

The Start of High School Doesn't Have to Be Stressful

A) This month, more than 4 million students across the nation will begin high school. Many will do well. But many will not. Consider that nearly two-thirds of students will experience the "ninth-grade shock," which refers to a dramatic drop in a student's academic performance. Some students cope with this shock by avoiding challenges. For instance, they may drop difficult coursework. Others may experience a hopelessness that results in failing their core classes, such as English, science and math.

B) This should matter a great deal to parents, teachers and policymakers. Ultimately it should matter to the students themselves and society at large, because students' experience of transitioning to the ninth grade can have long-term consequences not only for the students themselves but for their home communities. We make these observations as research psychologists who have studied how schools and families can help young people thrive.

C) In the new global economy, students who fail to finish the ninth grade with passing grades in college preparatory coursework are very unlikely to graduate on time and go on to get jobs. One study has calculated that the lifetime benefit to the local economy for a single additional student who completes high school is half a million dollars or more. This is based on higher earnings and avoided costs in health care, crime, welfare dependence and other things.

D) The consequences of doing poorly in the ninth grade can impact more than students' ability to find a good job. It can also impact the extent to which they enjoy life. Students lose many of the friends they turned to for support when they move from the eighth to the ninth grade. One study of ninth-grade students found that 50 percent of friendships among ninth graders changed from one month to the next, signaling striking instability in friendships.

E) In addition, studies find the first year of high school typically shows one of the greatest increases in depression of any year over the life span. Researchers think that one explanation is that ties to friends are broken while academic demands are rising. Furthermore, most adult cases of clinical depression first emerge in adolescence. The World Health Organization reports that depression has the greatest burden of disease worldwide, in terms of the total cost of treatment and the loss of productivity.

F) Given all that's riding on having a successful ninth grade experience, it pays to explore what can be done to meet the academic, social and emotional challenges of the transition to high school. So far, our studies have yielded one main insight: Students' beliefs about change — their beliefs about whether people are stuck one way forever, or whether people can change their personalities and abilities — are related to their ability to cope, succeed academically and maintain good mental health. Past research has called these beliefs "mindsets" with a "fixed mindset" referring to the belief that people cannot change and a "growth mindset" referring to the belief that people can change.

G) In one recent study, we examined 360 adolescents' beliefs about the nature of "smartness" — that is, their fixed mindsets about intelligence. We then assessed biological stress responses for students whose grades were dropping by examining their stress hormones. Students who believed that intelligence is fixed — that you are stuck being "not smart" if you struggle in school — showed higher levels of stress hormones when their grades were declining at the beginning of the ninth grade. If students believed that intelligence could improve — that is to say, when they held more of a growth mindset of intelligence — they showed lower levels of stress hormones when their grades were declining. This was an exciting result because it showed that the body's stress responses are not determined solely by one's grades. Instead, declining grades only predicted worse stress hormones among students who believed that worsening grades were a permanent and hopeless state of affairs.

H) We also investigated the social side of the high school transition. In this study, instead of teaching students that their smartness can change, we taught them that their social standing — that is, whether they are bullied or excluded or left out — can change over time. We then looked at high school students stress responses to daily social difficulties. That is, we taught them a growth mindset about their social lives. In this study, students came into the laboratory and were asked to give a public speech in front of upper-year students. The topic of the speech was what makes one popular in high school. Following this, students had to complete a difficult mental math task in front of the same upper-year students.

I) Experiment results showed that students who were not taught that people can change showed poor stress responses. When these students gave the speech, their blood vessels contracted and their hearts pumped less blood through the body — both responses that the body shows when it is preparing for damage or defeat after a physical threat. Then they gave worse speeches and made more mistakes in math. But when students were taught that people can change, they had better responses to stress, in part because they felt like they had the resources to deal with the demanding situation. Students who got the growth mindset intervention showed less-contracted blood vessels and their hearts pumped more blood — both of which contributed to more oxygen getting to the brain, and, ultimately, better performance on the speech and mental math tasks.

J) These findings lead to several possibilities that we are investigating further. First, we are working to replicate these findings in more diverse school communities. We want to know in which types of schools and for which kinds of students these growth mindset ideas help young people adapt to the challenges of high school. We also hope to learn how teachers, parents or school counselors can help students keep their on going academic or social difficulties in perspective. We wonder what would happen if schools helped to make beliefs about the potential for change and improvement a large feature of the over all school culture, especially for students starting the ninth grade.

Words & Expressions

shock/ʃɒk/ *n.* （对生活方式的）冲击，撞击
dramatic/drə'mætɪk/ *adj.* 突然的；巨大的；令人吃惊的
drop/drɒp/ *v.* 停止；终止；放弃
core/kɔː(r)/ *adj.* 最重要的；主要的；基本的
matter/'mætə(r)/ *v.* 事关紧要；要紧；有重大影响
striking/'straɪkɪŋ/ *adj.* 引人注目的；异乎寻常的；显著的
instability/ˌɪnstə'bɪləti/ *n.* 不稳定，不稳固
yield/jiːld/ *v.* 出产（作物）；产生（收益、效益等）；提供
insight/'ɪnsaɪt/ *n.* 洞察力，领悟力
mindset/'maɪndset/ *n.* 观念模式，思维倾向
hormone/'hɔːməʊn/ *n.* 激素，荷尔蒙
solely/'səʊlli/ *adv.* 仅；只；唯；单独地
bully/'bʊli/ *v.* 恐吓；伤害；胁迫

contract/'kɒntrækt/v. （使）收缩，缩小
pump/pʌmp/v. 用泵（或泵样器官等）输送
intervention/ˌɪntə'venʃ(ə)n/n. 干预，介入
replicate/'replɪkeɪt/v. 重复，复制
in terms of 依据；按照

Exercises

I. Comprehension of the Text

Read the text and answer the following questions. Write the answers on the lines.

1. What will the students do when they experience "ninth-grade shock"?

2. What are the consequences of doing poorly in ninth grade?

3. What does "growth mindset" refer to according to the passage?

4. Why does the first year of high school show one of the greatest increases in depression?

5. How did the students who were told they had growth mindset do in the experiment?

II. Main Details Comprehension

Each of the following statement contains information given in one of the paragraphs. Identify the paragraph from which the information is derived. You may choose a paragraph more than once. Each paragraph is marked with a letter. Answer the questions by marking the corresponding letter in the blanks.

____1. The number of people experiencing depression shows a sharp increase in the first year of high school.

____2. According to one study students academic performance is not the only decisive factor of their stress responses.

____3. Researchers would like to explore further how parents and schools can help ninth graders by changing their mindset.

____4. According to one study each high school graduate contributes at least 500,000 dollars to the local economy.

____5. In one study, students were told their social position in school is not unchangeable.

____6. It is reported that depression results in enormous economic losses worldwide.

____7. One study showed that friendships among ninth graders were far from stable.

____8. More than half of students will find their academic performance declining sharply when they enter the ninth grade.

＿＿＿9. Researchers found through experiments that students could be taught to respond to stress in a more positive way.

＿＿＿10. It is beneficial to explore ways to cope with the challenges facing students entering high school.

Ⅲ. Translation

Translate the five following sentences into English, using the words or expressions given in brackets.

1．这项公告对房屋价格产生了巨大的影响。（dramatic）

＿＿＿＿＿＿＿＿＿＿＿＿＿＿＿＿＿＿＿＿＿＿＿＿＿＿＿＿＿＿＿＿＿＿＿＿＿＿＿

2．我认为我们最好不要再谈这个话题。（drop）

＿＿＿＿＿＿＿＿＿＿＿＿＿＿＿＿＿＿＿＿＿＿＿＿＿＿＿＿＿＿＿＿＿＿＿＿＿＿＿

3．新商家在这一地区蓬勃兴起。（thrive）

＿＿＿＿＿＿＿＿＿＿＿＿＿＿＿＿＿＿＿＿＿＿＿＿＿＿＿＿＿＿＿＿＿＿＿＿＿＿＿

4．这项研究提供了有用的资料。（yield）

＿＿＿＿＿＿＿＿＿＿＿＿＿＿＿＿＿＿＿＿＿＿＿＿＿＿＿＿＿＿＿＿＿＿＿＿＿＿＿

5．这些变化带来的效果难以评估。（assess）

＿＿＿＿＿＿＿＿＿＿＿＿＿＿＿＿＿＿＿＿＿＿＿＿＿＿＿＿＿＿＿＿＿＿＿＿＿＿＿

Grammar
状语从句（Adverbial Clause）

一、时间状语从句

1．When，as，while 引导的时间状语从句

（1）When 引导时间状语从句时表示"当…的时候"，when 既可以指时间段也可指时间点，从句中既可用延续性动词又可用非延续性动词，且动作既可和主句的动作同时发生又可在主句的动作之前或之后发生。例如：

I owed Jack $100 when I was in London. 我在伦敦期间欠杰克 100 美元。

When I came home, my wife was cooking dinner. 我回家时，妻子在做晚饭。

（2）While 引导时间状语从句时表示"当…的时候"，它强调主句的动作与从句的动作同时持续地进行，用于这一用法时 while 引导的时间状语从句和主句中的谓语动词必须是延续性动词，或者主句的动作发生在从句动作的进行过程中，此时主句中的谓语动词通常是非延续性动词。例如：

I met her while I was on my way to school. 我在上学的路上遇见了她。

（3）As 引导时间状语从句时表示"当…时，一边…一边…"，侧重表示两个动作同时发生（包括一个主语同时进行两个动作），或者一种动作随着另一种动作的变化而变化。例如：

He jumps as he goes along. 他边走边跳。

2．Till, until（not...until/till...直到…才…）引导的时间状语从句

Till 和 until 这两个词作连词和介词时的意义和用法相同，一般可以换用（放在句首时通常用 until 的形式，till 在口语中更为常见）。Till 和 until 引导时间状语从句时跟主句中肯定形式或否定形式的、表示延续性动作的谓语动词连用表示"到…为止"，跟主句中否定形式的、表示非延续性动作的谓语动词连用表示"直到…才（开始）"。例如：

I'll stay here till/until Tom arrives. 我会待在这里直到汤姆到达。

He didn't go home till/until he had finished his homework. 直到完成作业他才回家。

注意：如果将"not until..."结构放在句首，那么主句要部分倒装。例如：

Not until the teacher came in did the students stop talking. 直到老师进来，学生们才停止讨论。

3．Before/since 引导的时间状语从句

（1）Before 本义为"在…之前"，可根据语境译为"还未…就…，…才…，趁…，还没来得及…"，since 表示"自…以来"。例如：

Please write it down before you forget it. 趁你没忘请把它记下来。

He hasn't been home since he graduated. 他毕业后没回过家。

（2）Before/since 常用句型。

It will be＋时间段＋before（从句用一般现在时）过…时间才…

It was not long before（从句用一般过去时）没过很长时间就…

It was＋时间段＋before（从句用一般过去时）过了…时间才…

It is/has been＋时间段＋since（从句用一般过去时）自…以来已经有多长时间了

It was＋时间段＋since（从句用过去完成时）自…以来已经有多长时间了

例如：

It was two years before he left the country. 过了两年他才离开了这个国家。

It was three years since we had been there. 我们在那儿已待了三年。

4．As soon as, immediately, the moment/minute, no sooner...than..., hardly/scarcely...when...均可引导时间状语从句，表示从句的动作一发生，主句的动作随即就发生，意为"一…就…"。no sooner...和 hardly/scarcely...位于句首时，主句要部分倒装。例如：

The moment I heard the voice, I knew my father was coming. 我一听到声音，就知道是父亲来了。

Hardly had I got home when it began to rain. 我一到家，天就开始下雨了。

5．Every time, each time, next time 引导的时间状语从句

名词词组用来引导时间状语从句，表示"每当…，每次…，下次…"。例如：

Every/Each time I was in trouble, he would come to help me out. 每次我遇到麻烦，他都会来帮我。

二、条件状语从句

1．If 和 unless

If 表示正面的条件，意为"如果"，unless（＝if not）表示负面的条件，意为"除非，

如果不"。例如：

If you ask him, he will help you. 如果你请求他，他会帮助你。

He is sure to come unless he has some urgent business. 他一定会来，除非他有急事。

2．In case, on condition that, providing, provided (that), supposing (that), as/so long as 这些引导词（词组）意思相近，表示"假如，假使，在…条件下，只要"。例如：

In case he comes, let me know. 如果他来的话，告诉我一声。

Supposing (that) he does not come, what shall we do? 他要是不来，我们该怎么办？

You may use the book so long as you return it on time. 只要你准时还，你就可以借这本书。

三、原因状语从句

（1）Because 引导的原因状语从句一般放于主句之后，because 表示直接原因，语气最强，最适合回答 why 引导的疑问句。例如：

- Why wasn't he present? 他为什么没来？
- Because he was ill. 因为他病了。

（2）Since 引导的原因状语从句一般放于主句前，表示已知的、显然的理由，翻译成"既然"，较为正式，语气比 because 弱。Seeing (that), now (that), considering (that) in that 引导原因状语从句，与 since 意思相近，表示"既然"。例如：

Since you're not interested, I won't tell you about it. 既然你不感兴趣，那我就不告诉你这件事了。

Now that everyone has been here, let's start our meeting. 既然大家都来了，我们开始开会吧。

She was fortunate in that she had friends to help her. 她很幸运，因为有一些朋友帮助她。

Seeing that it is eight o'clock, we'll wait no longer. 由于已经八点了，我们不再等了。

（3）As 引导原因状语从句时表示附带说明的"双方已知的原因"，语气比 since 弱，较为正式，位置较为灵活（常放于主句之前）。例如：

As I was in a hurry this morning, I left my key at home. 今天早晨因为太匆忙，我把钥匙忘在了家里。

四、地点状语从句

（1）地点状语从句表示地点、方位，这类从句通常由 where，wherever 引导。例如：

They will go where they are happy. 他们想到他们觉得快乐的地方去。

Wherever there is smoke, there is fire. 无火不生烟（无风不起浪）。

（2）区分 where 引导的定语从句与状语从句：where 引导状语从句时，where 是从属连词，where 引导的从句修饰主句的谓语动词，where 前面没有表示地点的先行词；where 引导定语从句时，where 是关系副词，在从句中作地点状语，其前面有表示地点的先行词，where 引导的从句修饰先行词。例如：

You'd better make a mark where you have any questions.（状语从句）

You'd better make a mark at the place where you have any questions.（定语从句）

你最好在有问题的地方做个记号。

五、目的状语从句

引导目的状语从句的连词有 in order that, so that, in case, lest, for fear that（lest, for fear that 后的目的状语从句一般要用"should＋动词原形"的虚拟语气形式；in case 后的目的状语从句多用虚拟语气，但也可用陈述语气）等。例如：

We used the computer in order that we could save time. 我们使用计算机是为了节省时间。

He's working hard for fear that he should fail. 他努力工作，唯恐失败。

Take an umbrella with you in case it should rain. 带把伞，以防下雨。

六、结果状语从句

（1）So that 可以引导目的状语从句，也可以引导结果状语从句。例如：

He worried so that he couldn't sleep. 他急得睡不着。

（2）表示"如此…以致…"的"so...that..."和"such...that..."均可引导结果状语从句，其中的 such 是形容词，修饰名词；so 是副词，修饰形容词或副词，具体的搭配形式如下：

① so＋*adj./adv.*＋that"，"so＋*adj.*＋a/an＋*n.*＋that

② such（＋a/an）（＋*adj.*）＋*n.*＋that

例如：

It is so fine today that we decide to go swimming. 今天天气很好,我们决定去游泳。

Our country has so much coal that she can export large quantities. 我们国家的煤炭非常丰富，可以大量出口。

So 与表示数量的形容词 many，few，much，little 等连用已经形成固定搭配，这些场合下不能换用 such 的对应结构表示。例如：

He's such a good person that we mustn't blame him. 他是这样好的人，我们不能怪他。

七、让步状语从句

让步状语从句表示前后句之间为让步关系。引导让步状语从句的连词主要有 though, although, even though, even if, while, as, whether, who (whom, what, which, when, where, how 等)＋-ever, no matter who (whom, what, how 等), whether...or...等。

（1）Though, although, even if 和 even though 引导让步状语从句。

四者皆有"虽然，即使，尽管"之语义，其中 even if 和 even though 语气较强，though 和 although 语气较弱，though 不如 although 正式。though 和 although 不与 but 连，但可与 yet 和 still 连用。例如：

Although it was so cold, he went out without an overcoat. 天气虽然很冷，但他没有穿大衣就出去了。

She carries on the job even though/even if she has a bad cold for several days. 尽管得重感冒几天了，但她仍坚守在工作岗位上。

Though they may not succeed, they will still try. 即使他们可能不会成功，但他们仍努

力尝试。

（2）No matter who（what, when, which, how, where 等）引导让步状语从句。

相当于"who（what, when, which, how, where 等）+-ever"，表示"无论何人（什么，何时，哪个/些，怎样，何地）"等。例如：

He keeps taking exercise in winter no matter how cold it is. 冬天不管有多冷，他一直坚持锻炼身体。

Whoever breaks the rule, he must be punished. 不管谁违反规定，都会被惩罚。

Whatever (=No matter what) you say, I will not change my mind. 无论你说什么，我也绝不改变主意。

（3）whether...or...引导让步状语从句意为"无论…还是…"。例如：

Whether she wins or loses, this is her last chance. 不管是赢是输，这都是她的最后一次机会。

（4）While 引导让步状语从句。意为"尽管，虽然"，相当于 although/though。例如：

While we don't agree on that, we continue to be friends. 虽然我们在那件事上意见不同，但我们仍然是朋友。

（5）让步状语从句的倒装。

Though 引导的让步状语从句可以倒装，也可以不倒装，但 as 引导的让步状语从句必须采用倒装结构，as 引导的倒装形式的让步状语从句的基本结构为：形容词/副词/名词（单数可数名词前一般不带冠词，有时也可见单数可数名词前形容词与不定冠词连用、形容词放在不定冠词前）/动词/过去分词+as+主语+谓语的其他部分。例如：

Bravely though we fought in the competition, we had no chance of winning. 尽管我们在竞赛中英勇拼搏，但胜利无望。

Try as he would, he could not lift the rock. 虽然尽了最大努力，但是他仍然不能搬动那块石头。

Great as the author was, he proved a bad model. 这位作者尽管了不起，到头来却成了一个坏榜样。

八、方式状语从句和比较状语从句

（1）方式状语从句常由 as, as if/as though 引导。例如：

Please do it as I told you. 请按照我告诉你的做。

（2）引导比较状语从句的从属连词为 as...as（和…一样），not as/so...as（和…不一样），than（比）。这类从句常以省略形式出现。例如：

The work is not so difficult as you imagine. 这工作不像你想象的那么困难。

You look younger than you are. 你看上去比你的实际年龄要年轻。

He doesn't work as hard as she (does). 他工作不像她那样努力。

九、状语从句的省略

当状语从句中的主语和主句的主语一致，或状语从句中的主语是 it，并且又含有 be 动词时，常可以省略从句中的主语和 be 动词。

状语从句的省略常出现在以下从句中：

Unit 7 Spirit and Mood

（1）在 as, before, till, once, when, while 等引导的时间状语从句中。例如：
While in Beijing, I paid a visit to the Summer Palace. 在北京时，我参观了颐和园。
（2）在 though, although 等引导的让步状语从句中。例如：
Though (they were) tired, they went on working. 虽然他们累了，但他们仍继续工作。
（3）在 if, unless (=if...not) 等引导的条件状语从句中。例如：
Unless (it is) necessary, you'd better not refer to the dictionary.
如果没有必要，你最好不要查字典。
（4）在 as, as if, as though 引导的方式状语从句中。例如：
He did as (he had been) told. 他按照被告知的那样去做了。
He paused as if (he was) expecting her to speak. 他停下来，好像是在期待她说话。
（5）在 as...as ..., than 引导的比较状语从句中。例如：
This car doesn't run as fast as that one (does). 这种小汽车不及那辆跑得快。

Exercises

Choose the best answer to the following sentences.

1. After the war, a new school building was put up _____ there had once been a theatre.
   A. that   B. where   C. which   D. when
2. I had just started back for the house to change my clothes _____ I heard the voices.
   A. as   B. after   C. while   D. when
3. The class went on with the story _____ they had left it before the holiday.
   A. where   B. which   C. in which   D. when
4. - Is Mr. Smith in the office?
   - Yes, _____ he is in charge of the office, he must be there.
   A. since   B. however   C. whether   D. for
5. Someone called me up in the middle of the night, but they hung up _____ I could answer the phone.
   A. as   B. since   C. until   D. before
6. John may phone tonight. I don't want to go out _____ he phones.
   A. as long as B. in order to C. in case   D. so that
7. ____others say, the expert is sure that his theory is correct.
   A. No matter   B. It doesn't matter C. Whatever D. What
8. Many places are flooded by heavy rainfalls, so they can't walk _____ they like these days.
   A. when   B. whenever   C. where   D. wherever
9. The roof fell _____ he had time to dash into the room to save his baby.
   A. before   B. as   C. after   D. until

10. - The thread of my kite broke and it flew away.
    - I had told you it would easily break _____ it was the weakest.
    A. when   B. where   C. unless   D. since
11. The crowd started cheering _____ he rose to speak.
    A. as   B. since   C. till   D. where
12. Scientists say it may be five or ten years _____ it is possible to test this medicine on human patients.
    A. since   B. before   C. after   D. when
13. ____ the Internet is bringing the distance between people, it may also be breaking some homes or will cause other family problems.
    A. When   B. If   C. As   D. Although
14. The two girls look ____ much alike ____ no one can tell them apart.
    A. so; that   B. so; and   C. as; that   D. such; that
15. John shut everybody out of the kitchen _____ he could prepare his grand surprise for the party.
    A. which   B. when   C. so that   D. as if
16. We must hurry up _____ catch the last train.
    A. that   B. so that to   C. in order that   D. in order to
17. No matter_____ hard it may be, I will carry it out.
    A. what   B. whatever   C. how   D. however
18. _____ you may do, you must do it well.
    A. Which   B. Whenever   C. Whatever   D. When
19. They went on working _____ it was late at night.
    A. even if   B. as if   C. however   D. as though
20. - Shall Brown come and play computer games?
    - No, _____ he has finished his homework.
    A. when   B. if   C. unless   D. once

Workshop
Reliving Pressure of College Students

I. Background

Today's college students are in face of pressure from all aspects, from parents' expectation, study, employment and all kinds of competitions. Although pressure, to some extent, can provide motivation, overdue pressure has a serious negative affect. Pressure can destroy a student's confidence. More seriously, it might make some students lose control of their emotions and behaviors. So it is very necessary for college students to know how to relieve the pressure and keep a balance between study and leisure.

II. Task

(1) Interview some classmates (including the ones who are not in the same class) to know what kind of pressure they are suffering and what do they do to relive their pressure.

(2) Category the solutions and report the findings to the whole class.

III. Process

Step 1: Complete the task in groups. Form small groups with 5 students respectively;

Step 2: Interview your classmates and classify the information;

Step 3: Finish a report on the reasons and solutions.

Unit 8 Social Media

Facebook

People are being lured onto Facebook with the promise of a fun, free service without realizing they're paying for it by giving up loads of personal information. Facebook then attempts to make money by selling their data to advertisers that want to send targeted messages.

Most Facebook users don't realize this is happening. Even if they know what the company is up to, they still have no idea what they're paying for Facebook because people don't really know what their personal data is worth.

The biggest problem, however, is that the company keeps changing the rules. Early on, you keep everything private. That was the great thing about Facebook — you could create your own little private network. Last year. The company changed its privacy rules so that many things — your city, your photo, your friends' names — were set, by default to be shared with everyone on the Internet.

According to Facebook's vice-president Elliot Schrage, the company is simply making changes to improve its service, and if people don't share information, they have a "less satisfying experience".

Some critics think this is more about Facebook looking to make more money. Its original business model, which involved selling ads and putting them at the side of the pages, totally failed. Who wants to look at ads when they're online connecting with their friends?

The privacy issue has already landed Facebook in hot water in Washington. In April, Senator Charles Schumer called on Facebook to change its privacy policy. He also urged the Federal Trade Commission to set guidelines for social-networking sites. "I think the senator rightly communicated that we had not been clear about what the new products were and how people could choose to use them or not to use them," Schrage admits.

I suspect that whatever Facebook has done so far to invade our privacy, it's only the beginning, which is why I'm considering deactivating my account. Facebook is a handy site, but I'm upset by the idea that my information is in the hands of people I don't know. That's too high a price to pay.

Unit 8 Social Media

Words & Expressions

lure/luə(r)/*v.* 劝诱；引诱；诱惑
attempt/ə'tempt/*v.* 努力，尝试；试图
targeted/'tɑːgɪtɪd/*adj.* 定向的；被定为攻击目标的
default/dɪ'fɔːlt/*n.* 默认，系统设定值
vice-president/ˌvaɪs 'prezɪdənt/*n.* （商业公司的）副总裁，副总经理
critic/'krɪtɪk/*n.* 批评家；评论家；评论员
privacy/'prɪvəsi/*n.* 隐私；私密
policy/'pɒləsi/*n.* 政策，方针
urge/ɜːdʒ/*v.* 敦促；催促；力劝
commission/kə'mɪʃ(ə)n/*n.* （通常为政府管控或调查某事的）委员会
suspect/ə'spekt/*v.* 疑有，觉得（尤指坏事可能属实或发生）
invade/ɪn'veɪd/*v.* 武装入侵；侵略；侵犯
deactivate/diː'æktɪveɪt/*v.* 使（仪器等）停止工作
account/ə'kaʊnt/*n.* （互联网、电子邮件等的）账户，账号
handy/'hændi/*adj.* 易使用的；容易做的；便利的
communicate/kə'mjuːnɪkeɪt/*v.* 传达，传递（想法、感情、思想等）
land sb./sth. in 使陷入（困境）
loads of 许多，大量
Federal Trade Commission 联邦贸易委员会

Exercises

Ⅰ. Comprehension of the Text

There are 5 questions in this section. For each of them there are four choices marked A, B, C and D. You should choose the best answer for each question.

1. What do we learn about Facebook from the first paragraph?
   A. It is a website that sends messages to targeted users.
   B. It makes money by putting on advertisements.
   C. It profits by selling its users' personal data.
   D. It provides loads of information to its users.

2. What does the author say about most Facebook users?
   A. They are reluctant to give up their personal information.
   B. They don't know their personal data enriches Facebook.
   C. They don't identify themselves when using the website.
   D. They care very little about their personal information.

3. Why does Facebook make changes to its rules according to Elliot Schrage?
   A. To render better service to its users.
   B. To conform to the Federal guidelines.
   C. To improve its users' connectivity.
   D. To expand its scope of business.
4. Why does Senator Charles Schumer advocate?
   A. Setting guidelines for advertising on websites.
   B. Banning the sharing of users' personal information.
   C. Formulating regulations for social-networking sites.
   D. Removing ads from all social-networking sites.
5. Why does the author plan to cancel his Facebook account?
   A. He is dissatisfied with its current service.
   B. He finds many of its users untrustworthy.
   C. He doesn't want his personal data abused.
   D. He is upset by its frequent rule changes.

II. Languages Focus

A. *Match the following words in left with their explanations in right.*

1. privacy
2. attempt
3. default
4. lure
5. suspect
6. urge
7. handy
8. deactivate
9. policy
10. invade

a. to make an effort or try to do sth., especially sth. difficult
b. easy to use or to do
c. to advise or try hard to persuade sb. to do sth.
d. a plan of action agreed or chosen by a political party, a business, etc.
e. to make sth. such as a device or chemical process stop working
f. what happens or appears if you do not make any other choice or change
g. to enter a country, town, etc. using military force in order to take control of it
h. the state of being alone and not watched or disturbed by other people
i. to have an idea that sth. is probably true or likely to happen, especially sth. bad, but without having definite proof
j. to persuade or trick sb. to go somewhere or to do sth. by promising them a reward

B. *Fill in the blanks with the words or expressions given below. Change the form where necessary.*

| attempt | communicate | policy | urge | loads of |
| privacy | lure | deactivate | default | land |

1. The prisoner _____ an escape, but failed.
2. She was longing for some peace and _____ .

3. The _____ option is to save your work every five minutes.
4. Do you know how to _____ the alarm.
5. The child was _____ into a car but managed to escape.
6. The company has adopted a firm _____ on shoplifting.
7. His hot temper has _____ him in trouble before.
8. He won _____ golds in gymnastics.
9. The report _____ that all children be taught to swim.
10. He was eager to _____ his ideas to the group.

III. Translation

Translate the following sentences into Chinese.

1. Facebook then attempts to make money by selling their data to advertisers that want to send targeted messages.

_____

2. The company changed its privacy rules so that many things — your city, your photo, your friends' names — were set, by default to be shared with everyone on the Internet.

_____
_____

3. Its original business model, which involved selling ads and putting them at the side of the pages, totally failed.

_____

4. The privacy issue has already landed Facebook in hot water in Washington.

_____

5. Facebook is a handy site, but I'm upset by the idea that my information is in the hands of people I don't know.

_____

IV. Discussion

Can you think of some ways to protect our privacy?

Fake Holiday Villa Websites Prompt Warning

A) During the British winter, the thought of two weeks in a coastal villa with soul-stirring views of the sea and a huge pool to enjoy is enough to offset the labor until the holidays start. For a growing number of people, however, their yearly break is turning into a nightmare as they find that the property they have paid thousands for does not exist and the website through which they booked it has disappeared.

B) Consumers have been warned to be aware of the potential for deception in this market, which is far from uncommon. In 2017 there were 1,632 cases of reported "villa fraud", with victims losing an average of £2,052, according to Action Fraud, the national center for reporting such frauds. "Millions of pounds are lost each year by holidaymakers," says Sean Tipton of the Association of British Travel Agents (ABTA).

C) The problem has ballooned in the last 10 years, with frauds becoming more and more sophisticated. The fake websites have authentic-sounding names involving a mix of keywords, typically including the place name, "summer" "villas" or "rentals". Details of legitimate villas are often stolen from other sites. "When the fraudsters first started it was unsophisticated — the websites looked amateur and there wasn't a lot of effort," says Tipton. "Now they are clever. They extensively rip off legitimate websites and use a different website name. They'll have pictures of a sales team and it might be a poor actor in New York that is down as their head of sales."

D) Fraudsters target popular seaside destinations for British tourists visiting Spain where prices can soar if demand exceeds supply. Prices are kept within reasonable ranges to avoid arousing suspicion. "A villa might cost £5,000 elsewhere and they will offer it at say £3,500. But a bit of a giveaway is that the villa will be cheaper than on other websites and there's unlimited availability," says Tipton. Fraudsters also invest in pay-per-click advertising to feature at the top of search engines when people type in phrases such as "Spanish seaside villas".

E) With such a degree of professionalism, how can consumers find out if the website they're looking to book with is trustworthy? "When people book holiday villas they are doing so through rose-colored glasses," says Tony Neate, chief executive of Get Safe Online. "They should be googling the property, and looking on websites like Google Maps and Street View to see if it's there. Also, speak to the person you're booking the villa with on a landline phone, as fraudsters tend to only use mobiles." He also suggests asking someone not going on the holiday to have a look at the website. "They might spot problems you don't spot." Another potential red flag is being asked to pay by bank transfer. "The problem is that when the money leaves your account it's in theirs straightaway and it's very hard to track it," says Barclays' head of digital safety, Jodie Gilbert. "We generally recommend other forms of payment, like credit card."

F) Little seems to be known about these fraudsters. "There is no way to definitely know who they are," says Neate. "It could be anyone. It could be your next-door neighbor or organized crime in Russia." Action Fraud says people should ensure the company renting the villa is a member of a recognized trade body such as ABTA.

G) "By working with industry partners such as ABTA and Get Safe Online, we are able to issue alerts about the latest threats they should be aware of. If you believe you have fallen victim to fraud or cyber crime, please report it to Action Fraud," it adds. ABTA says it is trying to combat the issue by running public awareness campaigns. "It's a growing problem and people can't stop fraudsters being dishonest," says Tipton. "They're still going to do it. It's not impossible to stop but as it's internet-based it's harder to pursue."

H) Nick Cooper, the founder and co-owner of villa booking company Villa Plus, estimates his company has uncovered more than 200 fake villa websites over the past two years, and doesn't believe enough is being done. "It is hopeless to report fake villa websites to the internet giants who host them," he says. "I found it impossible to speak to anyone. Also, once one bank account gets reported, they simply use another."

I) For now the only way to stop fraudsters appears ultimately to lie in the hands of the consumer. "When people book their holidays they get so emotionally involved, and when they find that villa at a good price with availability in peak season, they are an easy target," says Cooper. "The public has to learn to be far more aware they are a target for these sort of frauds." But it's not just the financial cost. "A family will turn up at villa and find out it doesn't exist or the owner doesn't know who you are," says Tipton. "The problem then is you have to find accommodation at short notice. It can be incredibly expensive but it's the emotional cost, too."

J) Carla O'Shaughnessy from Sydenham was searching last year for a good deal to book a villa in Majorca for a summer break for the family. I was comparing prices online and found one on that came in a bit cheaper than others," says O'Shaughnessy. She emailed the company via its website, asking how far the villa was from the airport and about local restaurants. "They came back with plausible answers; it was all very friendly and professional," she says. Happy with the responses, O'Shaughnessy paid the full amount of £3,000 via bank transfer into the travel agent's account and then forgot about it until a month before the booking.

K) "I tried logging on to the website and couldn't," she recalls. "I googled the agent's name and there were lots of complaints about him being a fraudster. If only I'd googled before but I never thought of it." Although she found another villa in time for their holiday, she admits she was much more cautious. "I paid through a secure third-party site and had phone conversations with the agent. But I wasn't able to relax until we turned up and I had the keys."

Words & Expressions

soul-stirring/'səul,stɔːrɪŋ/*adj*. 使人兴奋的；振奋人心的
deception/dɪ'sepʃn/*n*. 欺骗；蒙骗；诓骗
fraud/frɔːd/*n*. 欺诈罪；欺骗罪
victim/'vɪktɪm/*n*. 害者；罹难者；罹病者；牺牲品

balloon/bə'luːn/*v.*（突然）膨胀，涨大
fake/feɪk/*adj.* 假的
authentic/ɔː'θentɪk/*adj.* 真正的；真品的；真迹的
legitimate/lɪ'dʒɪtɪmət/*adj.* 正当合理的；合情合理的
amateur/'æmətə(r)/*adj.* 业余的
soar/sɔː(r)/*v.* 急升；猛增
availability/ə,veɪlə'bɪləti/*n.* 可用性，可得性
giveaway/'ɡɪvəweɪ/*n.*（公司为推销产品搭送的）随赠品
landline/'lændlaɪn/*n.*（电话的）陆地线路，陆线，固网
spot/spɒt/*v.* 看见；看出；注意到；发现
uncover/ʌn'kʌvə(r)/*v.* 发现；揭露；揭发
plausible/'plɔːzəb(ə)l/*adj.* 有道理的；可信的
log/lɒɡ/*v.* 把⋯载入正式记录；记录
rip off　偷窃
be aware of　知道
turn up　出现

Exercises

Ⅰ. Comprehension of the Text

Read the text and answer the following questions. Write the answers on the lines.

1. Why do people's yearly break turn into a nightmare?
_____

2. What do the fraudsters do to make their website authentic?
_____

3. What should people do when they book holiday villas?
_____

4. Is bank transfer recommended and why?
_____

5. What should people do when they have fallen victim to fraud or cyber crime?
_____

Ⅱ. Main Details Comprehension

Each of the following statement contains information given in one of the paragraphs. Identify the paragraph from which the information is derived. You may choose a paragraph more than once. Each paragraph is marked with a letter. Answer the questions by marking the corresponding letter in the blanks.

_____1. Fraudsters often steal villa-booking information from authentic holiday websites.

____2. Fraudsters keep changing their bank accounts to avoid being tracked.

____3. It is suggested that people not going on the holiday might help detect website frauds.

____4. More and more British holidaymakers find the seaside villas they booked online actually nonexistent.

____5. By checking an agent's name online before booking a villa holidaymakers can avoid falling into traps.

____6. Fraudsters are difficult to identify according to an online safety expert.

____7. Holidaymakers have been alerted to the frequent occurrence of online villa-booking frauds.

____8. It is holidaymakers that can protect themselves from falling victim to frauds.

____9. Holidaymakers are advised not to make payments by bank transfer.

____10. Fraudsters advertise their villas at reasonable prices so as not to be suspected.

Ⅲ. Translation

Translate the five following sentences into English, using the words or expressions given in brackets.

1．为补偿原料成本的增加而提高了价格。（offset）
_____

2．她被控告信用卡欺骗罪。（fraud）
_____

3．他们终于在近午夜时出现了。（turn up）
_____

4．邻居们发现有烟从这所房子里冒出来。（spot）
_____

5．层次较高的学生必须意识到词语搭配的重要性。（be aware of）
_____

Part C Grammar

倒装（Inversion）

倒装是一种语法手段，用于表示一定的句子结构或强调某一句子成分。倒装句有部分倒装和完全倒装两种。

一、部分倒装

（1）当句首为否定或半否定词 never, neither, nor, little, seldom, hardly, scarcely, in no way, few, not, no 等时，应用部分倒装，句子结构是否定/半否定词＋助动词＋主语＋谓语。例如：

I shall never forgive him. →Never shall I forgive him. 永远不会宽恕他。

She hardly has time to listen to music. →Hardly does she have time to listen to music. 她几乎没有时间听音乐。

He did not make a single mistake. →Not a single mistake did he make. 他不犯一个错。

注意：某些起副词作用的介词短语，由于含有否定词，若位于句首，其后要用部分倒装；但是，in no time（立即，马上）位于句首时，其后无须用倒装语序。例如：

On no accounts must this switch be touched. 这个开关是绝不能触摸的。

Under no circumstances will I lend money to him. 无论如何我也不会借钱给他。

In no time he worked out the problem. 他马上就算出了那道题。

（2）Only 修饰时间、地点、方式、原因等状语位于句首时，应用部分倒装。例如：

Only then did he realize that he was wrong. 到那时他意识到他错了。

Only in this way can we solve the problem. 只有这样，我们才能解决这个问题。

Only when you told me did I know her name. 直到你告诉我，我才知道她的名字。

注意：如果 only 修饰的不是状语，则句子不倒装。例如：

Only Uncle Li knows how it happened. 只有李叔叔知道这件事是怎么发生的。

（3）"so＋形容词/副词"和 such 及 "such＋形容词+名词"置于句首时，应用部分倒装。例如：

So fast does light travel that we can hardly imagine its speed. 光速很快，我们几乎没法想象它的速度。

Such good players are they that they often win. 他们是好队员，所以他们经常获胜。

（4）表示对前者的陈述也适用后者时，肯定倒装用 "so＋助动词/情态动词＋后者"，否定倒装用 "neither/nor＋助动词/情态动词＋后者"。例如：

She likes music and so do I. 她喜欢音乐，我也喜欢。

If she doesn't go there tomorrow, neither/nor will I. 如果她明天不去那儿，我也不去。

注意："so＋助动词/情态动词＋主语"与"so＋主语＋助动词/情态动词"的区别为前者表示所说的主语和前面主语的情况一样，所谈到的是两个人或物，意为"…也是这样"；后者所谈为同一人或物，说话者表示同意前者的观点，意为"的确如此"。例如：

- Li Lei likes sports. 李雷喜欢运动。

- So he does and so do I. 他的确喜欢，我也是。

（5）由 not only...but also...引起的并列句，若将 not only 置于句首，该分句应部分倒装，but also 引导的分句不倒装。而由 neither...nor...引起的并列句，neither 和 nor 置于句首时两个分句都倒装。例如：

Not only is he a teacher, but he is also a poet. 他不仅是一位教师，而且是一位诗人。

Neither does he watch TV, nor does he see films in the evening. 他晚上既不看电视也不看电影。

（6）在句型 no sooner...than, scarcely...when, hardly...when 中，主句应倒装，从句不倒装。例如：

Hardly had they gone out of the classroom when it began to rain. 他们刚刚离开教室就下起雨了。

No sooner had we reached the airport than the plane took off. 我们刚到机场，飞机就起

飞了。

（7）对于 not...until 句型，当 not until...位于句首时其后的主句要用倒装语序。例如：
Not until the rain stopped did he leave the room. 雨停了之后他才离开这房间。

（8）当 if 引导的虚拟条件从句中含有 had, were, should 等时，如将 if 省略，则要将 had, were, should 等移到主语前构成倒装句。例如：
Had you come yesterday, you would have seen him. 若你昨天来，你就会见到他了。
Were it not for your help, I would still be homeless. 要是你的帮助，我会仍然无家可归。

注意：省略 I 后提前的 had 不一定是助动词。例如：
Had I money, I would buy it. 假若我有钱，我就会买它。

二、完全倒装

（1）以 here, there, now, then, out, in, up, down, off, away 等地点、时间或方向性副词开头的句子，且句子主语是名词时，句子用完全倒装。即整个句子成了"状语＋谓语＋主语"结构。例如：
Here comes the bus. 公交车来了。
Then came a new difficulty. 这时又产生了一个新的困难。
The door opened and in came Mr Li. 门开了，李先生进来了。

注意：若主语为代词，则不用倒装。例如：
The door opened and in she came. 门开了，她走了进来。

（2）当表示地点的介词短语位于句首，且主语为名词时，应用完全倒装。例如：
On a hill in front of them stands a great castle. 在他们面前的山上矗立着一座巨大的城堡。
Around the lake are some tall trees. 湖的四周有些高树。
In front of the tower flows a stream. 塔前有条小溪。

（3）作表语的形容词、现在分词、过去分词等较短，而主语相对比较长，为了保持句子平衡而将表语前置时，句子的主谓也应完全倒装。例如：
Gone are the days when we Chinese were looked down upon. 中国人民被轻视的日子已成为过去。
Present at the meeting were the manager, all the designers and the writer. 出席会议的有经理、所有设计师和作者。

（4）在 there be 结构中，be 动词之后为句子的主语，属于完全倒装，be 应与主语保持一致。除 be 动词以外，能与 there 连用的动词还有 seem, exist, happen, appear, live, stand 等。例如：
There were a lot of people in the park last Sunday. 上周日公园里有很多人。
Once there lived a king who was cruel to his people. 从有一位对人民很残暴的国王。

（5）某些表示祝愿的句子也可用完全倒装（或部分倒装）。例如：
May you succeed! 祝你成功!

（6）As 引导的让步状语从句。例如：
Old as he was, he insisted on going with us. 尽管他很老了，他仍坚持与我们同行。

Hard as he worked, he failed. 尽管他很刻苦，他仍失败了。

Exercises

Choose the best answer to the following sentences.

1. Which of the following sentences is correct? _____
   A. In the teacher came
   B. In did come the teacher
   C. In did the teacher come
   D. In came the teacher
2. _____, he is honest.
   A. As he is poor   B. Poor is he   C. Poor as he is   D. Poor as is he
3. So carelessly _____ that he almost killed himself.
   A. he drives   B. he drove   C. does he drive   D. did he drive
4. Only when you realize the importance of foreign languages _____ them well.
   A. you can learn   B. can you learn   C. you learned   D. did you learn
5. Not only _____ to stay at home, but he was also forbidden to see his friends.
   A. he was forcing   B. he was forced   C. was he forcing   D. was he forced
6. Never before _____ seen such a stupid man.
   A. am I   B. was I   C. have I   D. shall I
7. Rarely _____ such a silly thing.
   A. have I heard of   B. I have heard of   C. am I heard of   D. had I heard of
8. No sooner _____ asleep than she heard a knock at the door.
   A. she had fallen   B. had she fallen   C. she had fell   D. had she fell
9. She did not see Smith. _____.
   A. Neither did I   B. Nor didn't I   C. Neither I did   D. So didn't I
10. Nearby _____ in which they had spent their summer vacation.
    A. was two houses
    B. two houses were
    C. were two houses
    D. are two houses
11. Not a single song _____ at yesterday's party.
    A. she sang   B. sang she   C. did she sing   D. she did sing
12. _____ had I finished my translation when the class was over.
    A. Never   B. No sooner   C. Hardly   D. How
13. Such _____ the results of the experiments.
    A. is   B. was   C. are   D. as be
14. _____, his mother will wait for him to have dinner together.
    A. However late is he
    B. However he is late
    C. However is he late
    D. However late he is
15. After that we never saw her again, nor _____ from her.
    A. did we hear
    B. we heard
    C. has we heard
    D. we have heard

16. She is a teacher and works at the college._____.
    A. So is Li Ming
    B. So does Li Ming
    C. So is it with Li Ming
    D. So it is with Li Ming
17. In front of the farmhouse _____.
    A. lay a peasant boy
    B. laid a peasant boy
    C. a peasant lay
    D. did a peasant boy lie
18. So tired _____ after a whole day's heavy work that I _____ stand on my feet.
    A. was I; could hardly
    B. was I felt; could hardly
    C. was I; couldn't hardly
    D. I was; hardly couldn't
19. _____ earlier you would have met him.
    A. If you came
    B. If you did come
    C. Did you come
    D. Had you come
20. _____ reading and speaking English every day, he would speak it well enough now.
    A. Had he practiced
    B. Did he practice
    C. Should he practice
    D. Were he to practice

Workshop
Effective Social Media Strategy

Ⅰ. Background

In today's digital age, social media has become an integral part of our personal and professional lives. Organizations of all sizes are leveraging social media platforms to engage with their target audience, build brand awareness, and drive business growth. However, creating and executing an effective social media strategy requires careful planning and understanding of the best practices.

Ⅱ. Task

During this workshop, participants will work individually and in groups to create a comprehensive social media strategy for a hypothetical organization. The task involves the following steps:

Step 1: Understanding goals and target audience
- Define the organization's goals and objectives for social media engagement.
- Identify the target audience and their preferences and behaviors.

Step 2: Platform selection and content strategy
- Evaluate various social media platforms and select the most suitable ones based on the target audience and organizational goals.

Step 3: Engagement and community building

- Explore methods to encourage user-generated content, increase interactions, and foster a sense of community.

III. Process

1. Introduction

- Overview of the workshop objectives, agenda, and expectations.
- Highlight the importance of social media strategy in today's digital landscape.

2. Presentation and group discussions

- Present key concepts and best practices related to social media strategy.
- Facilitate group discussions on each step of the task, encouraging participants to share their insights and experiences.

3. Group activity: strategy development

- Divide participants into small groups.
- Allocate time for groups to work on each step of the task, providing guidance and support as needed.
- Encourage groups to brainstorm ideas, collaborate, and develop a comprehensive social media strategy.

4. Group presentations and feedback

- Each group presents their social media strategy to the rest of the participants.
- Facilitate constructive feedback and discussions, allowing participants to learn from different approaches and perspectives.

5. Summary and wrap-up

- Summarize the key learning and insights from the workshop.
- Provide participants with additional resources and references for further exploration.

Unit 9 Culture

Writing on It All

Most kids grow up learning they cannot draw on the walls. But it might be time to unlearn that training — this summer, group of culture addicts, artists and community organizers are inviting New Yorkers to write all over the walls of an old house on Governor's Island.

The project is called Writing On It All, and it's a participatory writing project and artistic experiment that has happened on Governor's Island every summer since 2013.

"Most of the participants are people who are just walking by or are on the island for other reasons, or they just kind of happen to be there," Alexandra Chasin, artistic director of Writing On It All, tells Smithsonian.com.

The 2016 season runs through June 26 and features sessions facilitated by everyone from dancers to domestic workers. Each session has a theme, and participants are given a variety of materials and prompts and asked to cover surfaces with their thoughts and art. This year, the programs range from one that turns the house into a collaborative essay to one that explores the meaning of exile.

Governor's Island is a national historic landmark district long used for military purposes. Now known as "New York's shared space for art and play," the island, which lies between Manhattan and Brooklyn in Upper New York Bay, is closed to cars but open to summer tourists who flock for festivals, picnics, adventures, as well as these "legal graffiti" sessions.

The notes and art scribbled on the walls are an experiment in self-expression. So far, participants have ranged in age from 2 to 85. Though Chasin says the focus of the work is on the activity of writing, rather than the text that ends up getting written, some of the work that comes out of the sessions has stuck with her.

"One of the sessions that moved me the most was state violence on black women and black girls," says Chasin, explaining that in one room, people wrote down the names of those killed because of it. "People do beautiful work and leave beautiful messages."

unlearn/ˌʌnˈlɜːn/ v. 故意忘却（尤指学到的错事或坏事）；抛弃
addict/ˈædɪkt/ n. 吸毒成瘾的人；瘾君子

participatory /pɑːˌtɪsɪˈpeɪtəri/ *adj.* 参与式的
feature /ˈfiːtʃə(r)/ *v.* 以⋯为特色
session /ˈseʃ(ə)n/ *n.* （某项活动的）一段时间
facilitate /fəˈsɪlɪteɪt/ *v.* 使更容易，使便利；促进，推动
prompt /prɒmpt/ *n.* （给演员的）提词；（计算机屏幕上显示准备接受指令的）提示
exile /ˈeksaɪl/ *n.* 流放；被流放者，流亡者
district /ˈdɪstrɪkt/ *n.* 地区，区域；行政区，辖区
military /ˈmɪlətri/ *adj.* 军事的，军队的
flock /flɒk/ *v.* 群集，蜂拥
graffiti /ɡrəˈfiːti/ *n.* （公共场所墙上等处的）涂鸦，胡写乱画（graffito 的复数形式）
scribble /ˈskrɪb(ə)l/ *v.* 潦草地写，匆匆地写；乱涂，乱画
self-expression /ˌself ɪkˈspreʃn/ *n.* 自我表达
stuck /stʌk/ *adj.* 被困住，陷入困境；难以继续的，被难倒的
happen to 碰巧，偶然发生
range from 从⋯到⋯变动；从⋯到⋯范围
turn...into... 变成

Notes

Governor's Island

总督岛位于美国纽约市的上纽约湾，曼哈顿岛南端约 1 千米处，与布鲁克林相隔巴特米尔克水道，其坐标为 40°41′29″N、74°0′58″W。在 20 世纪初该岛南侧扩大了 33 公顷（82 英亩）的垃圾填埋场，使得全岛总面积达到 70 公顷（173 英亩）。

Exercises

Ⅰ. Comprehension of the Text

There are 5 questions in this section. For each of them there are four choices marked A, B, C and D. You should choose the best answer for each question.

1. What does the project Writing On It All invite people to do?
    A. Unlearn their training in drawing.
    B. Participate in a state graffiti show.
    C. Cover the walls of an old house with graffiti.
    D. Exhibit their artistic creations in an old house.

2. What do we learn about the participants in the project?
    A. They are just culture addicts.
    B. They are graffiti enthusiasts.
    C. They are writers and artists.
    D. They are mostly passers-by.

3. What did the project participants do during the 2016 season?
   A. They were free to scribble on the walls whatever came to their mind.
   B. They expressed their thoughts in graffiti on the theme of each session.
   C. They learned the techniques of collaborative writing.
   D. They were required to cooperate with other creators.
4. What kind of place is Governor's Island?
   A. It is a historic site that attracts tourists and artists.
   B. It is an area now accessible only to tourist vehicles.
   C. It is a place in Upper New York Bay formerly used for exiles.
   D. It is an open area for tourists to enjoy themselves year round.
5. What does Chasin say about the project?
   A. It just focused on the sufferings of black females.
   B. It helped expand the influence of graffiti art.
   C. It has started the career of many creative artists.
   D. It has created some meaningful artistic works.

II. Languages Focus

A. *Match the following words in left with their explanations in right.*

1. unlearn	a. a person who is unable to stop taking harmful drugs
2. addict	b. to include a particular person or thing as a special feature
3. facilitate	c. to write sth. quickly and carelessly, especially because you do not have much time
4. prompt	d. used in the home; connected with the home or family
5. exile	e. to go or gather together somewhere in large numbers
6. flock	f. to deliberately forget sth. that you have learned, especially sth. bad or wrong
7. scribble	g. to make an action or a process possible or easier
8. feature	h. not knowing what to do in a particular situation
9. stuck	i. the state of being sent to live in another country that is not your own, especially for political reasons or as a punishment
10. domestic	j. a word or words said to an actor, to remind them what to say next when they have forgotten

B. *Fill in the blanks with the words or expressions given below. Change the form where necessary.*

addict	flock	facilitate	unlearn	turn...into...
range from	scribble	happen to	collaborative	domestic

1. Thousands of people _____ to the beach this weekend.
2. I _____ be working on a similar project at the moment.

3. You'll have to _____ all the bad habits you learned with your last piano teacher.
4. The new trade agreement should _____ more rapid economic growth.
5. The _____ trend is true across scientific disciplines.
6. She is a TV _____ and watches as much as she can.
7. For lovers of the great outdoors, activities _____ canoeing to bird watching.
8. When Caroline was five she _____ on a wall.
9. Women are still the main victims of _____ violence.
10. Sometimes, an entire boathouse is _____ a dwelling.

Ⅲ. Translation

Translate the following sentences into Chinese.

1. Most of the participants are people who are just walking by or are on the island for other reasons, or they just kind of happen to be there.

2. The 2016 season runs through June 26 and features sessions facilitated by everyone from dancers to domestic workers.

3. Governor's Island is a national historic landmark district long used for military purposes.

4. This year, the programs range from one that turns the house into a collaborative essay to one that explores the meaning of exile.

5. Though Chasin says the focus of the work is on the activity of writing, rather than the text that ends up getting written, some of the work that comes out of the sessions has stuck with her.

Ⅳ. Discussion

Can you think of some ways to express your thoughts?

Part B

Why Are Asian Americans Missing from Our Textbooks?

A) I still remember my fourth-grade social studies project. Our class was studying the

Gold Rush, something all California fourth-graders learned. I was excited because I had asked to research Chinese immigrants during that era. Growing up in the San Francisco Bay Area, I had always know that "San Francisco" translated to "Gold Mountain" in Chinese. The name had stuck ever since Chinese immigrants arrived on the shores of Northern California in the 1850s, eager to try their luck in the gold mines. Now I'd have the chance to learn about them.

B) My excitement was short-lived. I remember heading to the library with my class and asking for help. I remember the librarian's hesitation. She finally led me past row after row of books, to a corner of the library where she pulled an oversized book off the shelf. She checked the index and turned over to a page about early Chinese immigrants in California. That was all there was in my entire school library in San Francisco, home of the nation's first Chinatown. That was it.

C) I finally had the opportunity to learn about Asian Americans like myself, and how we became part of the fabric of the United States when I took an introductory class on Asian-American history in college. The class was a revelation. I realized how much had been missing in my textbooks as I grew up. My identity had been shaped by years of never reading, seeing, hearing, or learning about people who had a similar background as me. Why, I wondered, weren't the stories, histories, and contributions of Asian Americans taught in K-12 schools, especially in the elementary schools? Why are they still not taught?

D) Our students-Asian, Latino, African American, Native American, and, yes, white — stand to gain from a multicultural curriculum. Students of color are more engaged and earn better grades when they see themselves in their studies. Research has also found that white students benefit by being challenged and exposed to new perspectives.

E) For decades, activists have called for schools to offer anti-racism or multicultural curricula. Yet a traditional American K-12 curriculum continues to be taught from a Eurocentric point of view. Being multicultural often falls back on weaving children of color into photographs, or creating a few supporting characters that happen to be ethnic — an improvement, but superficial nonetheless. Elementary school classrooms celebrate cultural holidays — Lunar New Year! Red envelopes! Lion dancers! — but they're quick to gloss over the challenges and injustices that Asian Americans have faced. Most students don't, for example, learn about the laws that for years excluded Asians from immigrating to the U.S. They don't hear the narratives of how and why Southeast Asian refugees had to rebuild their lives here.

F) Research into what students learn in school has found just how much is missing in their studies. In an analysis, Christine Sleeter, a professor in the College of Professional Studies at California State University, Monterey Bay, reviewed California's history and social studies framework, the curriculum determined by state educators that influences what is taught in K-12 classrooms. Of the nearly 100 Americans recommended to be studied, 77% were white, 18% African American, 4% Native American, and 1% Latino. None were Asian American.

G) Worse, when Asian Americans do make an appearance in lesson books, it is often laced with problems. "There hasn't been much progress," says Nicholas Hartlep, an assistant professor at Metropolitan State University. His 2016 study of K-12 social studies textbooks and teacher manuals found that Asian Americans were poorly represented at best, and subjected to racist caricatures at worst. The wide diversity of Asian Americans was overlooked; there was very little mention of South Asians or Pacific Islanders, for example. And chances were, in the images, Asian Americans appeared in stereotypical roles, such as engineers.

H) Teachers with a multicultural background or training could perhaps overcome such curriculum challenges, but they're few and far between. In California, 65% of K-12 teachers are white, compared with a student population that is 75% students of color. Nationwide, the gap is even greater. It isn't a requirement that teachers share the same racial or ethnic background as their students, but the imbalance poses challenges, from the potential for unconscious bias to a lack of knowledge or comfort in discussing race and culture.

I) How race and ethnicity is taught is crucial, says Allyson Tintiangco-Cubales, an Asian-American studies professor at San Francisco State University. She added that it's not so much about the teacher's background, but about training. "You can have a great curriculum but if you don't have teachers dedicated to teaching it well." she says, "it won't work as well as you want it to."

J) Some teachers are finding ways to expose students to Asian-Amenican issues — if not during school hours, then outside of them. This summer, Wilson Wong will lead a class of rising fifth-graders at a day camp dedicated to Chinese culture and the Chinese-American community in Oakland, California. His students, for instance, will learn about how Chinese immigrants built the railroads in California, and even have a chance to "experience" it themselves: They will race each other to build a railroad model on the playground, with some students being forced to "work" longer and faster and at cheaper wages. Wong, a middle school teacher during the school year, hopes he's exposing the students to how Chinese Americans contributed to the U.S., something that he didn't get as a student growing up in the San Francisco Bay Area. "I planted the seeds early," he says. "That's what I'm hoping for."

K) And, despite setbacks, the tide may finally be turning. California legislators passed a bill last year that will bring ethnic studies to all its public high schools. Some school districts, including San Francisco and Los Angeles, already offer ethnic studies at its high schools. High schools in Portland, Chicago, and elsewhere have either implemented or will soon introduce ethnic studies classes. And, as more high schools begin teaching it, the door could crack open for middle schools and perhaps inevitably, elementary schools, to incorporate a truly more multicultural curriculum. Doing so will send an important message to the nation's youngest citizens: Whatever your race or ethnicity, you matter, your history matters, and your story matters.

Words & Expressions

immigrant/'ɪmɪgrənt/ *n.* 移民，外侨
short-lived/ˌʃɔːt 'lɪvd/ *adj.* 短暂的
head/hed/ *v.* 朝（某方向）行进
fabric/'fæbrɪk/ *n.* （社会、机构等的）结构
revelation/ˌrevə'leɪʃ(ə)n/ *n.* 启示
stand/stænd/ *v.* 很有可能做某事
anti-racism/'ænti 'reɪsɪzəm/ *n.* 反种族主义
weave/wiːv/ *v.* 将（素材等）编入（故事或设计中）
refugee/ˌrefju'dʒiː/ *n.* 难民，避难者
narrative/'nærətɪv/ *n.* 叙事
manual/'mænjuəl/ *n.* 使用手册，说明书
caricature/'kærɪkətʃʊə(r)/ *n.* 夸张的描述
stereotypical/ˌsteriə'tɪpɪkl/ *adj.* 模式化的
bias/'baɪəs/ *n.* 偏见
dedicated/'dedɪkeɪtɪd/ *adj.* 专注的
setback/'setbæk/ *n.* 挫折，阻碍
bill/bɪl/ *n.* 议案，法案
crack/kræk/ *v.* 破裂，裂开
lace/leɪs/ *v.* 使编织（或交织、缠绕）在一起
gloss over 掩盖，掩饰
exclude...from 防止…发生
few and far between 稀少，不常发生
be subjected to 受到…，经受…

Exercises

Ⅰ. Comprehension of the Text

Read the text and answer the following questions. Write the answers on the lines.

1. Why was the author's excitement short-lived when he went to the library for books about immigrants?

_____

2. What challenges does the imbalance of teachers and students with different racial background bring?

_____

3. What did Nicholas Hartlep find in his study of K-12 social studies textbooks and teacher manuals?

4. What will Wilson Wong do to expose his students to Asian-American issues?

5. What message will be sent to the youngest citizens by exposing to ethnic studies?

Ⅱ. Main Details Comprehension

Each of the following statement contains information given in one of the paragraphs. Identify the paragraph from which the information is derived. You may choose a paragraph more than once. Each paragraph is marked with a letter. Answer the questions by marking the corresponding letter in the blanks.

_____1. While cultural holidays are celebrated, the injustices experienced by Asian Americans are not exposed in elementary school classrooms.

_____2. Little information can be found about Chinese immigrants in the author's school library.

_____3. A middle school teacher is making a great effort to help students learn about the contributions made by Chinese immigrants to America.

_____4. No Asian Americans were included in the list of historical figures recommended for study in K-12 classrooms.

_____5. There is an obvious lack of teachers with a multicultural perspective to meet the curriculum challenges in America.

_____6. Students of ethnic backgrounds learn better from a multicultural curriculum.

_____7. Now more and more high schools in America are including ethnic studies in their curriculums.

_____8. A study of some K-12 textbooks and teacher manuals showed that Asian Americans were inadequately and improperly represented in them.

_____9. When taking a class in college, the author realized that a lot of information about Asian Americans was left out of the textbooks he studied.

_____10. An Asian-American studies professor placed greater emphasis on teacher training than on teachers' background.

Ⅲ. Translation

Translate the five following sentences into English, using the words or expressions given in brackets.

1. 他的思想深受战时经历的影响。(be shaped by)

2. 该公司的年度报告试图掩盖近期的严重亏损。(gloss over)

3. 全力照料动物的动物园不应遭受不公正的批评。(be subjected to)

4. 成功的女政治家少之又少。(few and far between)

5. 他不想向任何人显露他的恐惧与不安。(expose)

Grammar
虚拟语气（Subjunctive Mood）

一、概念

动词虚拟语气表示说话人的愿望、假设、猜测、建议、请求、意图、设想等未能或不可能成为事实的情况，或者在说话人看来实现可能性很小的情况，而不表示客观存在的现实。

二、表现形式

通过句中谓语动词的特殊形式来表现。这些特殊形式与谓语动词的某些时态相同，但它们只表示语气，而不表示时态，但含有一定的时间概念。

三、用法

（一）虚拟语气在非真实条件句中的用法

使用虚拟语气的含条件句的复合句称为非真实条件句。

1. 针对当前事实的虚拟

表示违背当前事实，在现在条件下不可能发生或者实现的可能性极小。基本表达规则：在表示假设的条件句中，谓语动词的形式为一般过去时；在表示结果的主句中，谓语动词的形式为 would（或 could，might，should）＋动词原形。例如：

If I had more time, I should study computer better. 如果我有更多时间，我会把计算机学得更好。

If he were not so busy, he would attend the meeting this afternoon. 如果他不忙的话他会参加今天下午的会议。

If they didn't take exercises every day, they wouldn't be so healthy. 如果他们不每天锻炼的话就不会很健康。

2. 针对过去事实的虚拟

表达违背过去已经发生的事实。基本表达规则：在条件从句中，谓语动词的形式为过去完成时；在表示结果的主句中，谓语动词的形式为 would（或 could，might，should）＋现在完成时。例如：

If electronic computers had not been invented, many problems on space flight could not have been solved. 如果没有发明电子计算机，许多关于宇宙的问题就不可能得到解决。

If you had taken the teacher's advice, you would not have failed in the exam. 如果你听了老师的建议，你就不会考试不及格了。

3. 针对未来事实的虚拟

表明在未来条件下不具备实现的可能性，或者实现的可能性极小。基本表达规则：条件从句中谓语动词的形式为 should（或 were to）接动词原形；在主句中，谓语动词的形式为 would（或 could, might, should）＋动词原形。例如：

If we should miss the train, we would have to wait an hour at the station. 如果我们误了火车，就得在车站等一个小时。

If the sun were to rise in the west tomorrow, I would marry you. 如果明天太阳从西边升起，我就和你结婚。

4. 错综时间虚拟

错综时间虚拟，是指条件从句的情况和主句中的情况在时间上不同步，常见的是：条件从句针对过去，而主句针对现在，表示"如果过去怎样，那么现在会如何"。例如：

Do you think the event would be just as memorable if you hadn't won? 你觉得假如当时你没有获胜，这次比赛还会一样难忘吗？

5. 虚拟语气在非真实条件句中用法的几个变体

（1）在书面语中，如果条件从句中的谓语中有 were，had，should 等词，可将 if 省略，而把 were，had，should 放在句首。例如：

Were I you (=If I were you), I would get up very early. 如果我是你，我会起得很早。

Had you arrived (=If you had arrived) at the station ten minutes earlier yesterday, you could have caught the train. 如果你早到车站 10 分钟，你就能赶上火车了。

（2）假设的条件不以条件从句，而以其他方式如介词短语、从句等表达出来，这种句子称为含蓄条件句。例如：

What would you do with a million dollars? =…if you had a million dollars? 如果你有一百万你会做什么？

Without/But for music, the world would be a dull place. =If there were not music,…? 如果没有音乐，世界将会枯燥无味。

He would have given you more help, but he has been so busy. (事实)=He has been so busy, otherwise/or, he would have given you more help. 他本应给你更多的帮助，但是他太忙了。

（二）虚拟语气在状语从句中的用法

（1）在 even if/though 引导的让步状语从句中，若表示与事实相反，可用虚拟语气形式，主从句的谓语动词形式与非真实条件句相同。例如：

Even if I were rich, I would work. 即使我很富有，我也要工作。

（2）在 as if/though 引导的方式状语从句中，表示与事实情况相反的猜测，常用虚拟语气。

①表示与现在事实相反或对现在情况有所怀疑，谓语用过去式。例如：

She looked as if she were ill. 她看起来好像病了。

②表示与过去事实相反的情况，as if/though 从句谓语用过去完成式。例如：
The machines operated as if it had been repaired. 机器运行起来好像被修理过一样。
（3）在 so that, in order that 引导的目的状语从句中，从句表目的性，谓语使用情态动词+动词原形。例如：
We took a taxi in order that we could get there on time. 我们打了出租车这样可以准时到达。

（三）虚拟语气在主语从句中的用法
如果表示说话人的看法，想法或意见，在句型"It is/was + adj. + that 从句"中可用虚拟语气。主语从句中谓语动词用 should do 表示现在或将来情况，用 should have done 表示过去情况。例如：
It is necessary that you should clean the lab before you left. 你很有必要在离开前把实验室打扫干净。
It was very strange that he should have left without say goodbye. 真奇怪，他竟然不告而别。

（四）虚拟语气在宾语从句中的用法
（1）在 wish 引导的宾语从句中，通常表示不可能实现或没有实现的愿望，常用虚拟语气。
①Wish 的宾语从句用过去式，表示现在或将来没有实现或不可能实现的愿望。例如：
I wish it were spring here all the year round. 我希望这里四季如春。
②Wish 引导的宾语从句用过去完成式，表示过去没有实现或不可能实现的愿望。例如：
We wish we had got the film tickets last night. 我们真希望昨晚弄到了电影票。
③Wish 引导的宾语从句若用 would，则一般表示请求，对现状不满或希望未来有所改变。例如：
I wish the prices would come down. 我希望价格可以降下来。
（2）在 suggest, advise, demand, require, order, insist 等表示建议、命令等动词后的宾语从句中，谓语动词常用（should）+动词原形的虚拟语气形式。例如：
I suggested that we (should) go there at once. 我建议我们立刻去那。
I demand that he should answer me at once. 我要求他立刻答复我。
（3）用在 would rather/prefer 后的 that 从句中表示现在或将来情况谓语动词用过去时形式，表示过去情况动词用过去完成时形式。例如：
I would rather he came next Saturday. 我宁愿他下周六来。
I would prefer you had seen the film yesterday. 我倒希望你昨天就看过那部电影。

（五）虚拟语气在特殊句式中的用法
（1）在 It is (about/high) time that...句式中，that 从句中的谓语动词用过去式。例如：
It is time that you studied the problem carefully. 你该认真考虑这个问题了。
（2）在 if only 引导的感叹句中表示但愿，要是…就好了，其中谓语动词形式与 wish 的宾语从句相同。例如：
If only he didn't drive so fast! (=I wish he didn't drive so fast.) 要是他不开那么快就好了。

If only he had taken the doctor's advice. (=I wish he had taken the doctor's advice.) 她要是听医生的建议就好了。

If only the rain would stop! (=I wish the rain would stop.) 要是雨停了就好了。

Exercises

Choose the best answer to the following sentences.

1. The movie bored me to death I wish I _____ to it.
   A. have not gone   B. did not go
   C. could not have gone   D. had not gone
2. Because she had a fever, his father insisted that she _____ to school.
   A. mustn't go   B. not go   C. do not go   D. would not go
3. It is important that the customs of all nations _____ respected.
   A. be   B. are   C. must be   D. will be
4. I wished it _____ , but it did.
   A. occurred not   B. did not occur
   C. had not occurred   D. would not occur
5. The sun rises in the east and sets in the west, so it seems as if the sun _____ round the earth.
   A. circles   B. is circling   C. be circling   D. were circling
6. If only I _____ how to operate an electronic computer as you do.
   A. had known   B. would know   C. should know   D. knew
7. _____ the snow, we should have reached the station.
   A. Because of   B. In case of   C. In spite of   D. But for
8. If the sea _____ 500 feet, India would become an island.
   A. is to rise   B. were risen   C. has risen   D. were to rise
9. Were it not for the foggy weather, we _____ all right.
   A. would be   B. would have been   C. were   D. may be
10. _____ more careful, his ship would not have sunk.
    A. If he were   B. Had he been
    C. Should he be   D. If he would have been
11. If he _____ me tomorrow, I would let him know.
    A. should call   B. should not have been able
    C. were not able   D. are not able
12. If you asked your mother, you _____ permission.
    A. may get   B. might get   C. should have got   D. maybe get
13. _____ today, he would get there by Friday.
    A. Would he leave   B. Was he leaving   C. Were he to leave   D. If he leaves
14. _____ I you, I would go with him to the party.
    A. Was   B. Had been   C. Will be   D. Were

15. The millions of calculations involved, had they been done by hand, _____ all practical value by the time they were finished.
    A. could lose
    B. would have lost
    C. might lose
    D. ought to have lost
16. Had Tom received six more votes in the last election, he _____ our chairman now.
    A. must have been   B. would have been   C. were   D. would be
17. If you _____ Jerry Brown until recently, you'd think the photograph on the right was strange.
    A. shouldn't contact
    B. didn't contact
    C. weren't to contact
    D. hadn't contacted
18. Look at the terrible situation I am in! If only I _____ your advice.
    A. Follow
    B. would follow
    C. had followed
    D. have followed
19. If you had told me in advance, I _____ him at the airport.
    A. would meet
    B. would had met
    C. would have meet
    D. would have met
20. I can't stand him. He always talks as though he _____ everything.
    A. knew   B. knows   C. has known   D. had known

Workshop
Traditional Chinese Culture Introduction

I. Background

Traditional Chinese culture has gained an increasing popularity nowadays. Elements of traditional Chinese culture such as Martial Arts, Peking Opera, Chinese Calligraphy and traditional costumes can be seen everywhere.

II. Task

(1) Choose one topic you are interested in;
(2) Search information online;
(3) Make a presentation in front of the class.

III. Process

Step 1: Complete the task in groups. Form small groups with 5 students respectively;

Step 2: Each group can choose one topic above and use the search engine to know the related news, comments and pictures or videos about this topic;

Step 3: Make a presentation in front of the whole class.

Unit 10　Internet security

Internet-Connected Security Camera

Roughly the size of a soda can, sitting on a bookshelf, a relatively harmless gadget may be turning friends away from your home. The elephant in your living room is your Internet-connected security camera, a device people are increasingly using for peace of mind in their homes. But few stop to think about the effect these devices may have on house guests. Should you tell your friends, for instance, that they're being recorded while you all watch the big game together?

"It's certainly new territory, especially as home security cameras become easier to install," says Lizzie Post, president of the Emily Post Institute, America's foremost manners advisors. "I think it will be very interesting to see what etiquette emerges in terms of whether you tell people you have a camera or not, and whether guests have a right to ask that it be turned off, if it's not a security issue."

Post wants to make clear that she's not talking about legal rights, but rather personal preference. She also wants to explain that there are no right or wrong answers regarding manners on this front yet, because the technology is just now becoming mainstream. Besides, the Emily Post Institute doesn't dictate manners.

When it comes to security cameras, Post says it's a host's responsibility to make sure guests feel comfortable within their home. "I'm always a fan of being open and honest." For instance, if the host casually acknowledges that there is a camera in the room by telling a story about it, that may be enough to provide an opening for a guest to say if they are uncomfortable.

However, if a contractor is working in your home, you don't need to tell them that there are cameras watching. Then again, the air of accountability that the camera generates can also work in contractors' favor. "If anything does go wrong while they're in the house, they don't want to be blamed for it," she says. "In fact, the camera could be the thing that proves that they didn't steal the $20, or knock the vase off the table."

Words & Expressions

gadget/'gædʒɪt/n. 小器具；小装置
territory/'terətri/n.（个人、群体、动物等占据的）领域，管区，地盘

install/ɪnˈstɔːl/v. 安装；设置
foremost/ˈfɔːməʊst/adj. 最重要的；最著名的；最前的
etiquette/ˈetɪkət/n. 礼节，规矩
emerge/ɪˈmɜːdʒ/v. 浮现，出现
preference/ˈprefrəns/n. 偏爱，偏好
front/frʌnt/n. 方面，领域
dictate/dɪkˈteɪt/v. 命令，规定
contractor/kənˈtræktə(r)/n. 承包商，立约人
acknowledge/əkˈnɒlɪdʒ/v. 承认；认可
accountability/əˌkaʊntəˈbɪləti/n. 责任，责任心，可说明性
regarding/rɪˈɡɑːdɪŋ/prep. 关于，至于
knock/nɒk/v. （常为无意地）碰，撞

Exercises

I. Comprehension of the Text

There are 5 questions in this section. For each of them there are four choices marked A, B, C and D. You should choose the best answer for each question.

1. For what reason may your friends feel reluctant to visit your home?
    A. The security camera installed may intrude into their privacy.
    B. They don't want their photos to be circulated on the Internet.
    C. The security camera may turn out to be harmful to their health.
    D. They may not be willing to interact with your family members.
2. What does Lizzie Post say is new territory?
    A. The effect of manners advice on the public.
    B. Cost of applying new technologies at home.
    C. The increasing use of home security devices.
    D. Etiquette around home security cameras.
3. What is Lizzie Post mainly discussing with regard to the use of home security cameras?
    A. Legal rights.
    B. Moral issues.
    C. Likes and dislikes of individuals.
    D. The possible impact on manners.
4. What is a host's responsibility regarding security cameras, according to Lizzie Post?
    A. Making their guests feel at ease.
    B. Indicating where they are.
    C. Turning them off in time.
    D. Ensuring their guests' privacy.

5. In what way can the home security camera benefit visitors to your home?

   A. It can satisfy their curiosity.

   B. It can prove their innocence.

   C. It can help them learn new technology.

   D. It can make their visit more enjoyable.

II. Languages Focus

A. *Match the following words in left with their explanations in right.*

1. install
2. foremost
3. emerge
4. preference
5. dictate
6. acknowledge
7. generate
8. regarding
9. etiquette
10. contractor

a. a greater interest in or desire for sb./sth. than sb./sth. else
b. to produce or create sth.
c. to tell sb. what to do, especially in an annoying way
d. to fix equipment or furniture into position so that it can be used
e. the most important or famous; in a position at the front
f. concerning sb./sth.; about sb./sth.
g. to come out of a dark, confined or hidden place
h. a person or company that has a contract to do work or provide goods or services for another company
i. to accept that sth. is true
j. the formal rules of correct or polite behaviour in society or among members of a particular profession

B. *Fill in the blanks with the words or expressions given below. Change the form where necessary.*

| generate | in terms of | dictate | acknowledge | install |
| regarding | territory | knock | preference | foremost |

1. They have refused to allow UN troops to be stationed in their _____.
2. Call me if you have any problems _____ your work.
3. Did the experiment find any differences _____ what children learned?
4. We need someone to _____ new ideas.
5. What right do they have to _____ how we live our lives?
6. Many people expressed a strong _____ for the original plan.
7. Be careful you don't _____ your head on this low beam.
8. This question has been _____ in our minds recently.
9. She refuses to _____ the need for reform.
10. The hotel chain has recently _____ a new booking system.

III. Translation

Translate the following sentences into Chinese.

1. Roughly the size of a soda can, sitting on a bookshelf, a relatively harmless gadget may be turning friends away from your home.

_____

2. The elephant in your living room is your Internet-connected security camera, a device people are increasingly using for peace of mind in their homes.

_____

3. When it comes to security cameras, Post says it's a host's responsibility to make sure guests feel comfortable within their home.

_____

4. Post wants to make clear that she's not talking about legal rights, but rather personal preference.

_____

5. In fact, the camera could be the thing that proves that they didn't steal the $20, or knock the vase off the table.

_____

IV. Discussion

Can you tell the advantages and disadvantages of installing a camera in our house?

Can Burglars Jam Your Wireless Security System?

A) Any product that promises to protect your home deserves careful examination. So it isn't surprising that you'll find plenty of strong opinions about the potential vulnerabilities of popular home-security systems.

B) The most likely type of burglary by far is the unsophisticated crime of opportunity, usually involving a broken window or some forced entry. According to the FBI, crimes like these accounted roughly two-thirds of all household burglaries in the US in 2013. The wide majority of the rest were illegal, unforced entries that resulted from something like a window being left open. The odds of a criminal using technical means to bypass a security system are so small that the FBI doesn't even track those statistics.

C) One of the main theoretical home-security concerns is whether or not a given system is vulnerable to being blocked from working altogether. With wired setups, the fear is that a burglar might be able to shut your system down simply by cutting the right cable. With a wireless setup, you stick battery-powered sensors up around your home that keep an eye on windows, doors, motion, and more. If they detect something wrong while the system is armed, they'll transmit a wireless alert signal to a base station that will then raise the alarm. That approach will eliminate most cord-cutting concerns — but what about their wireless equivalent, jamming? With the right device tuned to the right frequency, what's to stop a thief from jamming your setup and blocking that alert signal from ever reaching the base station?

D) Jamming concerns are nothing new, and they're not unique to security systems. Any device that's built to receive a wireless signal at a specific frequency can be overwhelmed by a stronger signal coming in on the same frequency. For comparison, let's say you wanted to "jam" a conversation between two people — all you'd need to do is yell in the listener's ear.

E) Security devices are required to list the frequencies they broadcast on — that means that a potential thief can find what they need to know with minimal Googling. They will, however, need so know what system they're looking for. If you have a sign in your yard declaring what setup you use, that'd point them in the right direction, though at that point, we're talking about a highly targeted, semi-sophisticated attack, and not the sort forced-entry attack that makes up the majority of burglaries. It's easier to find and acquire jamming equipment for some frequencies than it is for others.

F) Wireless security providers will often take steps to help combat the threat of jamming attacks. SimpliSafe, winner of our Editor's Choice distinction, utilizes a special system that's capable of separating incidental RF interference from targeted jamming attacks. When the system thinks it's being jammed, it'll notify you via push alert（推送警报）. From there, it's up to you to sound the alarm manually.

G) SimpliSafe was singled out in one recent article on jamming, complete with a video showing the entire system being effectively bypassed with handheld jamming equipment. After taking appropriate measures to contain the RF interference to our test lab, we tested the attack out for ourselves, and were able to verify that it's possible with the right equipment. However, we also verified that SimpliSafe's anti-jamming system works. It caught us in the act, sent an alert to my smartphone, and also listed our RF interference on the system's event log. The team behind the article and video in question make no mention of the system, or whether or not in detected them.

H) We like the unique nature of that software. It means that a thief likely wouldn't be able to Google how the system works, then figure out a way around it. Even if they could, SimpliSafe claims that its system is always evolving, and that it varies slightly from system to system, which means there wouldn't be a universal magic formula for cracking it. Other systems also seem confident on the subject of jamming. The team at Frontpoint addresses the issue in a blog on its site, citing their own jam protection software and claiming that there aren't any documented cases of successful jam attack since the company began offering wireless security sensors in the 1980s.

I) Jamming attacks are absolutely possible. As said before, with the right equipment and the right know-how, it's possible to jam any wireless transmission. But how probable is it that someone will successfully jam their way into your home and steal your stuff?

J) Let's imagine that you live in a small home with a wireless security setup that offers a functional anti-jamming system. First, a thief is going to need to target your home, specifically. Then, he's going to need to know the technical details of your system and acquire the specific equipment necessary for jamming your specific setup. Presumably, you keep your doors locked at night and while you're away. So the thief will still need to break in. That means defeating the lock somehow, or breaking a window. He'll need to be jamming you at this point, as a broken window or opened door would normally release the alarm. So, too, would the motion detectors in your home, so the thief will need to continue jamming once he's inside and searching for things to steal. However, he'll need to do so without tripping the anti-jamming system, the details of which he almost certainly does now have access to.

K) At the end of the day, these kinds of systems are primarily designed to protect against the sort of opportunistic smash-and-grab attack that makes up the majority of burglaries. They're also only a single layer in what should ideally be a many-sided approach to securing your home, one that includes common sense things like sound locks and proper exterior lighting at night. No system is impenetrable, and none can promise to eliminate the worst case completely. Every one of them has vulnerabilities that a knowledgeable thief could theoretically exploit. A good system is one that keeps that worst-case setting as improbable as possible while also offering strong protection in the event of a less-extraordinary attack.

Words & Expressions

burglar/ˈbɜːglə(r)/ n. 破门盗贼；入室窃贼
jam/dʒæm/ v. （使）卡住，不能动弹，不能运转
wireless/ˈwaɪələs/ adj. 无线电收音机
unsophisticated/ˌʌnsəˈfɪstɪkeɪtɪd/ adj. 基本的；简单的；不复杂的
account/əˈkaʊnt/ v. （数量上、比例上）占
odds/ɒdz/ n. （事物发生的）可能性，概率，几率，机会
bypass/ˈbaɪpɑːs/ v. 绕过；避开
track/træk/ v. 跟踪；追踪
theoretical/ˌθɪəˈretɪk(ə)l/ adj. 理论上的
block/blɒk/ v. 堵塞；阻塞
setup/ˈsetʌp/ n. （计算机硬件或软件的）安装
cable/ˈkeɪb(ə)l/ n. （系船用的）缆绳；（支撑桥梁等用的）钢索
battery/ˈbætri/ n. 电池，蓄电池
sensor/ˈsensə(r)/ n. （探测光、热、压力等的）传感器，敏感元件，探测设备
detect/dɪˈtekt/ v. 发现；查明；侦察出
arm/ɑːm/ v. 武装；装备；备战
transmit/trænzˈmɪt/ v. 传送；输送；发射；播送

alert/əˈlɜːt/*adj.* 警觉的；警惕的；戒备的
eliminate/ɪˈlɪmɪneɪt/*v.* 排除；清除；消除
equivalent/ɪˈkwɪvələnt/*adj.* （价值、数量、意义、重要性等）相等的，相同的
combat/ˈkɒmbæt/*v.* 防止；减轻
utilize/ˈjuːtəlaɪz/*v.* 使用；利用；运用；应用
notify/ˈnəʊtɪfaɪ/*v.* （正式）通报，通知
opportunistic/ˌɒpətjuːˈnɪstɪk/ 机会致病性的（对免疫系统差的人有害）
exploit/ɪkˈsplɔɪt/*v.* 运用；利用；发挥
impenetrable/ɪmˈpenɪtrəb(ə)l/*adj.* 不可进入的；穿不过的；无法透视的
trip/trɪp/*v.* 绊；绊倒
exterior/ɪkˈstɪəriə(r)/*adj.* 外面的；外部的；外表的

Exercises

Ⅰ. Comprehension of the Text

Read the text and answer the following questions. Write the answers on the lines.

1. What is the most common type of burglary?
_____

2. What is a potential vulnerability of wired home-security setups, and how does wireless setup address this concern?
_____

3. What is jamming, and how can it be used to block wireless alert signals from home-security sensors?
_____

4. How can a thief find out what frequencies a wireless security system broadcasts on, and why might they need to know this information?
_____

5. What are some other factors that should be considered when securing a home besides a home-security system?
_____

Ⅱ. Main Details Comprehension

Each of the following statement contains information given in one of the paragraphs. Identify the paragraph from which the information is derived. You may choose a paragraph more than once. Each paragraph is marked with a letter. Answer the questions by marking the corresponding letter in the blanks.

____1. It is possible for burglars to make jamming attacks with the necessary equipment and skill.

____2. Interfering with a wireless security system is similar to interfering with a conversation.

____3. A burglar has to continuously jam the wireless security device to avoid triggering the alarm, both inside and outside the house.

____4. SimpliSafe provides devices that are able to distinguish incidental radio interference from targeted jamming attacks.

____5. Only a very small proportion of burglaries are committed by technical means.

____6. It is difficult to crack SimpliSafe as its system keeps changing.

____7. Wireless devices will transmit signals so as to activate the alarm once something wrong is detected.

____8. Different measures should be taken to protect one's home from burglary in addition to the wireless security system.

____9. SimpliSafe's device can send a warning to the house owner's cellphone.

____10. Burglars can easily get a security device's frequency by Internet search.

Ⅲ. Translation

Translate the five following sentences into English, using the words or expressions given in brackets.

1. 一条新路绕城镇而过。（bypass）

_____

2. 有了信用卡就用不着携带很多现金。（eliminate）

_____

3. 八千米约等于五英里。（equivalent）

_____

4. 罗马人首先使用混凝土作建筑材料。（utilize）

_____

5. 这些检查旨在早期查出疾病。（detect）

_____

Part C

Grammar
省略（Ellipsis）

省略是为了避免重复、突出新信息并使上下文紧密连接的一种语法修辞手段。省略在语言中，尤其在对话中，是一种十分普遍的现象。

1. 简单句中的省略

（1）感叹句中常省略主语和谓语。例如：

What a hot day (it is)! 多热的天啊!

（2）在一些口语中可以省略某些句子成分。例如：

(Will you) Have a smoke? 你抽烟吗？

(Is there) Anything else to say? 还有别的要说吗？

2．并列句中的省略

（1）在一些并列句中，由于前面已经出现了相同的主语，为了避免重复，后一个分句的主语也常常省略。例如：

Danny gave up smoking for a while, but (he) soon returned to his old habit. 丹尼戒了一阵子烟，可很快又开始抽了。

（2）如果主语不同，而谓语中的一部分相同，则省略谓语中相同的部分。例如：

John was the winner in 1994 and Bob (was the winner) in 1998. 约翰是 1994 年的获胜者，鲍勃是 1998 年的获胜者。

（3）主语相同，谓语也相同，则两者都可以省略。例如：

He advised me not to say anything until (I am) asked. 他劝我什么都别说，除非有人要我说。

3．复合句中的省略

（1）宾语从句中的省略：在宾语从句中常省略连词 that。但当及物动词之后跟两个或两个以上的宾语从句时，只有第一个连词 that 可以省略。例如：

I know (that) she is a teacher and that she is an excellent writer. 我知道她是一个老师，也是一个优秀的作家。

（2）状语从句中的省略：在一些状语从句中，如果谓语动词是 be，主语又和主句的主语一致，或者主语是 it，常常可以把从句中的主语和 be 省略掉。例如：

Though (they were) tired, they went on working. 虽然累了，但他们继续工作。

You shouldn't come to his party unless (you are) invited. 除非你被邀请，否则你不应来参加他的晚会。

（3）在比较状语从句中通常把和主句重复的部分省掉。例如：

He is working harder than (he worked) before. 他现在工作比过去努力多了。

4．定语从句中的省略

（1）一般说来，在限制性定语从句中，作宾语的关系代词 that, which, who, whom 可以省略；而在非限制性定语从句中作宾语的关系代词不可以省略。例如：

The man (whom) you saw yesterday fell ill. 你昨天见到的那个人病倒了。(whom 可以省)

The man, whom you saw yesterday, fell ill. 那个人病倒了，你昨天见到他了。(whom 不可以省)

（2）当先行词是 way，并且引导词在定语从句中作方式状语时，引导词可以用 in which 或 that，也可以省略。例如：

The way (in which/that) these comrades treat problems is wrong. 这些同志看待问题的方式是错误的。

5．不定式 to 后省略动词

动词不定式中动词原形部分是否省略，主要看上文是否出现过同样的动词。如果上文出现过同样的动词，为了避免重复，后面的不定式常省略动词，而保留不定式符号 to。例如：

I asked him to see the film, but he didn't want to (see the film). 我请他去看电影，但他不想去。

They may go if they wish to (go). 如果他们想去，他们就可以去。

6．介词的省略

一些与动词、名词或形容词一起搭配的介词常常被省略，而保留其后的动名词，常见句型有 have difficulty/trouble (in) doing sth., be busy (in) doing sth., stop/prevent sb. (from) doing sth.等。例如：

The heavy rain prevented him (from) arriving there on time. 大雨使得他没准时到达那里。

7．冠词的省略

两个名词并列时，第二个名词前的冠词常可省略。作同位语、补语等的表独一无二的职位、头衔的名词前也省略冠词。此外，在英语新闻标题、告示中，经常省略冠词。例如：

They elected John (the) monitor of the class. 他们选约翰当班长。

Exercises

Choose the best answer to the following sentences.

1. Some students are going to China in summer vacation, and _____.
   A. some are to America   B. some going to America
   C. some to America   D. some America

2. _____ the road, don't forget to look both ways.
   A. As crossing   B. While you cross   C. While crossing   D. Cross

3. - What's the matter with Jack?
   - He didn't win the game, but he still _____.
   A. hopes so   B. hopes to   C. hopes it   D. hopes that

4. - She must look like a very pretty girl.
   - Yes, imagine _____.
   A. to   B. that   C. it   D. so

5. This is an illness that can result in total blindness _____ left untreated.
   A. after   B. if   C. since   D. unless

6. - What will John Smith be doing in the fall of this year?
   - _____ mathematics at a high school.
   A. Teaching   B. To teach   C. Be teaching   D. Teach

7. - Better not have the operation right now.
   - _____.
   A. I mustn't   B. I shouldn't   C. I won't   D. I can't

8. - Will you go to the party?
   - Of course I will if _____.
   A. I was invited   B. invited
   C. having invited   D. I will be invited

9. The special medicine for the disease was difficult to find though _____ everywhere.
   A. sought   B. having sought

C. being sought　　　　　　　　　　　D. having been sought

10. Take such of medicine, if _____, will possibly do you great harm.

　　A. continue　　　B. to continue　　　C. continued　　　D. continuing

11. He is not easy to get along with, but the friendship of his, _____, will last forever.

　　A. once gained　　　　　　　　　　B. to be gained
　　C. after gained　　　　　　　　　　D. while gaining

12. - Don't forget to take the message to my teacher.
　　- _____.
　　A. Yes, I will　　　　　　　　　　　B. No, I won't
　　C. I don't think so　　　　　　　　 D. Sorry, I don't

13. The road is designed for only motor vehicles, so once _____, bicycles are not allowed to go along it.

　　A. opens　　　B. having opened　　　C. opening　　　D. opened

14. The teacher told us not to take the equipment out of the laboratory until _____.

　　A. allowing to take　　　　　　　　B. allowing to
　　C. allowed to be taken　　　　　　　D. allowed to

15. - Will you go home tomorrow evening?
　　- No, I am going to a lecture, or at least, I'm planning _____.
　　A. so　　　B. to　　　C. it　　　D. that

16. Would you read my letter and correct the mistakes if _____?

　　A. some　　　B. ever　　　C. any　　　D. never

17. When _____ where he was born, the old man was afraid to give his address.

　　A. asking　　　B. asked　　　C. was asked　　　D. ask

18. Don't speak to anyone when you are in a strange situation unless _____.

　　A. you will be spoken　　　　　　　B. you speak to
　　C. spoken　　　　　　　　　　　　D. you spoken to

19. - Will the Smith be going abroad this summer?
　　- No, they finally decided _____.
　　A. not to be　　　B. not to do　　　C. not going　　　D. not to

20. - How do you think Mary managed to improve her French in such a short time?
　　- _____ 4 hours on it every morning.
　　A. Because of spending　　B. By spending　　C. Spent　　　D. To spend

Part D

Workshop
Survey on Internet Security

Ⅰ. Background

Human beings are stepping into the information society. Information industry develops rapidly, so do hackers and fraudsters. The question of how stay safely online raises a lot of discussion in our country. We must take measures to protect our privacy and property effectively in the age of the rapid development of network.

Ⅱ. **Task**

(1) Interview your classmates or the people around you to learn about their experiences about information security in social media;

(2) Search information online to know more cases about this topic;

(3) Make a research on how to avoid ourselves from similar cases.

Ⅲ. **Process**

Step 1: Complete the task in groups. Form small groups with 5 students respectively;

Step 2: Interview your classmates to learn about their experiences about being involved in information security in social media and how do they cope with such cases;

Step 3: Search more information online about the measures to avoid similar cases;

Step 4: Make a research on the measures to protect our privacy and property effectively.

Unit 11 AI in Education

Artificially Intelligent Teaching Assistant

Professor Ashok Goel of Georgia Tech developed an artificially intelligent teaching assistant to help handle the enormous number of student questions in the online class, Knowledge-Based Artificial Intelligence. This online course is a core requirement of Georgia Tech's online Master of Science in Computer Science program Professor Goel already had eight teaching assistants, but that wasn't enough to deal with the overwhelming number of daily questions from students.

Many students drop out of online courses because of the lack of teaching support. When students feel isolated or confused and reach out with questions that go unanswered, their motivation to continue begins to fade. Professor Goel decided to do something to remedy this situation and his solution was to create a virtual assistant named Jill Watson, which is based on the IBM Watson platform.

Goel and his team developed several versions of Jill Watson before releasing her to the online forums. At first, the virtual assistant wasn't too great. But Goel and his team sourced the online discussion forum to find all 40,000 questions that had ever been asked since the class was launched. Then they began to feed Jill with the questions and answers. After some adjustments, and sufficient time, Jill was able to answer the students' questions correctly 97% of the time. The virtual assistant became so advanced and realistic that the students didn't know she was a computer. The students, who were studying artificial intelligence, were interacting with the virtual assistant and couldn't tell it apart from a real human being. Goel didn't inform them about Jill's true identity until April 26. The students were actually very positive about the experience.

The goal of Professor Goel's virtual assistant next year is to take over answering 40% of all the questions posed by students on the online forum. The name Jill Watson will, of course, change to something else next semester. Professor Goel has a much rosier outlook on the future of artificial intelligence than, say, Elon Musk, Stephen Hawking, Bill Gates or Steve Wozniak.

intelligent/ɪnˈtelɪdʒənt/ *adj.* 聪明的；有智力的；智能的

Unit 11　AI in Education

handle/ˈhænd(ə)l/*v*. 应付（局面），处理（难题），对待（某人）
assistant/əˈsɪstənt/*n*. 助理，助手，店员
enormous/ɪˈnɔːməs/*adj*. 巨大的，极大的
artificial/ˌɑːtɪˈfɪʃ(ə)l/*adj*. 人造的，人工的，人为的
overwhelm/ˌəʊvəˈwelm/*v*. 压垮，打败，压倒
isolate/ˈaɪsəleɪt/*v*. 分离，隔离，孤立
confuse/kənˈfjuːz/*v*. 使迷惑，使糊涂，混淆
motivation/ˌməʊtɪˈveɪʃ(ə)n/*n*. 动力，积极性，干劲
fade/feɪd/*v*. 逐渐消失，褪色，凋谢
virtual/ˈvɜːtʃuəl/*adj*. 实质上的，虚拟的，模拟的
forum/ˈfɔːrəm/*n*. 讨论会，论坛
sufficient/səˈfɪʃ(ə)nt/*adj*. 足够的，充足的，充分的
outlook/ˈaʊtlʊk/*n*. 看法，前景，展望
launch/lɔːntʃ/*v*. 发起，发行，发射，启动
adjustment/əˈdʒʌstmənt/ 调整，校正，调节，适应
interact with　与…互动
drop out of　退出；退学
take over　接管

Notes

Artificial Intelligence
人工智能，英文缩写为 AI。它是研究、开发用于模拟、延伸和扩展人的智能的理论、方法、技术及应用系统的一门新的技术科学。人工智能是计算机科学的一个分支，它企图了解智能的实质，并生产出一种新的能以人类智能相似的方式做出反应的智能机器。

Exercises

I. Comprehension of the Text

There are 5 questions in this section. For each of them there are four choices marked A, B, C and D. You should choose the best answer for each question.

1. What do we learn about Knowledge-Based Artificial Intelligence?
    A. It is a robot that can answer students' questions.
    B. It is a course designed for students to learn online.
    C. It is a high-tech device that revolutionizes teaching.
    D. It is a computer program that aids student learning.
2. What problem did Professor Goel meet with?
    A. His students were unsatisfied with the assistants.

B. His course was too difficult for the students.

C. Students' questions were too many to handle.

D. Too many students dropped out of his course.

3. What do we learn about Jill Watson?

A. She turned out to be a great success.

B. She got along pretty well with students.

C. She was unwelcome to students at first.

D. She was released online as an experiment.

4. How did the students feel about Jill Watson?

A. They thought she was a bit too artificial.

B. They found her not as capable as expected.

C. They could not but admire her knowledge.

D. They could not tell her from a real person.

5. What does Professor Goel plan to do next with Jill Watson?

A. Launch different versions of her online.

B. Feed her with new questions and answers.

C. Assign her to answer more of students' questions.

D. Encourage students to interact with her more freely.

Ⅱ. Languages Focus

A. *Match the following words in left with their explanations in right.*

1. virtual	a. a place where people can exchange opinions on an issue
2. launch	b. extremely large
3. fade	c. the attitude to life and the world of a person or culture
4. overwhelm	d. made or produced to copy sth. natural
5. outlook	e. to let sb. come out of a place where they have been kept
6. forum	f. to disappear gradually
7. assistant	g. to defeat sb. completely
8. artificial	h. to start an activity, especially an organized one
9. release	i. almost or very nearly the thing described
10. enormous	j. a person who helps or supports sb., usually in their job

B. *Fill in the blanks with the words or expressions given below. Change the form where necessary.*

core	isolate	sufficient	motivation	interact with
confuse	remedy	handle	enormous	take over

1. There is _____ evidence to show that plastic bags have caused white pollution to the environment.

2. People need leadership, guidance, _____, reward and sense of mission in order to

achieve peak performance.

3. This scientist accessed _____ different files to find the correct information.

4. People are _____ about all the different labels on food these days.

5. Sleeping hills, while helpful for some, are not necessarily an effective _____ either.

6. Even though I'm supposed to be working by myself, there are other people who I can _____.

7. Patients will be _____ from other people for between three days and one month after treatment.

8. Concern for the environment is at the _____ of our policies.

9. There are now more than 20 big companies waiting in the wings to _____ some of its business.

10. She admitted to herself she didn't know how to _____ the problem.

III. Translation

Translate the following sentences into Chinese.

1. Professor Goel decided to do something to remedy this situation and his solution was to create a virtual assistant named Jill Watson, which is based on the IBM Watson platform.

_____

_____

2. The students, who were studying artificial intelligence, were interacting with the virtual assistant and couldn't tell it apart from a real human being.

_____

_____

3. When students feel isolated or confused and reach out with questions that go unanswered, their motivation to continue begins to fade.

_____

_____

4. The goal of professor Goel's virtual assistant next year is to take over answering 40% of all the questions posed by students on the online forum.

_____

_____

5. But Goel and his team sourced the online discussion forum to find all 40,000 questions that had ever been asked since the class was launched.

_____

_____

IV. Discussion

Please talk about the pros and cons of Artificial Intelligence in our daily life.

Some College Students Are Angry That They Have to Pay to Do Their Homework

A) Digital learning systems now charge students for access codes needed to complete coursework, take quizzes, and turn in homework. As universities go digital, students are complaining of a new hit to their finances that's replacing — and sometimes joining — expensive textbooks: pricey online access codes that are required to complete coursework and submit assignments.

B) The codes — which typically range in price from $80 to $155 per course—give students online access to systems developed by education companies like McGraw Hill and Pearson. These companies, which long reaped big profits as textbook publishers, have boasted that their new online offerings, when pushed to students through universities they partner with, represent the future of the industry.

C) But critics say the digital access codes represent the same profit-seeking ethos of the textbook business, and are even harder for students to opt out of. While they could once buy second-hand textbooks, or share copies with friends, the digital systems are essentially impossible to avoid.

D) "When we talk about the access code we see it as the new face of the textbook monopoly, a new way to lock students around this system," said Ethan Senack, the higher education advocate for the U. S. Public Interest Research Group, to BuzzFeed News. "Rather than $250 (for a print textbook) you're paying $120," said Senack. "But because it's all digital it eliminates the used book market and eliminates any sharing and because homework and tests are through an access code, it eliminates any ability to opt out."

E) Sarina Harpet, a 19-year-old student at Virginia Tech, was faced with a tough dilemma when she first started college in 2015 — pay rent or pay to turn in her chemistry homework. She told BuzzFeed News that her freshman chemistry class required her to use Connect, a system provided by McGraw Hill where students can submit homework, take exams and track their grades. But the code to access the program cost $120 — a big sum for Harper, who had already put down $450 for textbooks, and had rent day approaching.

F) She decided to wait for her next work-study paycheck, which was typically $150 ~ $200, to pay for the code. She knew that her chemistry grade may take a dive as a result. "It's a balancing act," she said. "Can I really afford these access codes now?" She didn't hand in her first two assignments for chemistry, which started her out in the class with a failing grade.

G) The access codes may be another financial headache for students, but for textbook businesses, they're the future. McGraw Hill, which controls 21% of the higher education market, reported in March that its digital content sales exceeded print sales for the first time in 2015. The company said that 45% of its $140 million revenue in 2015 "was derived from digital products".

H) A Pearson spokesperson told *BuzzFeed News* that "digital materials are less expensive and a good investment" that offer new features, like audio texts, personalized knowledge checks and expert videos. Its digital course materials save students up to 60% compared to traditional printed textbooks, the company added. McGraw Hill didn't respond to a request for comment, but its CEO David Levin told the *Financial Times* in August that "in higher education, the era of the printed textbook is now over".

I) The textbook industry insists the online systems represent a better deal for students. "These digital products aren't just mechanisms for students to submit homework, they offer all kinds of features," David Anderson, the executive director of higher education with the Association of American Publishers, told *BuzzFeed News*. "It helps students understand in a way that you can't do with print homework assignments."

J) David Hunt, an associate professor in sociology at Augusta University, which has rolled out digital textbooks across its math and psychology departments, told *BuzzFeed News* that he understands the utility of using systems that require access codes. But he doesn't require his students to buy access to a learning program that controls the class assignments. "I try to make things as inexpensive as possible," said Hunt, who uses free digital textbooks for his classes but designs his own curriculum. "The online systems may make my life a lot easier but I feel like I'm giving up control. The discussions are the things where my expertise can benefit the students most."

K) A 20-year-old junior at Georgia Southern University told *BuzzFeed News* that she normally spends $500-$600 on access codes for class. In one case, the professor didn't require students to buy a textbook, just an access code to turn in homework. This year she said she spent $ 900 on access codes to books and programs. "That's two months of rent," she said. "You can't sell any of it back. With a traditional textbook you can sell it for $30 ~ $50 and that helps to pay for your new semester's books. With an access code, you're out of that money."

L) Benjamin Wolverton, a 19-year-old student at the University of South Carolina, told *BuzzFeed News* that "it's ridiculous that after paying tens of thousands in tuition we have to pay for all these access codes to do our homework." Many of the access codes he's purchased have been required simply to complete homework or quizzes. "Often it's only 10% of your grade in class." he said. "You're paying so much money for something that hardly affects your grade—but if you didn't have it, it would affect your grades enough. It would be bad to start out at a B or C." Wolverton said he spent $500 on access codes for digital books and programs this semester.

M) Harper, a poultry science major, is taking chemistry again this year and had to buy a new access code to hand in her homework. She rented her economics and statistics textbooks for about $20 each. But her access codes for homework, which can't be rented or bought second-hand, were her most expensive purchases: $120 and $85.

N) She still remembers the sting of her first experience skipping an assignment due to the high prices. "We don't really have a missed assignment policy," she said. "If you miss it, you just miss it. I just got zeros on a couple of first assignments. I managed to pull everything back up. But as a scared freshman looking at their grades, it's not fun."

Words & Expressions

charge/tʃɑːdʒ/v. 收（费）；（向…）要价
access/'ækses/n. 通道；通路；入径
pricey/'praɪsi/adj. 昂贵的
submit/səb'mɪt/v. 提交，呈递（文件、建议等）
range/reɪndʒ/v.（在一定的范围内）变化，变动
reap/riːp/v. 取得（成果）；收获
associate/ə'səʊsieɪt/adj. 非正式的；准的；副的
boast/bəʊst/v. 自夸；自吹自擂
ethos/'iːθɒs/n.（某团体或社会的）道德思想，道德观
opt/ɒpt/v. 选择；挑选
monopoly/mə'nɒpəli/v. 垄断；专营服务；被垄断的商品（或服务）
expertise/ˌekspɜː'tiːz/n. 专门知识；专门技能；专长
approach/ə'prəʊtʃ/v.（在距离或时间上）靠近，接近
exceed/ɪk'siːd/v. 超过（数量）
poultry/'pəʊltri/n. 家禽
sting/stɪŋ/v. 刺；蜇；叮
partner with 与…合作
roll out 推出，展开

Notes

Buzz Feed News

Buzz Feed News 是 Buzz Feed 旗下的一个新闻部门。Buzz Feed 是一个美国的新闻聚合网站，2006 年由乔纳·佩雷蒂创建于美国纽约，致力于从数百个新闻博客那里获取订阅源，通过搜索、发送信息链接，为用户浏览当天网上的热门事件提供方便，被称为媒体行业的颠覆者。*Buzz Feed News* 在新闻报道的方式和风格上可能与传统的新闻机构有所不同，其更倾向于采用轻松、易懂和具有吸引力的方式来呈现新闻。

Exercises

I. Comprehension of the Text

Read the text and answer the following questions. Write the answers on the lines.
1. What are digital learning systems, and how do they impact students financially?

2. How much do online access codes typically cost per course, and what do they give

students access to?

3. Can students opt out of using digital access codes, and if not, why?

4. What new features do digital materials offer, according to Pearson?

5. Why does David Hunt use free digital textbooks for his classes but designs his own curriculum?

II. Main Details Comprehension

Each of the following statement contains information given in one of the paragraphs. Identify the paragraph from which the information is derived. You may choose a paragraph more than once. Each paragraph is marked with a letter. Answer the questions by marking the corresponding letter in the blanks.

_____1. A student's yearly expenses on access codes may amount to their rent for two months.

_____2. The online access codes may be seen as a way to tie the students to the digital system.

_____3. If a student takes a course again, they may have to buy a new access code to submit their assignments.

_____4. McGraw Hill accounts for over one-fifth of the market share of college textbooks.

_____5. Many traditional textbook publishers are now offering online digital products, which they believe will be the future of the publishing business

_____6. One student complained that they now had to pay for access codes in addition to the high tuition.

_____7. Digital materials can cost students less than half the price of traditional printed books according to a publisher.

_____8. One student decided not to buy her access code until she received the pay for her part-time job.

_____9. Online systems may deprive teachers of opportunities to make the best use of their expertise for their students.

_____10. Digital access codes are criticized because they are profit-driven just like the textbook.

III. Translation

Translate the five following sentences into English, using the words or expressions given in brackets.

1. 他只收我半价。(charge)

2. 完成的方案必须在 3 月 10 日前交上来。（submit）
_____

3. 超过建议使用的剂量会有危险。（exceed）
_____

4. 现在，他们的辛劳全部得到了回报。（reap）
_____

5. 我们听见一辆汽车加速的声音。（approach）
_____

 Part C

Grammar
强　　调

英语中常见的强调方法有以下 7 种。
（1）用助动词"do (does/did)＋动词原形"来表示强调。例如：
He does know the place well. 他的确很熟悉这个地方。
Do write to me when you get there. 你到那儿后务必给我来信。
（2）用形容词 very, only, single, such 等修饰名词来加强语气。例如：
That's the very textbook we used last term. 这正是我们上学期用过的教材。
You are the only person here who can speak Chinese. 你是这里唯一会讲汉语的人。
Not a single person has been in the shop this morning. 今天上午这个商店里连一个人都没有。
（3）用 ever, never, very, just 等副词和 badly, highly, really 等带有-y 的副词来进行强调。例如：
He never said a word the whole day. 一整天，他一句话也没说。
You've got to be very, very careful. 你一定得非常、非常小心。
This is just what I wanted. 这正是我所要的。
I really don't know what to do next. 我的确不知道下一步该怎么做。
（4）用 in the world, on earth, at all, not in the least 等介词短语可以表达更强的语气（常用于疑问句）。例如：
Where in the world could he be? 他到底会在哪儿?
What on earth is it? 它究竟是什么?
（5）用倒装句（也就是将被强调的部分置于句首）来加强语气。例如：
On the table were some flowers. 桌上摆着一些花。
Many a time have I climbed that hill. 我多次翻过那座山。
Only in this way can we solve this problem. 只有这样我们才能解决这个问题。
Not until the opera had begun did he arrive at the theatre. 戏剧开演了他才赶到剧院。
（6）"It＋be＋强调部分＋that/who"强结构。例如：
It was in 1989 that he got enrolled in university. 他是在 1989 年考进大学的。

Unit 11　AI in Education

这个结构可以强调主语、宾语、状语。在此结构中，当被强调的部分指人时，用 who/that；当被强调的部分为物时，用 that。例如：

It was he who/that opened the door. 是他开的门。（强调主语）

It was trees that we planted at the gate. 我们在门口种的是树。（强调宾语）

It was through his carelessness that the key was lost. 正是由于他的粗心，钥匙才丢了。（强调状语）

It was not until dark that she realized it was too late to go home. 直到黄昏她才意识到太晚了无法赶回家。

（7）用 if 来表示强调。

① If 从句＋I don't know who/what, etc. does/is/has, etc；主语部分也可以用 nobody does/is/has, etc. 或 everybody does/is/has, etc. 来代替。例如：

If he can't do it, I don't know who can. 要是他做不了这件事，我不知道还有谁能做。

② If 从句＋it be 主句。例如：

If anyone knew the truth , it was Tom. 如果说有人了解事实的真相，那便是汤姆。

③ 主语从句＋be＋被强调部分，主语从句要用 what 引导。例如：

What John wants is a ball. 约翰想要的是一个球。

What Mary does every day is (to) give piano lessons. 玛丽每天从事的工作是教钢琴。

Exercises

Choose the best answer to the following sentences.

1. It was after he had made a thorough investigation ＿＿＿＿ he came to know the actual state of affairs.
　　A. where　　　　　　B. when　　　　　　C. that　　　　　　D. and
2. It was not until she had arrived home ＿＿＿＿ remembered her appointment with the doctor.
　　A. when she　　　　B. that she　　　　　C. and she　　　　D. she
3. It must have been ＿＿＿＿ who gave the signal.
　　A. them　　　　　　B. they　　　　　　　C. theirs　　　　　　D. these
4. It was the way he said rather than what he actually said ＿＿＿＿ completely upset her.
　　A. what　　　　　　B. that　　　　　　　C. who　　　　　　D. whom
5. It was the clothes she created ＿＿＿＿ changed the way women looked and how they looked at themselves.
　　A. that　　　　　　　B. then　　　　　　　C. so that　　　　　D. therefore
6. ＿＿＿＿ she first heard of the man referred to as a specialist.
　　A. That was from Stephen　　　　　　　B. It was Stephen whom
　　C. It was from Stephen that　　　　　　D. It was Stephen that
7. ＿＿＿＿ that the trade between the two countries reached its high point.
　　A. During the 1960s　　　　　　　　　B. It was in the 1960s
　　C. That it was in the 1960s　　　　　　D. It was the 1960s
8. She said she would go and she ＿＿＿＿ go.

A. didn't　　　　　B. did　　　　　C. really　　　　　D. would

9. - Were all the three people in the car injured in the accident?
   - No, _____ only the two passengers who got hurt.
   A. there were　　　B. it were　　　C. there was　　　D. it was

10. She _____ you a new cup.
    A. did buy　　　　B. do buy　　　C. has buy　　　　D. have buy

11. It was _____ who broke the window.
    A. him　　　　　　B. her　　　　　C. he　　　　　　D. hi

12. It is _____ I know well, not his brother.
    A. he　　　　　　　B. him　　　　　C. his　　　　　　D. himself

13. It was _____ the next morning that my brother began to think about where he was going.
    A. before　　　　　B. after　　　　C. when　　　　　D. not until

14. It _____ people, not things, that _____ decisive.
    A. is is　　　　　　B. are are　　　C. is are　　　　　D. are is

15. It _____ his new ties that we want to see.
    A. is　　　　　　　B. are　　　　　C. were　　　　　D. has

16. _____ they met each other and became fast friends.
    A. It was in the lake area in the north of the country that
    B. It was in the lake area in the north of the country when
    C. Being in the lake area in the north of the country
    D. It was in the lake area in the north of the country

17. It might have been John _____ bought a new book for Mary yesterday afternoon.
    A. therefore　　　　B. who　　　　　C. so that　　　　D. which

18. I really don't know _____ I had my money stolen.
    A. where is it that　　　　　　　　B. when it is that
    C. where is was that　　　　　　　D. it was where that

19. - Was _____ that I saw last night at the concert?
    - No, it wasn't.
    A. it you　　　　　　B. not you　　　C. you　　　　　　D. that yourself

20. _____ find my wallet, Tom?
    A. Where did you that　　　　　　B. Where was it you
    C. Where have you　　　　　　　D. Where was it that you

Workshop
Exploring the Significance of Artificial Intelligence

Ⅰ. Background

Artificial Intelligence (AI) is a rapidly evolving field with significant implications for various industries and society as a whole. Understanding the concepts, applications, and implications of AI is essential for professionals across different domains. This workshop aims to provide participants with a comprehensive overview of AI, its significance, and its potential impact on their respective fields.

Ⅱ. Task

The workshop will consist of discussions, and hands-on activities to help participants grasp the fundamentals of AI and explore its significance. Participants will have the opportunity to delve into various AI applications and engage in group exercises to understand AI's transformative potential.

Ⅲ. Process

Step 1: Complete the task in groups. Form small groups with 5 students respectively.

Step 2: Search online or work in group to try to complete the following tasks: Understanding the historical background and evolution of AI; Exploring the impact of AI on the education, life, and other aspects; Addressing concerns and misconceptions surrounding AI; Group discussions on potential AI applications in participants' specific domains.

Step 3: Conduct a research and make a presentation.

Ⅳ. Appreciation of Classics

1. 尖端科技同飞跃，文人积习消除却。《菩萨蛮·其二十八》

Cutting-edge technology eliminate the long-standing practice of literati.

释义：指先进的技术正在相互跳跃，并扫除了文人的积习。

2. 欲为生民销战伐，首凭科技占优先。《江南好·其二》

To fight for the people, technology is the first priority.

释义：指想要为了百姓战争，但首先科技要排第一。

3. 黄鹤一去不复返，白云千载空悠悠。《黄鹤楼》

Once gone, the yellow crane will never on earth alight; Only white clouds still float in vain from year to year.

释义：黄鹤一去再也没有返回这里，千万年来只有白云飘飘悠悠。

4. 闲云潭影日悠悠，物换星移几度秋。《滕王阁诗》

Leisurely clouds hang over still water all day long; Stars move from spring to autumn in changless sky.

释义：悠闲的浮云影子倒映在江水中，整天悠悠然地漂浮着；时光易逝，人世变迁，不知已经度过几个春秋。

5. 锦江春色来天地，玉垒浮云变古今。《登楼》

The colors of spring arrive, bringing changes to the world.

释义：锦江的春色从天地边际迎面扑来，从古到今玉垒山的浮云变幻莫测。

Unit 12 Food

How to Affect Calories Consumption?

Can you remember what you ate yesterday? If asked, most people will be able to give a vague description of their main meals: breakfast, lunch, dinner. But can you be sure you've noted every snack bar in your car, or every handful of nuts at your desk? Most people will have a feeling that they've missed something out.

We originally had this suspicion back in 2016, puzzled by the fact that national statistics showed calorie consumption falling dramatically over past decades. We found reliable evidence that people were drastically under-reporting what they ate.

Now the Office for National Statistics has confirmed that we are consuming 50% more calories than our national statistics claim.

Why is this happening? We can point to at least three potential causes. One is the rise in obesity levels itself. Under-reporting rates are much higher for obese people, because they simply consume more food, and thus have more to remember.

Another cause is that the proportion of people who are trying to lose weight has been increasing over time. People who want to lose weight are more likely to under-report their eating — regardless of whether they are overweight or not. This may be driven partly by self-deception or "wishful thinking".

The final potential cause is an increase in snacking and eating out over recent decades — both in terms of how often they happen and how much they contribute to our overall energy intake. Again, there is evidence that food consumed out of the home is one of the most poorly recorded categories in surveys.

So, what's the message conveyed? For statistics, we should invest in more accurate measurement options. For policy, we need to focus on options that make it easy for people to eat fewer calories. If people do not know how much they are eating, it can be really hard for them to stick to a diet. Also, we should be looking for new ways to ensure what people eat wouldn't have much impact on their waistlines. If this works, it won't matter if they can't remember what they ate yesterday.

calorie/'kæləri/*n.* 卡（路里）（热量单位）

Unit 12　Food

drastically/'dræstɪkli/*adv.* （动作或变化）猛烈地，力度大地，极其
snack/snæk/*n.* 零食，点心，小吃
obesity/əʊ'bi:səti/*n.* 过度肥胖，肥胖症
overweight/ˌəʊvə'weɪt/*adj.* 肥胖的，超重的
impact/'ɪmpækt/*n.* 撞击，冲击力；巨大影响，强大作用
convey/kən'veɪ/*v.* 传送，运输，表达，传递
option/'ɒpʃ(ə)n/*n.* 可选择的事物，选择，选择权
reliable/rɪ'laɪəb(ə)l/*adj.* 可靠的，可信赖的，真实可信的
originally/ə'rɪdʒənəli/*adv.* 起初，原来，独创地，新颖地
analytical/ˌænə'lɪtɪk(ə)l/*adj.* 分析的，善于分析的
diet/'daɪət/*n.* 日常饮食，规定饮食
confirm/kən'fɜ:m/*v.* 确定，确认，证实
cause/kɔ:z/*n.* 原因，起因，动机
statistic/stə'tɪstɪk/*n.* 统计数字，统计资料，统计学
a handful of　一把，少量的，一小部分
the proportion of　…的比例
regardless of　不顾，不管
wishful thinking　一厢情愿
stick to　坚持，粘住
have impact on　对…有影响
contribute to　有助于，捐献，带来，促成
be likely to　倾向于，很有可能

Notes

Office for National Statistics
英国负责收集、分析和发布有关英国经济、社会和人口统计数据的独立机构。其主要职责包括大规模的调查和普查、检测和评估英国经济表现、发布各类统计报告和数据等。英国国家统计局的数据对于政府制定政策、评估政策效果、企业制订战略以及学术界进行研究都具有重要的参考价值。

Exercises

Ⅰ. Comprehension of the Text

There are 5 questions in this section. For each of them there are four choices marked A, B, C and D. You should choose the best answer for each question.

1. What did the author suspect back in 2016?
　　A. Calorie consumption had fallen drastically over the decades.

B. Most people surveyed were reluctant to reveal what they ate.

C. The national statistics did not reflect the actual calorie consumption.

D. Most people did not include snacks when reporting their calorie intake.

2. What has the Office for National Statistics verified?

A. People's calorie intake was far from accurately reported.

B. The missing out of main meal leads to the habit of snacking.

C. The nation's obesity level has much to do with calorie intake.

D. Calorie consumption is linked to the amount of snacks one eats.

3. What do we learn about obese people from the passage?

A. They usually keep their eating habits a secret.

B. They overlook the potential causes of obesity.

C. They cannot help eating more than they should.

D. They have difficulty recalling what they have eaten.

4. What often goes unnoticed in surveys on food consumption?

A. They growing trend of eating out.

B. The potential causes of snacking.

C. People's home energy consumption.

D. People's changing diet over the years.

5. What does the author suggest policymakers do about obesity?

A. Remind people to cut down on snacking.

B. Make sure people eat non-fattening food.

C. Ensure people don't miss their main meals.

D. See that people don't stick to the same diet.

Ⅱ. Languages Focus

A. *Match the following words in left with their explanations in right.*

1. cause a. a part or share of a whole
2. proportion b. to make ideas, feelings, etc., known to sb.
3. reliable c. not clear in a person's mind
4. option d. person or thing that makes sth. happen
5. convey e. a group of people or things in common
6. vague f. very fat in a way that is not healthy
7. category g. information shown in numbers
8. obesity h. correct and true in every detail
9. statistic i. something that you can choose
10. accurate J. that you can rely on

B. *Fill in the blanks with the words or expressions given below. Change the form where necessary.*

| confirm | impact | diet | regardless of | originally |
| overweight | calorie | reliable | stick to | snack |

1. Vitamin deficiency in the _____ can cause illness.
2. Our _____ plan was overtaken by events and we had to make a new one.
3. A survey of the British diet has revealed that a growing number of people are _____.
4. It has been _____ that the meeting will take place next week.
5. _____ the change by action is large or small, there is considerable happiness in heart.
6. This will improve your performance and help you burn off _____.
7. There are no _____ statistics for the number of deaths in the battle.
8. It is customary to offer a drink or a _____ to guests.
9. Though there was only a slim chance to win the game, all of the team members chose to _____ the end.
10. Cheating also has a destructive _____ on teachers.

Ⅲ. Translation

Translate the following sentences into Chinese.

1. People who want to lose weight are more likely to under-report their eating — regardless of whether they are overweight or not.

2. Now the Office for National Statics has confirmed that we are consuming 50% more calories than our national statistics claim.

3. One is the rise in obesity levels itself. Under-reporting rates are much higher for obese people, because they simply consume more food, and thus have more to remember.

4. Also, we should be looking for new ways to ensure what people eat wouldn't have much impact on their waistlines.

5. Again, there is evidence that food consumed out of the home is one of the most poorly recorded categories in surveys.

Ⅳ. Discussion

Discuss about connection between food with health in groups, and then write down your opinions.

The History of the Lunch Box

A) It was made of shiny, bright pink plastic with a Little Mermaid sticker on the front, and I carried it with me nearly every single day. My lunch box was one of my first prized possessions, a proud statement to everyone in my kindergarten: "I love Mermaid-Ariel on my lunch box."

B) That bulky container served me well through my first and second grades, until the live-action version of *101 Dalmatians* hit theaters, and I needed the newest red plastic box with characters like Pongo and Perdita on the front. I know I'm not alone here — I bet you loved your first lunch box, too.

C) Lunch boxes have been connecting kids to cartoons and TV shows and super-heroes for decades. But it wasn't always that way. Once upon a time, they weren't even boxes. As schools have changed in the past century, the midday meal container has evolved right along with them.

D) Let's start back at the beginning of the 20th century — the beginning of the lunch box story, really. While there were neighborhood schools in cities and suburbs, one-room schoolhouses were common in rural areas. As grandparents have been saying for generations, kids would travel miles to school in the countryside (often on foot).

E) "You had kids in rural areas who couldn't go home from school for lunch, so bringing your lunch wrapped in a cloth, in oiled paper, in a little wooden box or something like that was a very long-standing rural tradition," says Paula Johnson, head of food history section at the Smithsonian National Museum of American History in Washington, D.C..

F) City kids, on the other hand, went home for lunch and came back. Since they rarely carried a meal, the few metal lunch buckets on the market were mainly for tradesmen and factory workers.

G) After World War Ⅱ, a bunch of changes reshaped schools — and lunches. More women joined the workforce. Small schools consolidated into larger ones, meaning more students were farther away from home. And the *National School Lunch Act* in 1946 made cafeterias much more common. Still, there wasn't much of a market for lunch containers — yet. Students who carried their lunch often did so in a re-purposed bucket or tin of some kind.

H) And then everything changed in the year of 1950. You might as well call it the Year of the Lunch Box, thanks in large part to a genius move by a Nashville-based manufacturer, Aladdin Industries. The company already made square metal meal containers, the kind workers carried, and some had started to show up in the hands of school kids.

I) But these containers were really durable, lasting years on end. That was great for the consumer, not so much for the manufacturer. So, executives at Aladdin hit on an idea that would harness the newfound popularity of television. They covered lunch boxes with striking red paint and added a picture of TV and radio cowboy Hopalong Cassidy on the front.

J) The company sold 600,000 units the first year. It was a major "Ah-ha!" moment, and a wave of other manufacturers jumped on board to capitalize on new TV shows and movies. "The Partridge Family, the Addams Family, the Six Million Dollar Man, the Bionic Woman — everything that was on television ended up on a lunch box," says Allen Woodall. He's the founder of the Lunch Box Museum in Columbus, Georgia. "It was a great marketing tool because kids were taking that TV show to school with them, and then when they got home they had them captured back on TV," he says.

K) And yes, you read that right: There is a lunch box museum, right near the Chattahoochee River. Woodall has more than 2,000 items on display. His favorite? The *Green Hornet* lunch box, because he used to listen to the radio show back in the 1940s.

L) The new trend was also a great example of planned obsolescence, that is, to design a product so that it will soon become unfashionable or impossible to use and will need replacing. Kids would beg for a new lunch box every year to keep up with the newest characters, even if their old lunch box was perfectly usable.

M) The metal lunch box craze lasted until the mid-1980s, when plastic took over. Two theories exist as to why. The first — and most likely — is that plastic had simply become cheaper. The second theory — possibly an urban myth — is that concerned parents in several states proposed bans on metal lunch boxes, claiming kids were using them as "weapons" to hit one another. There's a lot on the internet about a state-wide ban in Florida, but a few days worth of digging by a historian at the Florida State Historical Society found no such legislation. Either way, the metal lunch box was out.

N) The last few decades have brought a new lunch box revolution, of sorts. Plastic boxes changed to lined cloth sacks, and eventually, globalism brought tiffin containers from India and *bento* boxes from Japan. Even the old metal lunch boxes have regained popularity. "I don't think the *heyday* has passed," says D. J. Jayasekara, owner and founder of *lunchbox.com*, a retailer in Pasadena, California. "I think it has evolved. The days of the ready-made, 'you stick it in a lunch box and carry it to school' are kind of done."

O) The introduction of backpacks changed the lunch box scene a bit, he adds. Once kids started carrying book bags, that bulky traditional lunch box was hard to fit inside. "But you can't just throw a sandwich in a backpack," Jayasekara says. "It still has to go into a container." That is, in part, why smaller and softer containers have taken off — they fit into backpacks.

P) And don't worry — whether it's a plastic *bento* box or a cloth bag, lunch containers can still easily be covered with popular culture. "We keep pace with the movie industries so we can predict which characters are going to be popular for the coming months," Jayasekara says. "You know, kids are kids."

Words & Expressions

backpack/'bækpæk/*n.* 背包，行囊
transformation/ˌtrænsfə'meɪʃ(ə)n/*n.* （彻底或重大的）改观，变化，转变
possession/pə'zeʃ(ə)n/*n.* 拥有，持有，个人财产，所有物
evolve/ɪ'vɒlv/*v.* 进化，演化，逐渐演变
rural/'rʊərəl/*adj.* 农村的，乡村的
consolidate/kən'sɒlɪdeɪt/*v.* 使巩固，使加强，合并，统一
durable/'djʊərəb(ə)l/*adj.* 持久的，耐用的，坚韧不拔的
popularity/ˌpɒpju'lærəti/*n.* 流行，普及，受欢迎
bucket/'bʌkɪt/*n.* 桶，铲斗，大量
metal/'met(ə)l/*n.* 金属，合金
regain/rɪ'geɪn/*v.* 恢复，重回，重新获得
unfashionable/ʌn'fæʃnəbl/*adj.* 过时的，不时髦的
claim/kleɪm/*v.* 声称，断言，索取
plastic/'plæstɪk/*n.* 塑料，信用卡
start back 返回，退缩
for generations 世世代代，祖祖辈辈
keep up with 赶得上，与……保持联系
keep pace with 跟上……，保持同步
end up 结束
fit into （使）适合，适应，符合

Notes

1. World War Ⅱ

第二次世界大战（1931 年 9 月 18 日至 1945 年 9 月 2 日），简称"二战"，也称世界反法西斯战争，以纳粹德国、意大利王国、日本帝国 3 个法西斯轴心国及仆从国与反法西斯同盟和全世界反法西斯力量进行的第二次全球规模的战争，战争范围从欧洲到亚洲，从大西洋到太平洋，先后有 60 个国家和地区、20 亿以上的人口被卷入战争。

2. National School Lunch Act

1946 年美国出台了《全国学校午餐法》，该法案的出台标志着"全国学校午餐计划"（National School Lunch Program，简称 NSLP）正式在全国范围内施行。该计划由美国联邦政府发起，旨在向中小学儿童发放廉价午餐，以保证贫困儿童身心健康的发展。

3. Lunch Box Museum

饭盒博物馆，坐落于美国佐治亚州哥伦布（Columbus）的第十大道上，馆内收藏了 2000 多只从 20 世纪 40 年代到 80 年代的饭盒，被称为全世界最大的饭盒博物馆。艾伦·伍道尔（Allen Woodall）是该馆的创始人。

Exercises

I. Comprehension of the Text

Read the text and answer the following questions. Write the answers on the lines.

1. Under what circumstance did the author change his bulky container into a new one?

_____

2. What was the origin of the lunch box at the beginning of 20th century?

_____

3. What an idea did executives at Aladdin come up with about lunch box after the company made durable metal container?

_____

4. How has the lunch box evolved from the year of 1950 to the age of globalization?

_____

5. What's the key factor for lunch containers to be popular in the future according to Jayasekara?

_____

II. Main Details Comprehension

Each of the following statement contains information given in one of the paragraphs. Identify the paragraph from which the information is derived. You may choose a paragraph more than once. Each paragraph is marked with a letter. Answer the questions by marking the corresponding letter in the blanks.

____1. Lunch containers were not necessary for school kids in cities.

____2. Putting TV characters on lunch boxes proved an effective marketing strategy.

____3. Smaller lunch boxes are preferred because they fit easily into backpacks.

____4. Lunch boxes have evolved along with the transformation of schools.

____5. Around the beginning of the nineteen fifties, some school kids started to use metal meal containers.

____6. School kids are eager to get a new lunch box every year to stay in fashion.

____7. Rural kids used to walk a long way to school in the old days.

____8. The author was proud of using a lunch box in her childhood.

____9. The most probable reason for the popularity of plastic lunch boxes is that they are less expensive.

____10. The durability of metal meal containers benefited consumers.

III. Translation

Translate the five following sentences into English, using the words or expressions given in brackets.

1. 这次会晤对巩固两国人民的友谊起了很大作用。(consolidate)
   _____
2. 这些学生正在设法适应新的环境。(fit into)
   _____
3. 一家成功的公司必须跟得上技术变革的步伐。(keep up with)
   _____
4. 有趣的是,汉字是由图画和符号演变而来的。(evolve)
   _____
5. 近年来她的小说很受欢迎。(popularity)
   _____

Practical Writing
询问信(Inquiry Letters)

询问信的主要目的是寻求所需信息,写信人也相信对方能够提供这样的信息,而且希望能尽快得到回复。询问信通常包括以下内容:首先表明写作意图,然后就具体问题进行询问,最后表明获取信息的急切心情,也可以提供联系方式以便收信人与你联系,并表达感谢之情。询问信的语言一般较正式,简洁清晰,语气礼貌恳切。

1. 常用表达

(1) 第一段(自我介绍、表明信息来源、表达对某话题的兴趣、说明写信目的、提出要求),例如:

I am writing to enquire about _____.

I am writing to ask if you could possibly _____.

I am now writing to inquire about the _____ to be held at _____.

I would like to obtain some useful information on _____.

I am interested in your advertisement in *China Daily* and I would like to have further information about _____.

I learn from _____ that there will be an art exhibition to be held at _____ tomorrow/next week/this Sunday.

I read/heard _____ and would like to know _____.

I am now writing to ask if you could do me a favor.

Could you please send me _____ at the address below/above?

(2) 第二段(提供相关背景情况,并具体询问相关事宜),例如:

Could you please send me your most recent brochure?

I wonder if you could _____.

I am also greatly concerned about _____.

I shall be grateful if you could offer me more detailed materials about _____.

Unit 12 Food   151

I would be grateful if you could send me full details of _____.
I would like to receive information regarding _____.
I would like to request materials for _____.
It would be highly appreciated if you could inform me what I have to do.
I would be more grateful if you could send information concerning/regarding _____.
（3）结尾段（希望对方就你的要求给予帮助，早日得到答复，并致以感谢），例如：
I look forward to hearing from you/receiving the information.
I am looking forward to a favorable reply at your earliest convenience.
I look forward to your immediate response.
I am exciting your early reply.
Your prompt attention to this letter would be highly appreciated.

2. 写作范例

Sample 1

Dear Mr. Guo,

　　My family and I have read in the traveling book *Lonely Planet* about your Happy Trails Horse Team. We are very much interested in going horse trekking with your team.

　　We want to choose the Ice Mountain route, which will take four days, from July 31 to August 3. What should we take with us? Will the guides provide accommodation for us? How much will the tour cost each of us?

　　We will reach Songpan on the afternoon of July 30 at about 5 o'clock. I hope it will not be too late when we arrive at your team.

　　I would be grateful to receive a prompt reply.

Yours faithfully,
Li Ming

Sample 2

Dear Professor Sun,

　　I'm a freshman of our university. I'm writing to know if it is possible for you to provide me with information regarding Image Processing and Pattern Recognition.

　　First of all, what is Image Processing and what is Pattern Recognition. Secondly, How to learn them carefully. Thirdly, to learn the two subjects well, which books or references should I borrow from the library or buy online.

　　I would also like to inquire which software must I master relevant to the above two subjects. It would be highly appreciated if you could give me some instructive advice and put forward relevant requirements during my study.

Sincerely yours,
Wang Lin

Sample 3

Dear Sir or Madam,

  I am organizing a group of students to pay a visit to the historical exhibition in your town. I am writing the letter in purpose of requesting information concerning the following aspects.

  First of all, what is the size of the exhibition, what is its theme and what objects are on display? Secondly, what are the dates between which the exhibition will be held, and what are the daily opening hours?

  I must point out that I hope to bring over students to the exhibition. So I would like to inquire if there is any discount available on entrance tickets for students. I look forward to your reply.

Yours sincerely,
Wu Jiang

Exercises

1. *Complete the following inquiry letter with the phrases or sentences listed below.*

a. if it is possible for you to offer a 3-month training course starting before or

b. the teaching staff and the possible schedule for this course

c. whether your company could offer a course on Quality Control for our managers

d. the Quality Control Training Course mentioned in the advert might be suitable for us

Dear Sir,

  I am writing to inquire (1)_____.

  I saw your advertisement in Daily News on Thursday, 26 May 2021, and (2) _____. I would like to know (3) _____, at the latest, on Tuesday, 14 June 2021, for a group of 20. Could you send some information about (4) _____?

  I am looking forward to receiving your reply.

Yours faithfully,
Charles Taylor

2. *Write an inquiry letter according to the information given below.*

假定你是吴江，正在英国参加短期语言培训，计划星期天开展一日游。互联网上的一则广告引起你的注意（如下），但一些具体信息不明确，请给该旅行社写一封信询问具体情况。

A Truly Exciting Day Tour!
Places to visit: Big Ben, The London Eye, Buckingham Palace
Transport: Bus
Price: $45
Start-time: 6:30 am
Pick-up: Anywhere in Oxford
For more information, contact:
Tel: 01865-783279
E-mail: CTravel@service.uk

Workshop
Cultural Introduction

Ⅰ. Appreciation of Classics

1. 民以食为天，食以安为先。《史记·郦生陆贾列传》

Food is the first necessity of the people, safety is the top priority of food.

释义：物质是一切的基础，人民的物质基础问题很重要，食物又以安全为主要，强调食品安全。

2. 一箪食，一瓢饮，在陋巷，人不堪其忧，回也不改其乐。《论语》

A handful of rice to eat, a gourdful of water to drink, living in a mean street. Others would have found it unendurable depressing, but to Hui's cheerfulness it made no difference at all.

释义：一箪饭，一瓢水，住在简陋的小屋里，其他人都忍受不了这种穷困清苦，颜回却没有改变他好学的乐趣。

3. 食不言，寝不语。《论语》

Chew with mouth closed, lay silent.

释义：吃饭和睡觉时不要说话聊天，有利于健康。

4. 饭后百步走，活到九十九。《凉月如眉挂柳湾》

A walk after dinner makes one live to 99.

释义：饭后多走动，利于健康。

5. 食之无味，弃之可惜。《三国志·魏志·武帝纪》

Unappetizing and yet not bad enough to be thrown away.

释义：形容东西吃起来没有什么味道。比喻事情进行下去没有太大必要，就此放手又舍不得。也形容进退两难，犹豫不决，无可奈何。

II. Appreciation of Chinese Poetry

Drinking Alone under the Moon
Li Bai

Amid the flowers, from a pot of wine
I drink without a companion of mine.
I raise my cup to invite the Moon who blends
Her light with my Shadow and we're three friends.
The Moon does not know how to drink her share;
In vain my Shadow follows me here and there.
Together with them for the time I stay,
And make merry before spring's spent away.
I sing and the Moon lingers to hear my song;
My Shadow's a mess while I dance along.
Sober, we three remain cheerful and gay;
Drunken, we part and each may go his way.
Our friendship will outshine all earthly love;
Next time we'll meet beyond the stars above.

月下独酌
李白

花间一壶酒，独酌无相亲。
举杯邀明月，对影成三人。
月既不解饮，影徒随我身。
暂伴月将影，行乐须及春。
我歌月徘徊，我舞影零乱。
醒时同交欢，醉时各分散。
永结无情游，相期邈云汉。

III. Cultural Tips

《月下独酌》是唐代诗人李白的组诗作品，本首诗是第一首，也是流传最广的一首。该诗组的四首诗写的都是诗人在月夜花下独酌、无人亲近的冷落情景。诗人心中愁闷，遂以月为友，对酒当歌，及时行乐。组诗运用丰富的想象，表达出诗人由孤独到不孤独，再由不孤独到孤独的一种复杂感情。表面看来，诗人真能自得其乐，可是深处却有无限的凄凉。

Unit 13　Recreation and Entertainment

A Growth Mindset of Internet Can Spark Innovative Thinking

From climate change to the ongoing pandemic and beyond, the issues facing today's world are increasingly complex and dynamic. Yet solving problems like these requires new approaches that extend beyond traditional ways of thinking. A study led by Yale Professor of Psychology, Paul O'Keefe, found that having a growth mindset of interest may spark this type of innovation.

Professor O'Keefe established in earlier studies that people hold different beliefs about the nature of interest. Those with a growth mindset of interest tend to believe that interests can be developed and cultivated, while those with a fixed mindset of interest tend to believe that interests are inherent and simply need to be "found". Building on these findings, the latest research examined how a growth mindset of interest can boost integrative thinking across the traditional disciplinary boundaries of arts and sciences.

For example, in one task, research participants were instructed to create new college majors by combining two or more existing academic Arts or Science programs at their university. After coding and analyzing the ideas they generated, the team found that people with a growth mindset of interest were more likely to bridge programs across the Arts and Sciences to create new majors like Computational Economics rather than creating majors that drew from only one of those areas, like Computational Chemistry.

As Professor O'Keefe pointed out, "This research provides a useful direction for organizations whose products and services call for integrated and creative solutions. Take smartphones for example. You need not only computer science and engineering knowledge, but also an understanding of psychology and visual design to create a better product. Employees with a growth mindset may be more likely to devise innovative ideas that bridge multiple areas of knowledge to achieve better solutions."

The benefits of a growth mindset of interest may also extend to those seeking employment. This is a pressing issue because many people are becoming unemployed due to the COVID-19 pandemic. Having a growth mindset of interest can help job seekers expand their interests and become more adaptable to different fields, and take the initiative to learn new skills.

Words & Expressions

pandemic/pæn'demɪk/*adj.* （疾病）大规模流行的
inherent/ɪn'herənt/*adj.* 与生俱来的，内在的，固有的
dynamic/daɪ'næmɪk/*adj.* 充满活力的，精力充沛的，动态的
innovation/ˌɪnə'veɪʃ(ə)n/*n.* 新事物，创新，革新
fixed/fɪkst/*adj.* 固定的，确定的，不变的
integrative/'ɪntɪɡreɪtɪv/*adj.* 综合的
generate/'dʒenəreɪt/*v.* 产生，引起
seek/siːk/*v.* 寻找，寻求
issue/'ɪʃuː/*n.* 议题，争论点
spark/spɑːk/*v.* 引发，触发
employment/ɪm'plɔɪmənt/*n.* 就业，就业人员，雇用
expand/ɪk'spænd/*v.* 扩大，增加，扩展
be adaptable to 适应…
take the initiative 采取主动，带头
tend to 倾向，易于…
call for 要求，需要
extend to 延伸至，扩展至…
draw from 从…中得到，从…提取
point out 指出，指明

Notes

1. Psychology

心理学是一门研究人类心理现象及其影响下的精神功能和行为活动的科学，兼顾突出理论性和应用性。心理学包括基础心理学与应用心理学，其研究涉及知觉、认知、情绪、思维、人格等许多领域，也与日常生活的许多领域——家庭、教育、健康、社会等发生关联。

2. Computational Economics

计算经济学是一门涉及计算机科学、经济学、数学、博弈论、社会科学等领域的交叉学科。

Exercises

I. Comprehension of the Text

There are 5 questions in this section. For each of them there are four choices marked A,

B, C and D. You should choose the best answer for each question.

1. What does the author say about the world today?
    A. It faces problems that are getting more varied and complicated.
    B. It has done away with many of the traditional ways of thinking.
    C. It is undergoing radical and profound changes.
    D. It is witnessing various types of innovations.
2. What did Professor O'Keefe find in his earlier studies?
    A. People's interests tend to change with age.
    B. People's interests determine their mindsets.
    C. People are divided about the nature of interest.
    D. People of different ages have different mindsets.
3. What is the focus of Professor O'Keefe's recent research?
    A. How boundaries can be removed between Arts and Science disciplines.
    B. How feasible it is to create new disciplines like Computational Economics.
    C. How students in Arts and Sciences view the two types of mindset of interest.
    D. How a growth mindset of interest can contribute to cross-disciplinary thinking.
4. What does the author want to illustrate with the example of smartphones?
    A. Hi-tech products are needed in interdisciplinary research.
    B. Improved technology gives birth to highly popular products.
    C. Making innovative products needs multidisciplinary knowledge.
    D. Hi-tech products can boost people's integrative thinking.
5. What is the author's suggestion to those who are seeking employment?
    A. Learning practical skills.
    B. Broadening their interests.
    C. Staying safe in the pandemic.
    D. Knowing their pressing issues.

II. Languages Focus

A. *Match the following words in left with their explanations in right.*

1. cultivate   a. a tiny bright piece of burning material
2. generate   b. look for sth./sb.
3. spark   c. staying the same
4. participant   d. a person who take part in an activity or event
5. issue   e. come near to sb./sth. in distance or time
6. dynamic   f. prepare and use land for growing plants or crops
7. seek   g. an important subject that people are discussing
8. fixed   h. produce or create sth.
9. innovation   i. full of energy and exciting ideas
10. approach   j. a new way of doing sth.

B. *Fill in the blanks with the words or expressions given below. Change the form where necessary.*

| employment | issue | call for | cultivate | point out |
| expand | innovation | tend to | boost | take the initiative |

1. Officials used the loud hailer to _____ calm.

2. It makes them feel valued and _____ their confidence, and it's part of being a good leader.

3. The party believes education is the most important _____ facing the government.

4. Don't worry too much about what she said — she _____ dramatize things.

5. You can also _____ to adopt certain behaviors and do some activities that have real value for change and success.

6. More than 3,000 local workers are _____ in the tourism industry.

7. As your horizons _____, these new ideas can give a whole new meaning to life.

8. We should develop _____ thinking abilities in the classrooms by giving students opportunities to generate new ideas.

9. It _____ that many parents still limit electronic reading, mainly due to concerns about increased screen time.

10. When kids participate in sport games just for fun, they will gain pleasure from the games, _____ friendship with others and develop team spirit.

Ⅲ. Translation

Translate the following sentences into Chinese.

1. Those with a growth mindset of interest tend to believe that interests can be developed and cultivated, while those with a fixed mindset of interest tend to believe that interests are inherent and simply need to be "found."

_____

2. A study led by Yale professor of Psychology, Paul O'Keefe, found that having a growth mindset of interest may spark this type of innovation.

_____

3. This research provides a useful direction for organization whose products and services call for integrated and creative solutions.

_____

4. Employees with a growth mindset may be more likely to devise innovative ideas that bridge multiple areas of knowledge to achieve better solutions.

_____
_____

Unit 13   Recreation and Entertainment   159

5. Having a growth mindset of interest can help job seeker expand their interests and become more adaptable to different fields, and take the initiative to learn new skills.

_____

_____

IV. Discussion

Can you come up with some tips on how to cultivate the growth mindset of interest in your life?

Team Spirit

A) Teams have become the basic building blocks of organizations. Recruitment advertisements routinely call for "team players". Business schools grade their students in part on their performance in group projects. Office managers knock down walls to encourage team building. Teams are as old as civilization, of course: even Jesus had 12 co-workers. But a new report by Deloitte, "Global Human Capital Trends", based on a survey of more than 7,000 executives in over 130 countries, suggests that the fashion for teamwork has reached a new high. Almost half of those surveyed said their companies were either in the middle of restructuring or about to embark on it; and for the most part, restructuring meant putting more emphasis on teams.

B) Companies are abandoning conventional functional departments and organising employees into cross-disciplinary teams that focus on particular products, problems or customers. These teams are gaining more power to run their own affairs. They are also spending more time working with each other rather than reporting upwards. Deloitte argues that a new organisational form is on the rise: a network of teams is replacing the conventional hierarchy.

C) The fashion for teams is driven by a sense that the old way of organising people is too rigid for both the modem marketplace and the expectations of employees. Technological innovation places greater value on agility. John Chambers, chairman of Cisco Systems Inc., a worldwide leader in electronics products, says that "we compete against market transitions, not competitors. Product transitions used to take five or seven years; now they take one or two." Digital technology also makes it easier for people to co-ordinate their activities without resorting to hierarchy. The "millennials" who will soon make up half the workforce in rich countries were raised from nursery school onwards to work in groups.

D) The fashion for teams is also spreading from the usual corporate suspects (such as GE and IBM) to some more unusual ones. The Cleveland Clinic, a hospital operator, has reorganised its medical staff into teams to focus on particular treatment areas; consultants, nurses and others collaborate closely instead of being separated by speciality and rank. The US Army has gone the same way. In his book, *Team of Teams* General Stanley McChrystal describes how the army's hierarchical structure hindered its operations during the early stages of the Iraq war. His solution was to learn something from the insurgents it was fighting: decentralise authority to self-organizing teams.

E) A good rule of thumb is that as soon as generals and hospital administrators jump on a management bandwagon, it is time to ask questions. Leigh Thompson of Kellogg School of Management in Illinois warns that, "Teams are not always the answer—teams may provide insight, creativity and knowledge in a way that a person working independently cannot; but teamwork may also lead to confusion, delay and poor decision-making." The late Richard Hackman of Harvard University once argued, "I have no question that when you have a team, the possibility exists that it will generate magic, producing something extraordinary... But don't count on it."

F) Hackman (who died in 2013) noted that teams are hampered by problems of co-ordination and motivation that chip away at the benefits of collaboration. High-flyers forced to work in teams may be undervalued and free-riders empowered. Groupthink may be unavoidable. In a study of 120 teams of senior executives, he discovered that less than 10% of their supposed members agreed on who exactly was on the team. If it is hard enough to define a team's membership, agreeing on its purpose is harder still.

G) Profound changes in the workforce are making teams trickier to manage. Teams work best if their members have a strong common culture. This is hard to achieve when, as is now the case in many big firms, a large proportion of staff are temporary contractors. Teamwork improves with time: America's National Transportation Safety Board found that 73% of the incidents in its civil-aviation database occurred on a crew's first day of flying together. However, as Amy Edmondson of Harvard points out, organisations increasingly use "team" as a verb rather than a noun: they form teams for specific purposes and then quickly disband them.

H) The least that can be concluded from this research is that companies need to think harder about managing teams. They need to rid their minds of sentimentalism: the most successful teams have leaders who are able to set an overall direction and take immediate action. They need to keep teams small and focused: giving in to pressure to be more "inclusive" is a guarantee of dysfunction. Jeff Bezos, Amazon's boss, says that "If I see more than two pizzas for lunch, the team is too big." They need to immunize teams against group-think: Hackman argued that the best ones contain "deviants" who are willing to do something that maybe upsetting to others.

I) A new study of 12,000 workers in 17 countries by Steelcase, a furniture-maker which also does consulting, finds that the best way to ensure employees are "engaged" is to give them more control over where and how they do their work—which may mean liberating them from having to do everything in collaboration with others.

J) However, organisations need to learn something bigger than how to manage teams better: they need to be in the habit of asking themselves whether teams are the best tools for the job. Teambuilding skills are in short supply: Deloitte reports that only 12% of the executives they contacted feel they understand the way people work together in networks and only 21% feel confident in their ability to build cross-functional teams. Loosely managed teams can become hotbeds of distraction — employees routinely complain that they can't get their work done because they are forced to spend too much time in meetings or compelled to work in noisy offices. Even in the age of open-plan offices and social networks some work is best left to the individual.

Words & Expressions

recruitment/rɪ'kru:tmənt/n. 招募；招聘
civilization/ˌsɪvəlaɪ'zeɪʃn/n. 文明社会；文明
abandon/ə'bændən/v. 抛弃，遗弃
conventional/kən'venʃən(ə)l/adj. 依照惯例的，习惯的，常规的
affair/ə'feə(r)/n. 事情，事件
rigid/'rɪdʒɪd/adj. 僵化的，顽固的
agility/ə'dʒɪləti/n.（动作）敏捷，灵活
transition/træn'zɪʃ(ə)n/n. 过渡，转变
millennial/mɪ'leniəl/n. 千禧一代
speciality/ˌspeʃi'æləti/n. 专业，专长
extraordinary/ɪk'strɔ:d(ə)n(ə)ri/adj. 非凡的，卓越的
undervalue/ˌʌndə'vælju:/v. 看轻，轻视
define/dɪ'faɪn/v. 解释；阐明
membership/'membəʃɪp/n. 会员身份，（全体）会员
inclusive/ɪn'klu:sɪv/adj. 包含的，广阔的
executive/ɪg'zekjətɪv/n. 主管，经理，行政部门
contact/'kɒntækt/v. 联系，联络，接触
distraction/dɪ'strækʃn/n. 干扰，分心的事物
embark on 开始，着手
put emphasis on 强调，着重
count on 指望，依靠
liberate from 从…解放

Notes

Team of Teams

中文名为《赋能》，是 2015 年 5 月 Portfolio 出版的图书，作者是 General Stanley

McChrystal, Chris Fussell, Tantum Collins, David Silverman. 该书主要探讨复杂环境下敏捷团队的打造，关于个人、团队、组织的进化。

Exercises

Ⅰ. Comprehension of the Text

Read the text and answer the following questions. Write the answers on the lines.

1. What's the new report by Deloitte mainly about?
   _____
2. What factors influence the fashion for teams?
   _____
3. Why does Leigh Thompson argue that teams are not always about something better?
   _____
4. Why is it hard for team members to share the same culture so as to acheive the most effective teamwork?
   _____
5. What was Hackman's argument about the best team?
   _____

Ⅱ. Main Details Comprehension

Each of the following statement contains information given in one of the paragraphs. Identify the paragraph from which the information is derived. You may choose a paragraph more than once. Each paragraph is marked with a letter. Answer the questions by marking the corresponding letter in the blanks.

_____1. Successful team leaders know exactly where the team should go and are able to take prompt action.

_____2. Decentralisation of authority was also found to be more effective in military operations.

_____3. In many companies, the conventional form of organisation is giving way to a network of teams.

_____4. Members of poorly managed teams are easily distracted from their work.

_____5. Teamwork is most effective when team members share the same culture.

_____6. According to a report by Deloitte, teamwork is becoming increasingly popular among companies.

_____7. Some team members find it hard to agree on questions like membership and the team's purpose.

_____8. Some scholars think teamwork may not always be reliable, despite its potential to work wonders.

Unit 13　Recreation and Entertainment

____9. To ensure employees' commitment, it is advisable to give them more flexibility as to where and how they work.

____10. Product transitions take much less time now than in the past.

Ⅲ. Translation

Translate the five following sentences into English, using the words or expressions given in brackets.

1．他将会用自己的传统医学知识尽全力帮助他们。（conventional）
_____
2．你和你大学里的朋友还保持联系吗？（contact）
_____
3．为了拓展业务，他需要提高整个团队的管理技能和创新能力。（innovation）
_____
4．在古代，人们把幸福的生活定义为有食物、有住所的生活。（define）
_____
5．重构和分散注意力的技巧可以缓解抑郁、焦虑和愤怒。（distraction）
_____

Practical Writing
简历（Resume）

简历也称履历，译为 resume，该词来源于法语，意思是"总结"，即要求求职者对自己的生活经历、工作经历、个人技能、教育背景、个人资质和学业成绩等进行认真地总结，以便把精确的相关信息传递给未来的雇主，供其参考，然后据此决定是否雇佣该求职者。换句话说，简历或履历就是个人经历的文字记载，是求职者谋职时必不可少的文字依据。

一、简历的主要内容

（1）个人资料（personal information）及联系方式（contact information）：姓名（name）、住址（address）、固定电话（telephone number）、电子邮箱（email address）、国籍（nationality）等，通常置于简历开头部分中间位置。

（2）求职目标（objective）：即打算谋取的职位。

（3）教育背景（education background）：求职者就读学校、所学专业、主修课程和所学学位等。

（4）工作经历（previous employment and work experience）：即求职者以前从事过的主要工作和取得的成就。

（5）奖励情况（honors & awards）：求职者曾获得的奖励。

（6）技能（skill）：主要指求职者的外语和计算机使用能力（knowledge of English and of other languages, computer skill）。

（7）其他（other information）：如社会活动（activities）、兴趣爱好（interests & hobbies）、推荐人（references）等。

二、简历的注意事项

（1）动词开头：简历中尽量不要出现人称，句子直接以动词开头，秉持简洁性原则。

（2）使用省略句：简历里冠词、连词、介词等虚词使句子显得冗长，且不利于清楚表达意思，因此通常省略。

（3）使用行为动词：简历中避免使用助动词，因为助动词会减弱句子的可信度，因此尽量使用具体的行为动词。

（4）时态转换：描述现在从事的工作用现在时，过去从事的工作用过去时。

（5）使用简单句式：避免复杂句式。

Exercise

1. *Read the following resume and answer the questions that follow.*

Exer c. Science
66 Aerobic Place
Cardio City, AK 112233
TEL: 555-222-1111
Email: exercscience@163.com

Objective
　　A challenging position in cardiac rehabilitation where I can utilize my knowledge in exercise science to guide individuals toward active healthy lifestyles.

Education
　　Diploma in Exercise Science, May 2001
　　University of New Mexico, Albuquerque, NM
　　Related Course Work

EKC Interpretation	Stress Testing
Designs for fitness	Exercise Physiology Ⅰ & Ⅱ
Physical Activity and Agin	Physical Activity and Disease Prevention
Applied Nutrition and Exercise	

Experience
　　August 2000 — present　　Good Samaritan Hospital, Albuquerque, New Mexico
- Lead physician — prescribed exercise programs
- Provide daily care for disabled patients
- Administer medications
- Design muscular strength and flexibility programs for clients
- Perform initial health questionnaires and assessments
- Maintain hygiene of facility

- Promote positive business ethics

    September 1999 to July 2000
    Defined Fitness

Special Skills
- Electrocardiograms
- Maximal exercise stress tests
- Submaximal exercise stress tests
- Body composition: skinfold. hydrostatic weighing. bioelectrical impedance
- Blood pressure
- Flexibility

Computer Skills
- Microsoft Word. Power Point. Excel. Adobe Illustrator. WEB Design

Language
- Fluent in Spanish and German

Memberships
- American Society of Exercise Physiologists
- American College of Sports Medicine
- National Strength and Conditioning Organization

(1) What is Exer c. Science's career objective?

(2) When did he graduate from college?

(3) Which foreign language did he master?

(4) Where does he work at present?

(5) What are his computer skills?

2. *Complete the following resume by translating the Chinese in brackets into English.*

Name: Melvin
Address: ×××× Road, ××× Province, ××××××（邮编）
Telephone: (×××) ××××××××
Email: ×××@×××.com
Place of Birth: ××× Province
Nationality: China

Objective

To obtain a management position in which I will be able to (1) _____
_____(用我的组织能力和我的市场营销与英语知识).

Education

  2013.9—2017.7 Diploma in Business Management,
          ××××××（毕业院校）
  2010.9—2013.7 ××××××× High School

Skill

  （2）_____（组织能力强）
  Creative thinker who enjoys coming up with new and different ideas
  Strong work ethic, with ability to work well under tight timelines
  （3）_____（英语流利）
  （4）_____（熟练使用 Microsoft Word，Excel 和 PowerPoint）

Work Experience

  2017—present （5）_____（市场助理），Powell, Inc.. Duties include planning and implementing all advertising and promotion, responding to enquiries, monitoring students performance
  2016—2017 （6）_____（兼职编辑）with ××× *Evening Newspaper*
  August 2016 one-month internship in（7）_____（销售部）of ××× Publishing

Awards

  2014 Model Student Leader of the Institute
  2015 National Encouragement Scholarship

Interests

  Basketball（8）_____（校篮球队的队员), sailing and traveling

References

  Available on Request

3. *Write a resume, using the information provided below.*

为王明制作一份简历，内容包括：①个人信息（家庭地址、邮编、电话、电子邮件）；②求职目标；③教育背景（毕业学校，所学专业）；④（工作）经历；⑤外语和计算机能力；⑥兴趣爱好。

Workshop
Cultural Introduction

Ⅰ. Appreciation of Classics

1. 偷得浮生半日闲。《题鹤林寺僧舍》

Steal half a day in leisure from one's floating life.

释义：从烦闷、失意中解脱，到幽雅脱俗的地方，让身心得到休养。

2. 宝剑锋从磨砺出，梅花香自苦寒来。《警世贤文》

Sharpness of a precious dagger comes from whetting, and fragrance of a plum flower from chilling.

释义：宝剑经过打磨才能有锋利的利刃，梅花经过严寒才能开花。寓意为若想拥有某种珍贵的品质或获得成功，需要付出自己的努力，在痛苦中锤炼自己。

3. 长风破浪会有时。《行路难》

There will be a time when I harness the wind and sails across the waves.

释义：坚信乘风破浪的时机定会到来。

4. 知之者不如好之者，好之者不如乐之者。《论语》

He who knows the truth is not equal to him who loves it, and he who loves is not equal to him who delights in it.

释义：对于学习，了解学习的人，不如喜爱学习的人；喜爱学习的人，又不如以学习为乐的人。

5. 苟日新，日日新，又日新。《礼记·大学》

If you can improve yourself every day, do it yourself every day and in the following days.

释义：从勤于省身和动态的角度强调及时反省和不断革新，加强思想革命化的问题关键。

Ⅱ. Appreciation of Chinese poetry

Visiting an Old Friend's Cottage
Meng Haoran

My friend's prepared chicken and rice;
I'm invited to his cottage hall.
Green trees surround the village nice;
Blue hills slant beyond city wall.
Windows open to field and ground;
Over wine we talk of crops of grain.
On double ninth day I'll come around
for the chrysanthemums again.

过故人庄
孟浩然

故人具鸡黍，邀我至田家。
绿树村边合，青山郭外斜。
开轩面场圃，把酒话桑麻。
待到重阳日，还来就菊花。

Ⅲ. Cultural Tips

《过故人庄》是唐代诗人孟浩然创作的一首五言律诗,写的是诗人应邀到一位农村老朋友家做客的经过。在淳朴自然的田园风光之中,主客举杯饮酒,闲谈家常,充满了乐趣,抒发了诗人和朋友之间真挚的友情。这首诗初看平淡如水,细细品味就像一幅画着田园风光的中国画,将景、事、情完美地结合在一起,具有强烈的艺术感染力。

Unit 14 Travelling

The Olympic Class Ships

You probably know about the Titanic, but it was actually just one of three state-of-the art ocean ships back in the day. The Olympic class ships were built by the Harland & Wolff ship makers in Northern Ireland for the White Star Line company. The Olympic class included the Olympic, the Britannic and the Titanic. What you may not know is that the Titanic wasn't even the flagship of this class. All in all, the Olympic class ships were marvels of sea engineering, but they seemed cursed to suffer disastrous fates.

The Olympic launched first in 1910, followed by the Titanic in 1911, and lastly the Britannic in 1914. The ships had nine decks, and White Star Line decided to focus on marking them the most luxurious ships on the water.

Stretching 269.13 meters, the Olympic class ships were wonders of naval technology, and everyone thought that they would continue to be so for quite some time. However, all suffered terrible accidents on the open seas. The Olympic got wrecked before the Titanic did, but it was the only one to survive and maintain a successful career of 24 years. The Titanic was the first to sink after famously hitting a huge iceberg in 1912. Following this disaster, the Britannic hit a naval mine in 1916 and subsequently sank as well.

Each ship was coal-powered by several boilers constantly kept running by exhausted crews below deck. Most recognizable of the ship designs are the ship's smoke stacks, but the fourth stack was actually just artistic in nature and served no functional purpose. While two of these ships sank, they were all designed with double hulls believed to make them "unsinkable", perhaps a mistaken idea that led to the Titanic's and the Britannic's tragic end.

The Olympic suffered two crashes with other ships and went on to serve as a hospital ship and troop transport in World War I. Eventually, she was taken out of service in 1935, ending the era of the luxurious Olympic class ocean liners.

Words & Expressions

marvel/'mɑːv(ə)l/n. 奇迹，令人惊异的人（或事）
suffer/'sʌfə(r)/v. 经受，遭受（坏事）
disastrous/dɪ'zɑːstrəs/adj. 灾难性的，很糟的

launch/lɔ:ntʃ/v. 发动，发起，上市
deck/dek/n. 甲板
mark/mɑ:k/n. 标志，迹象，符号
luxurious/lʌɡˈʒʊəriəs/adj. 奢侈的，豪华的，舒适的
stretch/stretʃ/v. 拉长，伸展肢体，伸出
wonder/ˈwʌndə(r)/v. 想知道，好奇，感到惊讶
wreck/rek/v. （严重）破坏，造成（船舶）失事
survive/səˈvaɪv/v. 幸存，幸免于难，（经历事故、战争或疾病）后活下来
maintain/meɪnˈteɪn/v. 保持，维持，维修
sink/sɪŋk/v. 下沉，沉没，下降
hit/hɪt/v. 打，撞击，击中，命中
subsequently/ˈsʌbsɪkwəntli/adv. 后来，随后
constantly/ˈkɒnstəntli/adv. 总是，经常地，不断地
exhausted/ɪɡˈzɔ:stɪd/adj. 筋疲力尽的，耗尽的，枯竭的
crew/kru:/n. 全体船员，全体机组人员
stack/stæk/n. 一堆，大量，许多
crash/kræʃ/v. 撞车，坠毁，猛撞
eventually/ɪˈventʃuəli/adv. 最终，结果
in nature 本质上，事实上

Notes

1. the Olympic class ships

奥林匹克号邮轮（1911—1934），长 269.68 米，宽 28.19 米，载客 2 764 人，隶属于英国白星航运公司。

2. the Titanic

泰坦尼克号，又译作铁达尼号，是英国白星航运公司下辖的一艘奥林匹克级邮轮，是当时世界上体积最庞大、内部设施最豪华的客运轮机，有"永不沉没"的美誉。然而，1912 年 4 月 14 日 23 时 40 分左右，泰坦尼克号与一座冰山相撞，造成右舷船至船中部破裂，1517 人丧生，泰坦尼克号沉没事故为和平时期死伤人数最为惨重的一次海难。

Exercises

Ⅰ. Comprehension of the Text

There are 5 questions in this section. For each of them there are four choices marked A, B, C and D. You should choose the best answer for each question.

1. What does the passage say about the three Olympic class ships?

   A. They performed marvelously on the sea.

Unit 14　Travelling

    B. They could all break the ice in their way.

    C. They all experienced terrible misfortunes.

    D. They were models of modern engineering.

2. What did White Star line have in mind when it purchased the three ships?

    A. Their capacity of sailing across all waters.

    B. The utmost comfort passengers could enjoy.

    C. Their ability to survive disasters of any kind.

    D. The long voyages they were able to undertake.

3. What is said about the fourth stack of the ships?

    A. It was a mere piece of decoration.

    B. It was the work of a famous artist.

    C. It was designed to let out extra smoke.

    D. It was easily identifiable from afar.

4. What might have led to the tragic end of the Titanic and the Britannic?

    A. Their unscientific designs.

    B. Their captains' misjudgment.

    C. The assumption that they were built with the latest technology.

    D. The belief that they could never sink with a double-layer body.

5. What happened to the ship Olympic in the end?

    A. She was used to carry troops.

    B. She was sunk in World War I.

    C. She was converted into a hospital ship.

    D. She was retired after her naval service.

II. Languages Focus

A. *Match the following words in left with their explanations in right.*

1. wonder	a. a tiny bright piece of burning material
2. crew	b. to start an activity
3. sink	c. to be curious or in doubt about
4. stretch	d. a wonderful and surprising person or thing
5. marvel	e. the top outside floor of a ship or boat
6. subsequently	f. a group of people who work on a ship or aircraft
7. deck	g. very bad, harmful, or unsuccessful
8. mark	h. after sth. else has happened
9. launch	i. something with a particular word or symbol
10. disastrous	j. to extend in length

B. *Fill in the blanks with the words or expressions given below. Change the form where necessary.*

| maintain | suffer | survive | exhausted | luxurious |
| hit | crash | constantly | eventually | in nature |

1. _____ your child will leave home to lead her own life as a fully independent adult.
2. A truck went out of control and _____ into the back of a bus.
3. The rise of a major power is both economic and military _____.
4. To _____ her weight, she simply chooses fruits and vegetables over fat and sweets.
5. The business is still in crisis but it has _____ the worst of the recession.
6. I couldn't remember where I'd seen him before, and then it suddenly _____ me.
7. She was so weak and _____ that she had to lie back in the easy chair.
8. She _____ from severe depression after losing her job.
9. We must _____ adapt and innovate to ensure success in a growing market.
10. The millionaire has such _____ tastes that he found it hard to endure life when he had to live on an ordinary wage.

III. Translation

Translate the following sentences into Chinese.

1. What you may not know is that the Titanic wasn't even the flagship of this class.
   _____

2. The Olympic launched first in 1910, followed by the Titanic in 1911, and lastly the Britannic in 1914.
   _____

3. The Olympic got wrecked before the Titanic did, but it was the only one survive and maintain a successful career of 24 years.
   _____

4. Most recognizable of the ship designs are the ship's smoke stacks, but the fourth stack was actually just artistic in nature and served no functional purpose.
   _____
   _____

5. The Olympic suffered two crashes with other ships and went on to serve as a hospital ship and troop transport in World War I.
   _____

IV. Discussion

Discuss about the place that the most impressive one you've ever traveled to, and state your reasons.

As Tourists Crowd Out Locals, Venice Faces "Endangered" List

A) On a recent fall morning, a large crowd blocked the steps at one of Venice's main tourist sites, the Rialto Bridge. The Rialto Bridge is one of the four bridges spanning the Grand Canal. It is the oldest bridge across the canal, and was the dividing line between the districts of San Marco and San Polo. But on this day, there was a twist: it was filled with Venetians, not tourists.

B) "People are cheering and holding their carts in the air," says Giovanni Giorgio, who helped organize the march with a grass-roots organization called Generazione'90. The carts he refers to are small shopping carts — the symbol of a true Venetian. "It started as a joke," he says with a laugh. "The idea was to put blades on the wheels! You know? Like Ben Hur. Precisely like that, you just go around and run people down."

C) Venice is one of the hottest tourist destinations in the world. But that's a problem. Up to 90,000 tourists crowd its streets and canals every day — far outnumbering the 55,000 permanent residents. The tourist increase is one key reason the city's population is down from 175,000 in the 1950s. The outnumbered Venetians have been steadily fleeing. And those who stick around are tired of living in a place where they can't even get to the market without swimming through a sea of picture-snapping tourists. Imagine, navigating through 50,000 people while on the way to school or to work.

D) Laura Chigi, a grandmother at the march, says the local and national governments have failed to do anything about the crowds for decades, because they're only interested in tourism — the primary industry in Venice, worth more than $3 billion in 2015. "Venice is a cash cow," she says, "and everyone wants a piece."

E) Just beyond St. Mark's Square, a cruise ship passes, one of hundreds every year that appear over their medieval surroundings. Their massive wake creates waves at the bottom of the sea, weakening the foundations of the centuries-old buildings themselves. "Every time I see a cruise ship, I feel sad," Chigi says. "You see the mud it drags; the destruction it leaves in its wake? That hurts the ancient wooden poles holding up the city underwater. One day we'll see Venice break down."

F) For a time, UNESCO, the cultural wing of the United Nations, seemed to agree. Two years ago, it put Italy on notice, saying the government was not protecting Venice. UNESCO considers the entire city a World Heritage Site, a great honor that means Venice, at the cultural level, belongs to all of the world's people. In 2014, UNESCO gave Italy two years to manage Venice's flourishing tourism or the city would be placed on another list — World Heritage In Danger, joining such sites as Aleppo and Palmyra, destroyed by the war in Syria.

G) Venice's deadline passed with barely a murmur this summer, just as UNESCO was meeting in Istanbul. Only one representative, Jad Tabet from Lebanon, tried to raise the issue. "For several years, the situation of heritage in Venice has been worsening, and it has now reached a dramatic situation," Tabet told UNESCO. "We have to act quickly — there is not a moment to waste."

H) But UNESCO didn't even hold a vote. "It's been postponed until 2017," says Anna Somers, the founder and CEO of *The Art Newspaper* and the former head of Venice in Peril, a group devoted to restoring Venetian art. She says the main reason the U.N. cultural organization didn't vote to declare Venice a World Heritage Site In Danger is because UNESCO has become "intensely politicized. There would have been some back-room negotiations."

I) Italy boasts more UNESCO World Heritage Sites than any other country in the world, granting it considerable power and influence within the organization. The former head of the UNESCO World Heritage Centre, which oversees heritage sites, is Francesco Bandarin, a Venetian who now serves as UNESCO's assistant director-general for culture.

J) Earlier this year, Italy signed an accord with UNESCO to establish a task force of police art detectives and archaeologists to protect cultural heritage from natural disasters and terror groups, such as ISIS. The accord underlined Italy's global reputation as a good steward of art and culture.

K) But adding Venice to the UNESCO endangered list — which is dominated by sites in developing and conflict-ridden countries — would be an international embarrassment, and could even hurt Italy's profitable tourism industry. The Italian Culture Ministry says it is unaware of any government efforts to pressure UNESCO. As for the organization itself, it declined a request for an interview.

L) The city's current mayor, Luigi Brugnaro, has ridiculed UNESCO and told it to mind its own business, while continuing to support the cruise ship industry, which employs 5,000 Venice residents.

M) As for Venetians, they're beyond frustrated and hoping for a solution soon. "It's a nightmare for me. Some situations are really difficult with tourists around," says Giorgio as he navigates around a swelling crowd at the Rialto Bridge. "There are just so many of them. They never know where they are going, and do not walk in an orderly manner. Navigating the streets can be exhausting."

N) Then it hits him: This crowd isn't made up of tourists. They're Venetians. Giorgio says he's never experienced the Rialto Bridge this way in all his 22 years. "For once, we are the ones who are blocking the traffic," he says delightedly. "It feels unreal. It feels like we're some form of endangered species. It's just nice. The feeling is just pure." But, he worries, if tourism isn't managed and his fellow locals continue to move to the mainland, his generation might be the last who can call themselves native Venetians.

Unit 14　Travelling 　175

Words & Expressions

endanger/ɪnˈdeɪndʒə(r)/v. 使处于险境，危及
tourist/ˈtʊərɪst/n. 旅行者，观光客
precisely/prɪˈsaɪsli/adv. 精确地，准确地
destination/ˌdestɪˈneɪʃn/n. 目的地，终点，目标
permanent/ˈpɜːmənənt/adj. 永久的，永恒的
resident/ˈrezɪdənt/n. 居民，住户
outnumber/ˌaʊtˈnʌmbə(r)/vt. 数目超过，比…多
navigate/ˈnævɪɡeɪt/v. 导航，引路，浏览
primary/ˈpraɪməri/adj. 主要的，首要的，初级的
massive/ˈmæsɪv/adj. 大量的，大规模的
destruction/dɪˈstrʌkʃ(ə)n/n. 破坏，摧毁
heritage/ˈherɪtɪdʒ/n. 遗产，传统
barely/ˈbeəli/adv. 几乎不，勉强才能，仅仅
raise/reɪz/v. 提出，提及（某事），养育
restore/rɪˈstɔː(r)/v. 恢复，修复
intensely/ɪnˈtensli/adv. 强烈地，专注地，非常
dominate/ˈdɒmɪneɪt/v. 统治，支配，在…中占首要地位
tourism/ˈtʊərɪzəm/n. 旅游业，观光业
decline/dɪˈklaɪn/v. 下降，衰退，拒绝
delightedly/dɪˈlaɪtɪdli/adv. 高兴地，欣喜地
symbol/ˈsɪmb(ə)l/n. 象征，标志，符号
be filled with　被…充满
be tired of　厌烦
hold up　支撑，举起，阻挡
break down　分解，瓦解，发生故障，失败
make up of　构成，由…组成

Notes

1. Venice

威尼斯是意大利东北部著名的旅游与工业城市，也是威尼托地区（威尼托大区）的首府。威尼斯曾经是威尼斯共和国的中心，被称作"亚得里亚海明珠"，堪称世界最浪漫的城市之一。1987年，威尼斯被列入《世界遗产名录》。

2. UNESCO

联合国教育、科学及文化组织，简称联合国教科文组织（United Nations Educational, Scientific and Cultural Organization），成立于1945年11月16日，总部设于法国巴黎，

现有 195 个成员国。联合国教科文组织致力于推动各国在教育、科学和文化领域开展国际合作，以此共筑和平。其主要机构包括大会、执行局和秘书处。

 Exercises

Ⅰ. Comprehension of the Text

Read the text and answer the following questions. Write the answers on the lines.

1. What's the local and national government's attitude toward the crowds?
_____

2. How would UNESCO respond if Italian government failed to manage Venice's flourishing tourism?
_____

3. What did Jad Tabet think of the situation of heritage in Venice?
_____

4. Why didn't UNESCO hold a vote to declare Venice a World Heritage Site In Danger?
_____

5. What's Venetians' feeling toward the tourists?
_____

Ⅱ. Main Details Comprehension

Each of the following statement contains information given in one of the paragraphs. Identify the paragraph from which the information is derived. You may choose a paragraph more than once. Each paragraph is marked with a letter. Answer the questions by marking the corresponding letter in the blanks.

_____1. The passing cruise ships will undermine the foundations of the ancient buildings in Venice.

_____2. The Italian government has just reached an agreement with UNESCO to take measures to protect its cultural heritage.

_____3. The heritage situation in Venice has been deteriorating in the past few years.

_____4. The decrease in the number of permanent residents in Venice is mainly due to the increase of tourists.

_____5. If tourism gets out of control, native Venetians may desert the city altogether one day.

_____6. UNESCO urged the Italian government to undertake its responsibility to protect Venice.

_____7. The participants in the Venetian march used shopping carts to show they were 100% local residents.

_____8. Ignoring UNESCO's warning, the mayor of Venice maintains his support of the city's tourism industry.

_____9. One woman says that for decades the Italian government and local authorities have only focused on the revenues from tourism.

_____10. UNESCO has not yet decided to put Venice on the list of World Heritage Sites In Danger.

Ⅲ. Translation

Translate the five following sentences into English, using the words or expressions given in brackets.

1．这门课的主要目的是提高英语口语能力。（primary）

_____

2．这些古建筑是民族遗产的一部分。（heritage）

_____

3．这是一个固定职位，需要专心致志和勤奋工作。（permanent）

_____

4．祝愿你的生活充满爱、幸福和灵感。（be filled with）

_____

5．生活可以被比作一次不知目的的旅行。（destination）

_____

Practical Writing
辞职信（Resignation Letters）

辞职信是辞职者向工作单位辞去职务时写的书信，是辞职者在辞去职务时的必要程序，辞职信的内容一般包括辞职的岗位、时间，对公司、上司和同事的感谢，如有必要，还可以要求收信人给辞职者写封推荐信、辞职的理由以及表示保证协助做好交接工作等内容。

撰写辞职信时应注意以下要点：信的语气应客气，即使对所在工作单位、上司或同事不满，在信中也不要提及，不要批评他们或工作单位的一些做法。

一、常用表达

（一）开头（说明写信目的），例如：

Please accept this letter as notice of my resignation as staff accountant. My last day of employment will be _____ (date).

I am writing to formally announce my intention to resign from the job of _____ (position).

I am writing to inform you of my decision to resign from my post of Sales Administrator in the Bradford offices, effective 1 July, 2018.

（二）第二段（表达对雇主的感谢），例如：

I would like to take this opportunity to say how much I value the training, professional and personal support that I have received in my three years with _____ (person).

I cannot say enough wonderful things about Merck, about all the people I've encountered in my years of service with the company, and especially about you and all the others on the sales team. Your leadership has taken us all to new levels, and I have appreciated all your personal and professional advice over the years. It's my hope that we will stay in touch as I begin this new chapter in my life.

I would like to thank you for giving me a chance to gain work experience at _____ (company) with a superb team of professional and supportive coworkers. It would be greatly appreciated if you can provide me with a reference letter before I leave.

（三）第三段（表示协助做好交接工作），例如：

I would like to help with the transition of my accounting duties so that systems continue to function smoothly after my departure. I am available to help recruit and train my replacement, and I will make certain that all reporting and records are updated before my last day of work.

二、写作范例

Sample 1

Dear Board of Directors:

I have decided to resign my position as a member of the USAWKF Board of Directors effective today November 16, 2021.

I would like to thank all of you for giving me a chance to serve as a member of the Board of Directors.

Your support of me during the time I have participated much appreciated. I will continue to support the USAWKF to the best of my abilities.

Best wishes to all the board members and the USAWKF.

Sincerely,
Li Ming

Sample 2

To the Apple Board of Directors and the Apple Community,

I have always said if there ever came a day when I could no longer meet my duties and expectations as Apple's CEO., I would be the first to let you know. Unfortunately, that day has come.

I hereby resign as CEO of Apple. I would like to serve, if the Board sees fit, as Chairman of the Board, director and Apple employee.

As far as my successor goes, I strongly recommend that we execute our succession plan and name Tim Cook as CEO of Apple.

Unit 14 Travelling

I believe Apple's brightest and most innovative days are ahead of it. And I look forward to watching and contributing to its success in a new role.

I have made some of the best friends of my life at Apple, and I thank you all for the many years of being able to work alongside you.

Steve Jobs

Sample 3

Dear Mr. Smith,

As required by my employment contract, I hereby give you three weeks' notice of my intention to leave my position of sales manager.

I have decided that it is time to move on and have accepted a position elsewhere. This was not an easy decision and took a lot of consideration. However, I am confident that my new role will help me advance towards some of the goals I have for my career.

Please be assured that I will do all I can to assist in the smooth transfer of my responsibilities before leaving.

I wish both you and F.Wilson & Sons Ltd.. All the best in the future and would like to thank you for having included me as part of your team.

Yours sincerely,
Herbert Brown

 Exercise

1. *Complete the following resignation letters with the phrases or sentences listed below.*

a. as well as my regret for not being able to serve here any longer

b. I am so sorry to inform you by this letter that I plan to resign my present job in the next month

c. Qingdao is my hometown

d. I have had a very happy and enjoyable time working with you and other colleagues

Dear Mr. Smith,

(1) _____. The main reason is that I will move to Qingdao to live permanently with my family, as (2) _____.

Looking back upon my five-year experience in this organization, (3) _____, from whom I have received lots of help and have learned much.

Please accept my sincere gratitude, (4) _____.

Yours faithfully,
Wang Dali

a. Please make my resignation effective

b. Good luck to you in the years to come

c. this decision was not an easy one

d. I see no other alternative than to resign my position

Dear Manager,

　　After months of reviewing of the outlook for the company in the wake of this economic downturn, (5) _____ as chief financial officer with ABC company. Needless to say, after 12 years of service, (6) _____.

　　(7) _____ January 31, which is the end of my scheduled vacation. I will turn over all company books and settle my accounts prior to that date.

　　I look back on the experience gained and the friends made with much regard. My association with ABC company has been a valued part of my life.

　　(8) _____.

Sincerely,
Li Lei

---

2. *Write a resignation letter using the information given below.*

两个月前，你得到了杂志社的工作，但是现在发现这份工作与你的预期不符，你决定辞职。请给你的老板 Mr. Wang 写一封辞职信，告诉你的决定并说明理由。

Workshop
Cultural Introduction

Ⅰ. Appreciation of Classics

1. 读万卷书，行万里路。《画禅室随笔》

Read ten thousand books and travel ten thousand Li.

释义：比喻要努力读书，让自己的才识过人并让所学在生活中体现，同时增长见识，理论结合实际，学以致用。

2. 千里之行，始于足下。《老子》

A journey of a thousand miles begins with a single step.

释义：走一千里路，是从迈第一步开始的。比喻事情应从点滴小事做起，艰难的事情，只要坚持不懈地行动，必有所成。

3. 山重水复疑无路，柳暗花明又一村。《游山西村》

After endless mountains and rivers that leave doubt whether there is a path out, suddenly one encounters the shade of a willow, bright flowers and a lovely village.

释义：比喻在遇到困难一种办法行不通时，可以用另一种办法解决，通过探索去发现答案。

4. 路遥知马力，日久见人心。《事林广记》

Just as distance tests a horse's strength, time will reveal a person's sincerity.

释义：路途遥远才可以知道马的耐力大小，时间久了才可以看出人心的好坏。

5．路漫漫其修远兮，吾将上下而求索。《离骚》

Long, long is my road, and far, far is the journey; high and low, up and down, I'll search with will.

释义：在追寻真理方面，前方的道路还很漫长，但我将百折不挠、不遗余力地去追求和探索。

Ⅱ. Appreciation of Chinese Poetry

Fair South Recalled

Bai Juyi

Fair Southern shore
With scenes I much adore.
At sunrise riverside flowers more red than fire,
In spring green river waves grow as blue as sapphire,
Which I can't but admire.

忆江南

白居易

江南好，
风景旧曾谙。
日出江花红胜火，
春来江水绿如蓝。
能不忆江南？

Ⅲ. Cultural Tips

白居易曾担任杭州刺史，在杭州待了两年，后又任苏州刺史，任期也有一年有余。在他的青年时期，曾漫游江南，旅居苏杭，对江南有相当的了解，故江南在他的心中留有深刻印象。当他因病卸任苏州刺史，回到洛阳十二年后，写下三首忆江南，可见江南盛景仍在他心中栩栩如生。在该词中，白居易巧妙地用十几个字来概括江南春。他没有从描写江南惯用的"花""莺"着手，而是别出心裁地以"江"为中心下笔，又通过"红胜火"和"绿如蓝"，异色相衬，展现鲜艳夺目的江南春景。江南春色在白居易的笔下，从初日、江花、江水之中获得了色彩，又因烘染、映衬的手法形成了人们想象中的图画，色彩绚丽耀眼，层次丰富，几乎无须更多联想，江南春景便已跃然眼前。

Unit 15 Digital Age

Dilemma of Textbook Publishing in the Digital Age

Textbooks represent an 11 billion dollar industry, up from $8 billion in 2014. Textbook publisher Pearson is the largest publisher — of any kind — in the world.

It costs about $1 million to create a new textbook. A freshman textbook will have dozens of contributors, from subject-matter experts through graphic and layout artists to expert reviewers and classroom testers. Textbook publishers connect professors, instructors and students in ways that alternatives, such as open e-textbooks and open educational resources, simply do not. This connection happens not only by means of collaborative development, review and testing, but also at conferences where faculty regularly decide on their textbooks and curricula for the coming year.

It is true that textbook publishers have recently reported losses, largely due to students renting or buying used print textbooks. But this can be chalked up to the excessively high cost of their books — which has increased over 1,000 percent since 1977. A restructuring of the textbook industry may well be in order. But this does not mean the end of the textbook itself.

While they may not be as dynamic as an iPad, textbooks are not passive or lifeless. For example, over the centuries, they have simulated dialogues in a number of ways. From 1800 to the resent day, textbooks have done this by posing questions for students to answer inductively. That means students are asked to use their individual experience to come up with answers to general questions. Today's psychology texts, for example, ask: "How much of your personality do you think you inherited?" while ones in physics say: "How can you predict where the ball you tossed will land?"

Experts observe that "textbooks come in layers, something like an onion". For an active learner, engaging with a textbook can be an interactive experience: Readers proceed at their own pace. They "customize" their books by engaging with different layers and linkages. Highlighting, Post-It notes, dog-ears and other techniques allow for further customization that students value in print books over digital forms of books.

layout/'leɪaʊt/ *n.* 布局，设计，版面设计

Unit 15　Digital Age 183

collaborative/kəˈlæbərətɪv/*adj.* 合作的，协作的
excessively/ɪkˈsesɪvli/*adv.* 过分地，过量地，极度
simulate/ˈsɪmjuleɪt/*v.* 假装，冒充，模仿，模拟
pose/pəʊz/*v.* 造成，引起（威胁、危险），提出（问题）
inductively/ɪnˈdʌktɪvli/*adv.* 归纳地，诱导地
individual/ˌɪndɪˈvɪdʒuəl/*n.* 单独的，个别的，独特的，与众不同的
publisher/ˈpʌblɪʃə(r)/*n.* 出版者，出版商，发行人
inherit/ɪnˈherɪt/*v.* 继承（遗产），接手，承担
interactive/ˌɪntərˈæktɪv/*adj.* 交互式的，互动的，相互交流的
graphic/ˈɡræfɪk/*adj.* 详细的，生动的，绘画的，图形的
connection/kəˈnekʃn/*n.* 关系，联系，连接
general/ˈdʒen(ə)rəl/*adj.* 总体的，普遍的，一般的
personality/ˌpɜːsəˈnæləti/*n.* 个性，性格，魅力
print/prɪnt/*v.* 打印，印刷，出版
restructure/ˌriːˈstrʌktʃə(r)/*v.* 调整结构，改组，重组
by means of 通过，借助
come up with 提出，想出（计划、主意）
engage with 与…互动，进行交流或合作

Notes

Pearson

培生出版集团（Pearson plc）是一家全球化的媒体公司，于1844年创立于英国伦敦。它是全球最大的教育公司及书籍出版商。随着时间的推移，培生出版集团已经从传统的出版商慢慢过渡到数字化的新媒体服务公司。

Exercises

Ⅰ. Comprehension of the Text

There are 5 questions in this section. For each of them there are four choices marked A, B, C and D. You should choose the best answer for each question.

1. What does the passage say about open educational resources?
   A. They contribute to teaching as much as to learning.
   B. They don't profit as much as traditional textbooks do.
   C. They can't connect professors and students as textbooks do.
   D. They compete fiercely for customers with textbook producers.
2. What is the main cause of the publishers' losses?
   A. Failure to meet student need.

B. Emergence of e-books.

C. Industry restructuring.

D. Falling sales.

3. What does the textbook industry need to do?

    A. Reform its structures.

    B. Find replacements for printed textbooks.

    C. Cut its retail prices.

    D. Change its business strategy periodically.

4. What are students expected to do in the learning process?

    A. Think carefully before answering each question.

    B. Ask questions based on their own understanding.

    C. Answer questions using their personal experience.

    D. Give answers showing their respective personality.

5. What do experts say about students using textbooks?

    A. They can digitalize the prints easily.

    B. They can purchase customized versions.

    C. They can learn in an interactive way.

    D. They can adapt the material themselves.

Ⅱ. Languages Focus

A. *Match the following words in left with their explanations in right.*

1. inherit		a. to an excessive degree
2. print		b. receive property from sb. when they die
3. layout		c. connected with drawings and design
4. dynamic		d. approximately, but not exactly
5. graphic		e. a thing of two or more possibilities
6. pose		f. the plan, or design or arrangement
7. excessively		g. produce sth. in quantity using machine
8. alternative		h. to ask a question or create a threat
9. publisher		i. be full of energy or new ideas
10. general		J. a company that publishes book, etc.

B. *Fill in the blanks with the words or expressions given below. Change the form where necessary.*

personality	connection	dynamic	inherit	by means of
interactive	pose	simulate	come up with	collaborative

1. Tourism is an industry that has a necessarily close _____ with governments.

2. We _____ from our parents many of our physical characteristics.

3. The student is invited to test each item for himself _____ specific techniques.

4. That should create more _____ endeavors and help to develop projects aimed directly at solving global problems.

5. What's more, we can _____ our own ideas and learn more through discussion.

6. The scientist developed one model to _____ a full year of the globe's climate.

7. This _____ a threat to agriculture and the food chain, and consequently to human health.

8. The online classroom provides an innovative and _____ learning environment.

9. Is _____ the result of conditioning from parents and society, or are we born with it.

10. Our society needs to be able to imagine the possibility of someone utterly in tune with modern technology but able to make sense of a _____, confusing world.

Ⅲ. Translation

Translate the following sentences into Chinese.

1. Textbook publishers connect professors, instructors and students in ways that alternatives, such as open e-textbooks and open educational resources, simply do not.

_____

_____

2. Experts observe that "textbooks come in layers, something like on onion". For an active learner, engaging with a textbook can be an interactive experience.

_____

_____

3. A freshman textbook will have dozens of contributors, from subject-matter experts through graphic and layout artists to expert reviewers and classroom testers.

_____

_____

4. While they may not be as dynamic as an ipad, textbooks are not passive or lifeless. For example, over the centuries, they have simulated dialogues in a number of ways.

_____

_____

5. A restructing of the textbook industry may well be in order. But this does not mean the end of the textbook itself.

_____

Ⅳ. Discussion

Discuss about the question "What factors should be considered as for the excellent College English textbook?", and then write down your opinions.

When a Language Has No Words for Numbers

A) Numbers do not exist in all cultures. There are numberless hunter-gatherers in Amazonia, living along branches of the world's largest river tree. Instead of using words for precise quantities, these people rely exclusively on terms similar to "a few" or "some." In contrast, our own lives are governed by numbers. As you read this, you are likely aware of what time it is, how old you are, your checking account balance, your weight and so on. The exact numbers we think with impact everything in our lives.

B) But, in a historical sense, number-conscious people like us are the unusual ones. For the bulk of our species' approximately 200,000-year lifespan, we had no means of precisely representing quantities. What's more, the 7,000 or so languages that exist today vary dramatically in how they utilize numbers.

C) Speakers of anumeric, or numberless, languages offer a window into how the invention of numbers reshaped the human experience. Cultures without numbers, or with only one or two precise numbers, include the Munduruku and Piraha in Amazonia. Researchers have also studied some adults in Nicaragua who were never taught number words. Without numbers, healthy human adults struggle to precisely distinguish and recall quantities as low as four. In an experiment, a researcher will place nuts into a can one at a time and then remove them one by one. The person watching is asked to signal when all the nuts have been removed. Responses suggest that anumeric people have some trouble keeping track of how many nuts remain in the can, even if there are only four or five in total.

D) This and many other experiments have led to a simple conclusion: When people do not have number words, they struggle to make quantitative distinctions that probably seem natural to someone like you or me. While only a small portion of the world's languages are anumeric or nearly anumeric, they demonstrate that number words are not a human universal.

E) It is worth stressing that these anumeric people are cognitively normal, well-adapted to the surroundings they have dominated for centuries. As a child, I spent some time living with anumeric people, the Piraha who live along the banks of the black Maici River. Like other outsiders, I was continually impressed by their superior understanding of the ecology we shared. Yet numberless people struggle with tasks that require precise discrimination between quantities. Perhaps this should be unsurprising. After all, without counting, how can someone tell whether there are, say, seven or eight coconuts in a tree? Such seemingly straightforward distinctions become blurry through numberless eyes.

F) This conclusion is echoed by work with anumeric children in industrialized societies. Prior to being spoon-fed number words, children can only approximately discriminate quantities beyond three. We must be handed the cognitive tools of numbers before we can consistently and easily recognize higher quantities. In fact, acquiring the exact meaning of number words is a painstaking process that takes children years. Initially, kids learn numbers much like they learn letters. They recognize that numbers are organized sequentially, but have little awareness of what each individual number means. With time, they start to understand that a given number represents a quantity greater by one than the number coming before it. This "successor principle" is part of the foundation of our numerical cognition, but requires extensive practice to understand.

G) None of us, then, is really a "numbers person." We are not born to handle quantitative distinctions skillfully. In the absence of the cultural traditions that fill our lives with numbers from infancy, we would all struggle with even basic quantitative distinctions. Number words and their written forms transform our quantitative reasoning as they are introduced into our cognitive experience by our parents, peers and school teachers. The process seems so normal that we sometimes think of it as a natural part of growing up, but it is not. Human brains come equipped with certain quantitative instincts that are refined with age, but these instincts are very limited.

H) Compared with other mammals, our numerical instincts are not as remarkable as many assume. We even share some basic instinctual quantitative reasoning with distant non-mammalian relatives like birds. Indeed, work with some other species suggests they too can refine their quantitative thought if they are introduced to the cognitive power tools we call numbers.

I) So, how did we ever invent "unnatural" numbers in the first place? The answer is, literally, at your fingertips. The bulk of the world's languages use base-10, base-20 or base-5 number systems. That is, these smaller numbers are the basis of larger numbers. English is a base-10 or decimal language, as evidenced by words like 14 ("four"+ "10") and 31 ("three" × "10" + "one"). We speak a decimal language because an ancestral tongue, proto-Indo- Buropean, was decimally based. Proto-Indo-European, was decimally based. Proto-Indo- European was decimally oriented because, as in so many cultures, our ancestors' hands served as the gateway to the realization that "five fingers on one hand is the same as five fingers on the other." Such momentary thoughts were represented in words and passed down across generations. This is why the word "five" in many languages is derived from the word for "hand." Most number systems, then, are the by-product of two key factors: the human capacity for language and our inclination for focusing on our hands and fingers. This manual fixation — an indirect by-product of walking upright on two legs has helped yield numbers in most cultures, but not all.

J) Cultures without numbers also offer insight into the cognitive influence of particular numeric traditions. Consider what time it is. Your day is ruled by minutes and seconds, but these concepts are not real in any physical sense and are nonexistent to numberless people. Minutes and seconds are the verbal and written representations of an uncommon base-60 number system used in ancient Mesopotamia. They reside in our minds, numerical artifacts that not all humans inherit conceptually.

K) Research on the language of numbers shows, more and more, that one of our species' key characteristics is tremendous linguistic and cognitive diversity. If we are to truly understand how much our cognitive lives differ cross-culturally, we must continually explore the depths of our species' linguistic diversity.

Words & Expressions

precise/prɪ'saɪs/*adj.* 精确的，准确的，确切的
exclusively/ɪk'sklu:sɪvli/*adv.* 单独地，专门地
distinguish/dɪ'stɪŋgwɪʃ/*v.* 区别，分清，认出
quantity/'kwɒntəti/*n.* 数目，大量，大批
superior/su:'pɪərɪə(r)/*adj.* 优质的，上级的，更好的
initially/ɪ'nɪʃəli/*adv.* 开始，最初
extensive/ɪk'stensɪv/*adj.* 广阔的，广泛的，大量的
numerical/nju:'merɪk(ə)l/*adj.* 数字的，用数字表示的
transform/træs'fɔ:m/*v.* 使改观，使变形，使转化
instinct/'ɪnstɪŋkt/*n.* 本能，天性，直觉
remarkable/rɪ'mɑːkəb(ə)l/*adj.* 引人注目的，非凡的
inclination/ˌɪnklɪ'neɪʃn/*n.* 倾向，趋向，意愿
concept/'kɒnsept/*n.* 概念，观念
linguistic/lɪŋ'gwɪstɪk/*adj.* 语言的，语言学的
diversity/daɪ'vɜːsəti/*n.* 多样性，不同，差异
artifact/'ɑːtɪfækt/*n.* 人工制品，历史文物
rely on 依靠，依赖
in contrast 与此相反，相比之下
keep track of 记录，保持联系
prior to 在…之前
derive from 源自，源于

Notes

Amazonia
亚马孙河，位于南美洲北部，是世界上流量、流域最大，支流最多的河流。亚马孙河是世界第二长河，该河流共有 1.5 万条支流，分布在南美洲大片土地上，流域面积相当于澳大利亚国土面积。

Exercises

Ⅰ. Comprehension of the Text

Read the text and answer the following questions. Write the answers on the lines.

1. Why does the author say that "our lives are governed by numbers"?
_____

2. What kind of experiment was conducted by researchers to study the adults in Nicaragua?
_____

3. How does children acquire the exact meaning of number words?
_____

4. How does our quantitative reasoning transform?
_____

5. What are the two key factors of by-product for number systems?
_____

II. Main Details Comprehension

Each of the following statement contains information given in one of the paragraphs. Identify the paragraph from which the information is derived. You may choose a paragraph more than once. Each paragraph is marked with a letter. Answer the questions by marking the corresponding letter in the blanks.

____1. It is difficult for anumeric people to keep track of the change in numbers even when the total is very small.

____2. Human numerical instincts are not so superior to those of other mammals as is generally believed.

____3. The author emphasizes being anumeric does not affect one's cognitive ability.

____4. In the long history of mankind, humans who use numbers are a very small minority.

____5. An in-depth study of differences between human languages contributes to a true understanding of cognitive differences between cultures.

____6. A conclusion has been drawn from many experiments that anumeric people have a hard time distinguishing quantities.

____7. Making quantitative distinctions is not an inborn skill.

____8. Every aspect of our lives is affected by numbers.

____9. Larger numbers are said to be built upon smaller numbers.

____10. It takes great efforts for children to grasp the concept of number words.

III. Translation

Translate the five following sentences into English, using the words or expressions given in brackets.

1. 每一个国家都应该鼓励并且尽他们最大的努力保护生物多样性。(diversity)
_____

2. 他们称预期会议会对国家的未来产生显著影响。（impact）

_____

3. 尽管如此，有证据表明网络可以改变我们的日常交流。（transform）

_____

4. 新意常常源于研究方法的革新和发展。（derive from）

_____

5. 每个挑战都需要多个团队成员的洞察力和技能来完成。（insight）

_____

Practical Writing
名片（Business Card）

　　名片通常是现代人的自我介绍信和社交的联谊卡。它最基本的功能为自我介绍。在商务活动中，交换名片是一项很流行、很重要的活动。名片也可用于朋友间交流感情和结识新朋友。名片虽小，但方寸之间，透露着个人的重要信息。名片上的信息一般可分为8个部分，分别为：公司名称（the name of company）；本人姓名（person's name）；职位、职称、头衔（position, title）；公司地址（the address of your company）；电话号码（telephone number, mobile phone number）；传真号码（fax number）；电子邮箱（E-mail address）；公司网址（Web page address），其他名片上还可能印有公司或组织的标识（logo），甚至服务和产品介绍等。

一、常用表达

（一）部分职务的翻译
会计员，会计师 Accountant
会计部经理 Accounting Manager
会计主管 Accounting Supervisor
行政经理 Administration Manager
行政助理 Administrative Assistant
广告工作人员 Advertising Staff
总经理 General Manager
总监/主任 Director
设计师 Designer
系主任 Dean
主席/董事长 Chairman/President
总裁 Chief Executive Officer (CEO)
高级工程师 Senior Engineer
副教授 Associate Professor
教授 Professor

讲师 Instructor/Lecturer
技师 Technician
法律顾问 Legal Adviser
国际销售员 International Sales Staff
（二）部门的翻译
财务部 Accounts department
采购部 Purchasing department
企划部 Planning department
销售部 Sales department
广告部 Advertising department
商务部 Business department
客户服务部 Customer service section
会议室 Conference room
董事会 Board of directors
生产部 Production department
复印室 Photocopying room

二、写作范例

Sample 1

```
           The Great Wall Electronics Co. Ltd

                        Shen Liang
           Software Dept. Manager Electronics Engineer

 Address: 50 Changjiang Road,      Fax: 0431-4708558
          Binhai City
 Post code: 116 537
 Email: ya498@pub.bi.inpta.net.cn
 Tel: 0562-46732259                Mobile: 1302512564
```

Sample 2

```
            Zhejiang Sunshine Cashmere Co.,

                       Qiu Xiaoyun
                Business Assistant to General

 No.25 Kangtai Road, Huzhou        MP: 13905725312
 Zhejiang Province, China          Tel: 86-572-3177777
                                   Fax: 86-572-3177888
                                   E-mail: xiao@Sunshine.com
```

Exercise

1. Design an Englsih business card for Mr. Xin Wanfang based on the Chinese one given below.

```
              ××××××发展有限公司
                    鑫万方
                   销售经理
    地址：中国 ××市××路××号           邮编：××××××
    电话：（××）××× ×××× ××××         传真：（××）××× ×××× ××××
    电子邮件：xinmarketing@×××.com    手机：×××××××××××
```

2. Design an English business card according to the infromation given below.
王小斌：××××××有限公司（××××××× Co., Ltd.）市场营销部经理
公司地址：中国×××××3 号　　　　　　　邮编：××××××
公司电话号码：（××）×××-××××××××
公司传真号码：（××）×××-××××××××
手机号码：××××××××××
电子邮件地址：xali@×××.com

 Part D

Workshop
Cultural Introduction

Ⅰ. Appreciation of Classics

1. 温故而知新，可以为师矣。《论语》

If one can attain new understanding by reviewing old knowledge, he can qualify as a teacher.

释义：温习旧知识从而得知新的理解与体会，凭借这一点就可以成为老师了。说明人们的新知识、新学问往往都是在过去所学知识的基础上发展而来。

2. 学而不以，阖棺乃止。《韩诗外传》

There is no end of learning until one is encased in coffin.

释义：大千世界，茫茫宇宙，认识无止境，知识无止境。即使用尽毕生的时间来学习，也只能精通有限的知识。强调人应持之以恒地学习，永不满足。

3. 读书破万卷，下笔如有神。《奉赠韦左承丈二十二韵》

When you have read over ten thousand books, you can write like magic.

释义：读书只有读透书，博览群书，这样落实到笔下，运用起来才能得心应手，有如神功一般。

4. 好读书，不求甚解。《五柳先生传》
He takes delight in reading, but he does not bother about minor details.
释义：读书只求领会要旨，不刻意在字句上下功夫。
5. 万卷山积，一篇吟成。《续诗品·博习》
Unappetizing and yet not bad enough to be thrown away.
释义：只有积累丰厚学问，才能写出一首好诗。

Ⅱ. Appreciation of Chinese Poetry

The Book

Zhu Xi

There lies a glassy oblong pool,
Where light and shade pursue their course.
How can it be so clear and cool?
For water fresh comes from its source.

观书有感

朱熹

半亩方塘一鉴开，
天光云影共徘徊。
问渠那得清如许？
为有源头活水来。

Ⅲ. Cultural Tips

《观书有感》是一首借景喻理的名诗。全诗以方塘作比喻，形象地表达了一种微妙难言的读书感受。池塘并不是一泓死水，而是常有活水注入，因此像明镜一样，清澈见底，映照着天光云影。这种情景，与同一个人在读书中理通问题、获得新知而大有收益时的情形颇为相似。这首诗所表现的就是读书有悟有得时的那种灵气流动、思路明畅、精神清新活泼而自得自在的境界，也是作者作为一位大学问家切身的读书感受。诗中所表达的这种感受虽然仅就读书而言，却寓意深刻，内涵丰富。